DATE DUE

DEMCO 38-296

VIDEO ACQUISITIONS
AND CATALOGING

Recent Titles in
The Greenwood Library Management Collection

Automation in Library Reference Services: A Handbook
Robert Carande

Planning Second Generation Automated Library Systems
Edwin M. Cortez and Tom Smorch

Strategic Management for Academic Libraries: A Handbook
Robert M. Hayes

News Media Libraries: A Management Handbook
Barbara P. Semonche, editor

Reaching a Multicultural Student Community: A Handbook for Academic Librarians
Karen E. Downing, Barbara MacAdam, and Darlene P. Nichols

Library Records: A Retention and Confidentiality Guide
Shirley A. Wiegand

Managing Performing Arts Collections in Academic and Public Libraries
Carolyn A. Sheehy, editor

Video Collection Development in Multi-type Libraries: A Handbook
Gary P. Handman, editor

A Library Manager's Guide to the Physical Processing of Nonprint Materials
Karen C. Driessen and Sheila A. Smyth

The Challenge and Practice of Academic Accreditation: A Sourcebook for Library
Administrators
Edward D. Garten, editor

Information Services for People with Developmental Disabilities
Linda Lucas Walling and Marilyn M. Irwin, editors

Public Library Planning: Case Studies for Management
Brett Sutton

Video Acquisitions and Cataloging

A HANDBOOK

James C. Scholtz

THE GREENWOOD LIBRARY MANAGEMENT COLLECTION

GREENWOOD PRESS
Westport, Connecticut • London

Library of Congress Cataloging-in-Publication Data

Scholtz, James C.
    Video acquisitions and cataloging : a handbook / James C. Scholtz.
      p. cm.—(The Greenwood library management collection, ISSN
  0894–2986)
    Includes bibliographical references and index.
    ISBN 0–313–29345–7 (alk. paper)
    1. Acquisition of video recordings—United States. 2. Cataloging
  of video recordings—United States. I. Title. II. Series.
  Z692.V52S367   1995
  025.2'873—dc20   95–7536

British Library Cataloguing in Publication Data is available.

Library of Congress Catalog Card Number: 95–7536
ISBN: 0–313–29345–7
ISSN: 0894–2986

First published in 1995

Greenwood Press, 88 Post Road West, Westport, CT 06881
An imprint of Greenwood Publishing Group, Inc.

Printed in the United States of America

The paper used in this book complies with the
Permanent Paper Standard issued by the National
Information Standards Organization (Z39.48–1984).

10 9 8 7 6 5 4 3 2 1

Copyright Acknowledgments

The author and publisher are grateful for permission to reproduce the following copyrighted
material.

Figure 3.1, PBS Video Agreement (1994 PBS Video Catalog). Courtesy of Jon Cecil, PBS Video.

Figure 3.2, Ambrose Video Terms and Conditions Contract (Ambrose Video Publishing, Inc.,
1993 Catalog). Courtesy of William Ambrose, president, Ambrose Video Publishing, Inc.

Figure 4.3, Toledo-Lucas County (OH) Public Library Uniform Order Form. Courtesy of Pat
Lora, Toledo-Lucas County Public Library.

Figure 5.6, Instructional Video, Inc. Copyright Categories (Instructional Video, Inc., 1993-1994
Catalog). Courtesy of Joe McWilliams, president, Instructional Video, Inc.

This book is dedicated to my friend and golfing pal, PBS Video sales representative Paul Sweeny, who died in December 1991. He had a clarity of thought and a positive philosophical attitude that was unmatched, coupled with a flair for language, a sharp wit, and a tremendous (golf) slice. I think that I will miss his slice the most. I wish him well in the hereafter and hope that he looks upon this book with favor.

Contents

Illustrations

TABLES

Preface

The idea for this book grew from concerns expressed by media librarians across the country at the American Library Association's (ALA) annual meeting in Atlanta, Georgia in June 1991. During a Video Round Table (VRT) meeting, where members met to discuss the need for workshops and continuing education programs pertaining to videocassettes, the processes of acquisitions and cataloging were among those topics identified as being of paramount interest.

The term "acquisitions" has different connotations depending upon the type, size, and organizational structure of a library. To many librarians, the process of acquisitions covers that broad and rather vague spectrum of activities ranging from reading a review of a title through its purchasing and processing to cataloging and fund-accounting. Still other librarians regard acquisitions as a narrowly-defined, single-focus process, involving layers of activities which concentrate on purchasing materials that have already been identified as being needed by the library through a selection process. It is this latter, more focused definition that Chapters 1 through 3 will discuss.

Coexisting alongside the mainstream avenue of purchasing through recognized national jobbers, there are a wide variety of nonmainstream purchasing strategies, methods, and vendors. Lacking knowledge of these nonmainstream purchasing avenues, many librarians feel that they cannot fulfill their collection development obligations and are denying their patrons the richness and depth that exists within the broad mosaic of the video industry. Even when such materials are readily available, those same librarians often pay more for them than necessary. Lack of knowledge of the video industry, and its relationships with libraries, coupled with its increasing complexity has made video acquisitions a time-consuming, frustrating task.

Once videocassette titles are purchased, processed, and ready for circulation, how does a patron find a video on a particular topic, genre and/or subject? Historically, librarians have felt that their videocassette collections were largely an ephemeral, entertainment-only format. This notion was the primary driving force behind collection development—especially in public libraries where those collections, being comprised mainly of features, expanded and flourished under the premise of "patron demand." However, even as these collections grew, many librarians felt no obligation to provide their patrons with multiple access points through cataloging, treating them with less reverence than even their popular fiction collection. Today, primarily due to the burgeoning consumer, special interest videocassette market, the "information first, format appropriate" philosophy has been partly embraced by libraries, and librarians are in widespread agreement that all materials, including videocassettes, should be cataloged. However, there are many discrepancies in the standardization and inclusiveness of cataloging records, determination of access points, and views concerning alternative methods to the machine readable characters (MARC) format, especially when automated circulation/on-line public access catalogs (OPACs or PACs) are involved. To this end, this book will discuss the above topics, including difficulties, solutions, strategies, and options for cataloging videocassettes.

TOPIC INCLUSION

This book is a "how-to-do-it" manual for all librarians and library students interested in video acquisitions and cataloging. Before one can effectively acquire videocassettes, they must have a well-rounded understanding of the videocassette industry inclusive of the following knowledge: how both features and nonfiction videos are distributed; the pricing and discount structures; sales methods, purchasing avenues, and strategies; copyright; vendor choice; purchasing/vendor vocabulary; and the processes and procedures of ordering. This text will discuss those issues plus provide insight into the history, transformation, separation, and evolution of the video industry. As an offshoot of acquisitions, Chapter 6 will also address issues pertaining to cataloging and processing of videocassettes—more specifically, the availability and authoritativeness of MARC-based cataloging sources, as well as non-MARC catalogs and the interrelationship between acquisitions, cataloging, processing and circulation, and the problems of bibliographic access in the electronic environment.

ORGANIZATION

In an attempt to focus on practical use rather than theory, the text follows a chapter arrangement and includes sample procedures and forms currently in use in actual libraries. Application of theory is the primary thesis of this text; therefore, individual chapters will be arranged with the more immediately applicable, "how-to" mechanics information at the forefront and the theory placed at the end. Written for all librarians and their staff who purchase videocassettes, the purpose of this book is to make them more successful, effective, efficient, and prudent buyers. This book is not concerned with collection development or the selection process. However, the author fully understands that the development of any collection can only be measured by the librarian's success in obtaining the materials necessary for building or enhancing the collection. Finally, the text will not be concerned with a detailed description of the entire range of activities falling under acquisitions and cataloging but will focus on certain tasks involved in both processes. There are a great many books that provide adequate coverage of the broad and detailed work involved with print-based acquisitions. Many of these print-based acquisitions activities and processes can (and should) be transferred and readily adapted to videocassettes. Listed below are three of the best acquisitions texts which should be consulted for a thorough examination of the entire scope of the acquisitions process:

Eaglen, Audrey. *Buying Books: A How-To-Do-It Manual for Librarians* (New York: Neal-Schuman Publishers, Inc., 1989).
Magrill, Rose Mary and John Corbin. *Acquisitions Management and Collection Development in Libraries.* 2nd ed. (Chicago: ALA, 1989).
Schmidt, Karen A., ed. *Understanding the Business of Library Acquisitions* (Chicago: ALA, 1990).

Acknowledgments

Writing this book was like giving birth. Born out of passion, the writing process was time-consuming, laborious, often painful—simultaneously frustrating and intellectually stimulating. But, in the end, it *had* to be born! Starting in the autumn of 1992, the research and writing began but, due to an unforeseen job layoff, soon came to a screeching halt. The will to finish this work was present, but the time and perseverance were not. I thank my wife Suzi for having faith in me and keeping my ego afloat. Two positions later, in two different states and, after months of false starts, both time and perseverance returned with a vengence. I would like to thank all the people who helped me through the hard times—bolstering my belief in my subject knowledge and my writing/organizing abilities. Rolf Rasmussun, Sally Mason-Robinson, Irene Wood, Jean Kreamer, and Mark Richie deserve special thanks for their support. In terms of actual content and research assistance, I want to express my heartfelt appreciation to Linda Hansen, cataloger extraordinaire, of Professional Media Services; independent film/video representatives Gus Collins and George Jennings; and Bill Ambrose, president of Ambrose Video Publishing, Inc. Their knowledge of the volatile educational video market is unequalled. Without their input and insights, this book would not have been possible. I would also like to express my appreciation to Jon Cecil and Dan Hamby of PBS Video for their insights into the workings of that company. Lastly, I would like to give a big thank you to Dawn Mogle, audio visual department head for the Lake County Public Library (Merrilville, IN). She performed a great portion of the research, supplied many of the illustrative forms, and assisted in writing the text for the chapter on cataloging. She also proved to be an effective sounding board into the needs and demands of a technical services department in a large suburban library.

Introduction

Since the 1950s and the established, formal training of librarians, many books have been written about the acquisition of library materials. Most of these texts have focused upon print materials, giving audiovisual materials a few well-chosen paragraphs or perhaps a chapter, but not providing any in-depth coverage for specific audiovisual formats. In the past, that superficial coverage may have been sufficient because the average public librarian did not have to enter the world of filmstrips, audiocassettes, sixteen millimeter (16mm) films, and videocassettes—that world was reserved for the media librarian, armed with special skills, knowledge, and experience pertinent to that field.

Today, some fourteen years after the onslaught of the video revolution in libraries, videocassettes can be found in more than 85 percent of United States public libraries serving populations of 25,000 or more and 62.5 percent of all public libraries, as well as over 80 percent of public schools.[1] In 1985 alone, 1,197,000,000 books were checked out from public libraries, compared with over 1,200,000,000 videocassettes being loaned to patrons by those same libraries.[2] Many librarians are discovering that video is accounting for 15 to 43 percent of annual circulation; however, in those same libraries, videocassette budgets comprise only an average of 5 percent of the total materials budget.[3]

Videocassettes can be found in almost every library throughout the country, from the smallest school and public libraries to the largest university library. As a result, many traditionally print-based librarians are confronted with the seemingly monumental task of video collection development and acquisition without knowing much about the medium, title availability, vendors and pricing structures, public performance rights, or specific acquisition methods. Most graduate library schools compound the problem by not offering courses or continuing education classes in media librarianship or in emphasizing the changing role of media occurring in all types of libraries today.

Historically, only regional libraries, library systems, school cooperatives, colleges and universities, and large public libraries held collections of 16mm films because of per title costs, shelving space requirements, special handling, circulation, and maintenance concerns. Per-title costs ranged from $150 to $1,200 with an average in the vicinity of $500, and many feature titles were under long-term (5+ years), renewable leases at prices of $1,200 or more. As "home-use only" video evolved, this market has had a marked impact upon lowering the prices of both educational and independent video that had traditionally been influenced only by 16mm film trends. "Home-use only" video has made the video format both attractive and affordable to virtually every library and helped pave the way for the independent and educational distributors to market directly to the library building level rather than just the larger system or regional levels.

The current videocassette industry is very unique, being both complex and volatile but, at the same time, unstructured and undefined. Video librarians and acquisitions department personnel must learn to how to cope with a whole new set of rules, specialized vocabulary, and sometimes unorthodox procedures when dealing with video vendors. The video acquisitions librarian must possess a wealth of skills and attributes including a knowledge of economics and video distribution, superior prioritization, organization and communication skills, tenacity tempered with flexibility and a willingness to adapt to change, accounting/budgeting skills and, in today's technological world, computer skills. It is hoped that the reader of this book will come away with a greater understanding and appreciation of video acquisitions work, as well as a sense of perspective as to how video fits into the whole acquisitions picture.

NOTES

1. Ray Serebrin, "Video: Planning Backwards into the Future," *Library Journal* 120 (November 15, 1988): 33.

2. Randy Pitman, "A Librarian's View of Video in Libraries," in Martha Dewing, ed., *Home Video in Libraries: How Libraries Buy and Circulate Prerecorded Home Video* (Boston: G.K. Hall, 1988), p. 7.

3. Randy Pitman, "Rockefeller Foundation Videocassette Distribution Task Force: Final Report—Library Market" (Bremerton, WA, June 30, 1962, typewritten), p. 1.

1

The Video Industry— History and Evolution

HOW IT ALL STARTED

In order to truly appreciate today's complex video business, one must have an understanding and overview of its development and evolution. Simply stated, the history of video collections in public libraries can be divided into two periods—pre-1980 and post-1980. This chapter will address the changes and events during the pre-1980 period. Prior to 1980, public library involvement with video was generally in the area of cable television or building collections of videocassettes for in-house viewing. Few libraries loaned video tapes because patrons did not own or have access to VCR equipment. After 1980, the home video market began to expand exponentially and libraries responded by building circulating video collections. Prior to 1980, most of the video titles produced were film-to-video transfers from educational vendors like Encyclopaedia Britannica, Coronet/MTI, and Time-Life. All of these titles were more expensive than "home-use only" video and carried public performance rights, making them a group showing medium similar to film. However, at that time, no large screen or projection television systems existed to provide the video medium with a playback system conducive for group use. Even so, video was thought of as an extension of a film product, just in a different format. Home video changed the consumer's perception and use of video from educational, group use to private, individual entertainment. Today, those two perceptions are still juxtaposed; however, they are beginning to coalesce because of changes in the market. Most librarians describe the period since 1980 as "the video revolution." Others feel that it was more of a slow, long-term evolutionary process rather than a quick changeover "revolution." Former American Film and Video Association (AFVA) Executive Director Ron MacIntyre feels that it was neither a revolution nor an evolution, but rather a shift in technology and an acceptance of/demand on that technology by consumers to embrace an entirely new industry.[1] Regardless of the manner of change, video is here to stay, and technology is on the verge of changing video and television into true, large-group viewing mediums. Large-screen units and the emergence of consumer-market, affordable, three-tube, and liquid crystal display (LQD) front-projection televisions promise to deliver a large picture with superior picture resolution and sound clarity. Advances in High Definition Television (HDTV) are just around the corner and will most certainly have an impact on video technology as well, even though super-VHS faded out in the late 1980s. Advanced marketing concepts linked with sophisticated consumer-selected (or profiled) programming options, like the 1992 Summer Olympics Triplecast, pay-per-view Request Channel, and RCA's Direct TV promise a bright future for cable television and satellite companies, as well as the video sell-through market. These new technologies are expensive, and are creating societal and economic rifts between those viewers who can afford to pay for those services and those who take what they can get over "free" channels.

If one embraces the concept of video evolution, a timeline becomes helpful in understanding the history, marketing decisions, and trends as well as establishing a foundation for future decisions regarding video in libraries. Along this evolutionary line depicting the emergence of the videocassette and its subsequent acceptance as a viable collection item in libraries are many events, often occurring in chainlike fashion. These events have influenced our daily lives and changed the way we view technology, the consumer and retail markets, laws (copyright, intellectual freedom, and censorship), and methods of video distribution and sales. An event, for the purposes of this text, is defined as a documented historical happening, as well as a published article or monograph. When viewed together as part of a broader context, these events indicate and influence trends. Some events are insignificant, while others are monumental. Some small events acted as catalysts for larger, more consequential events. Most books dealing with acquisitions begin with a chapter covering the history of the book industry and its effects on library acquisitions. To be sure, these narrative descriptions are valuable, and the following timeline chronology should help bring those significant events into focus in similar fashion. This chronology provides a listing of the significant events, occurring in both the library and video industry worlds, that have helped shaped the way in which we use, view, and purchase video today.

VIDEOCASSETTE TIMELINE[2]

1970	Sony introduces the ¾-inch U-matic format—a self-contained two-reel videocassette.
	The Public Library Association (PLA) Audiovisual Committee publishes the first standards for public library media services, entitled *Guidelines for Audiovisual Materials and Services in Public Libraries.*
1972	In its November 1 issue, *Library Journal* reports that Learning Corporation of America (LCA) plans to make its educational films available in the videocassette format at prices comparatively lower than conventional film, with leasing also being considered as an option.
1973	Time-Life Multimedia starts distributing videocassettes like the *BBC Shakespeare* and *Ascent of Man* series in ¾-inch Sony U-matic format. Their video titles were priced at 70 percent of the 16mm film price.
	Reviews of video titles first appear in ALA's *Booklist* magazine in the November 1 issue when Angie Le Clerco compiled a list from three companies: LCA, Time-Life Multimedia, and Chelsea House—average price $280.
1974	The National Education Film Festival (NEFF) premieres in Oakland, California.
April 16, 1975	Sony introduces the ½-inch, self-contained videocassette and recording/playback units, the SL-7300 and the SL-6300, price $2,295.
	PLA Audiovisual Committee publishes an expansion/revision of its 1970 work, published in two parts, entitled *Recommendations for Audiovisual Materials and Services for Small and Medium-sized Public Libraries.*
1976	Senator Robert Kastenmeier (Rep. from Wisconsin) singlehandedly authors the Copyright Act, which will have far-reaching effects on the present and future use of videocassettes by the private individual, schools and colleges, and public libraries.
February 1976	Sony introduces Betamax, specifically designed for recording television programs off-air and playback at the user's convenience (phrase "timeshift recording" coined). Price $1,295, lowered to $1,095.
April 1976	Japan Victor Corporation (JVC) introduces its VHS ½-inch videocassette and recording/playback system, the VX-2000.
	The *Videophile* magazine classified-ad section includes an ad which reads, "get or give help in building collections of movies and television shows—trade and access to cable TV."

Andre Blay establishes Magnetic Video, the first video software sales company. Blay makes a deal with Twentieth Century Fox for nonexclusive rights to fifty feature films for transfer to videocassette, selling each title for $50.

1977

George Atkinson establishes the first video rental store in New York City, called Video Station. Later that year Jack Messer would start video rental stores in Los Angeles and New York City.

Matsushitsu and RCA develop the VHS unit, Selectavision—4-hour recording selling for $1,000.

February 1977

Magnavox introduces the video disc player.

April 1977

MCA/Universal sues Sony to prevent manufacture of prerecorded videotapes.

November 1977

Hi-Fi magazine publishers first recommended list of prerecorded videotapes for home use.

December 1977

Film producer charges New York BOCES with infringement of copyright in taping and retaining tapes off-air and making unauthorized copies.

March 1978

First issue of *Video Magazine* is published.

Time-Life Multimedia starts distributing its titles in VHS, Beta I, and Beta II formats. Video titles are priced at 50 percent of the 16mm film price.

Allied Artists begins distributing a line of 100 prerecorded titles in the ''home-use only'' market.

Time-Life Multimedia changes its name to Time-Life Video. This change is significant because it represents the first time a company recognizes that video is a separate, viable market.

The National Film Market is formed in 1978 as a place for vendors to showcase their films to librarians of system, regional, and educational AV collections for purchase.

Ted Grieder authors *Acquisitions: Where, What, and How*—destined to become one of the standard books on library acquisitions in the field.

December 1978

The first laserdisc player, the Magnavox Model 8000, is introduced.

1979

VHS models outsell Beta models 2 to 1.

March 1979

Congressional committee, headed by Wisconsin Congressman Rober Kastenmeier, establishes a set of standards for both the owners and users of copyrighted television programs entitled ''Guidelines for Off-air Recording of Broadcast Programming for Educational Purposes.''

Deirdre Boyle compiles first video review list for the Educational Film Library Association's (EFLA) serial publication, *Sightlines.*

Video Source Book, published by the National Video Clearinghouse and listing both "home-use only" and public performance videos, features, and nonfiction, appears.

New York City's Donnel Film Library concentrates on building a unique collection of ¾-inch videocassettes, at least one-half of which are produced independently.

The Milwaukee County Federated Library System has purchased over 900 ¾-inch videocassettes of primarily information titles which can be viewed in-house at twenty-three branch sites.

The Suburban Audio Visual Service (SAVS) in La Grange Park, Illinois, begins to develop a videocassette collection, offering videocassettes for loan to its member libraries.

Educational Film Library Association (EFLA) adopts Freedom to View statement.

1980   Disney tries a two-track marketing method of its "home-use only" titles—blue packaging (rental only); white packaging (sales only).

June 1980   Pioneer unveils its first laserdisc player, the VP-1000.

Morton Fink, president of Warner Home Video, proposes a rental plan that will allow movie studios to participate in rentals and gives the Warner packaging a distinctive "book-like" appearance, listing credits, photograph stills, and front and back liner notes.

Video Review magazine begins publication.

The Public Broadcasting Service creates a PBS Video subsidary to distribute some 2,800 programs on videocassette that are produced by television stations and independent producers for use in classrooms and libraries.

Billboard magazine premieres its "Top Videocassettes Rental" and "Sales Hit Charts." This event signals an acceptance in the entertainment industry that prerecorded videocassettes are to be taken seriously and video stores are a viable market.

1981   MCA, Pioneer, and Magnavox Video Productions introduces LaserVision's first interactive video disc, *The First National Kidisc.*

RCA introduces the new SelectaVision CED video disc system, the SGT 100.

Pat Machy writes an article for *Sightlines* (Summer 1981) entitled "Developing Video Collections," marking the first significant article to recognize video in libraries.

September 2, 1981   Warner Home Video unveils its video rental plan. Videocassette titles would be leased to rental stores on a weekly basis with declining rates over a six-week period, ranging from $8.25 to $4.40.

November 1981   Twentieth Century Fox announces a similar rental plan with a six-month window—$75 for blockbusters, $45 for all other titles.

December 1981   MGM/CBS initiates a rental plan with a four-month window, but also making their titles for sale.

Disney, Paramount, Columbia, and MGM follow Fox and Warner into the home video market. The studios were getting disgruntled because of the fact that they were not receiving any part of store rentals after the initial sale. A $79.95 sale price brought a royalty of about $10—a handsome profit multiplied by millions of consumers, but not so attractive when multiplied by only 10–15,000 video rental stores, who rent each title out hundreds of times at $5 per rental. The Video Software Dealer's Association (VSDA) announces a consumer market shift from sales to rentals.

Sightlines reports that 1981 should go down in American Film Festival history as the year in which video grew up. Deirdre Boyle presents a workshop, "Developing Video Collections," at the twenty-third annual American Film Festival.

Nancy B. Olson edits the book *Cataloging of Audiovisual Materials*, one of the first books to comprehensively cover the cataloging of prerecorded videocassettes for libraries.

1982   Two associations are formally established—the Video Software Retailer's Association and the Video Software Dealer's Association. The VSDA, originally a branch of the National Association of Recording Merchandisers (NARM), was initially organized in response to Hollywood's lobby efforts to have the First Sale Doctrine modified or repealed in order to claim a chunk of the growing rental market.

RCA ships the first capacitance electronic disc system (CED) videodisc players. These players use a stylus to electronically read video information encoded in record-like grooves on a twelve-inch disc.

Rating the Movies for Home Video, TV, Cable is published by the editors of *Consumer Guide*. It is the first guide for consumers on recommended features available on video.

Karl Video releases *Jane Fonda's Workout* with partial funding from RCA, selling over one million copies at $60 each to become the first special interest, sell-through hit. It was also the rock upon which the video how-to market was built.

Started in the spring of 1978, entrepreneur George Atkinson (Video Station of Los Angeles) has 500 affiliated video rental stores and also is a wholesaler of videocassettes.

The average retail price of a VCR is $470.

Deirdre Boyle compiles a "Documentary Video Classics" core collection list for EFLA's *Sightlines.*

Pioneer comes out with its laser disc and a library of feature films available on disc. Also, the spring 1983 issue of *Sightlines* reports use of an interactive videodisc system working with a computer to teach sign language.

October 1983

Universal v. Sony U.S. Supreme Court case. Basically, this case was brought about because Universal felt that timeshift recording by the public would prove damaging to the television and movie theater industry. Decision reached on January 17, 1984 in favor of Sony. Timeshift recording is permitted by law and is not against copyright.

March 1984

MGM/UA Home Entertainment Group, Inc. issues a public performance license to the Los Angeles County Public Library System for $100 to $225 per title permitting group and in-house showings for the 100-member library system. This license is the first of its kind issued by a major studio.

The U.S. Supreme Court issues a decision involving *Columbia Pictures v. Redd Horne*, finding a video store in violation of the copyright law because it allowed customers to watch "home-use only" videocassettes in-house. This ruling will have broad implications for libraries and schools in the use of video.

Billboard reports that the video market is kinder to a movie than the theatrical market, noting that *The Cotton Club* spent months on *Billboard*'s top rental charts after doing an abysmal business at the box office.

Billboard also notes that video is prone to obscene profits and is assisting theatrical productions, citing a specific incidence where Twentieth Century Fox, needing a $75 million loan, borrowed it from CBS/Fox Video rather than from a bank.

The 1969 publication *Audio Visual Market Place* changes its name to *Audio Video Market Place* to embrace the emerging video technology, offering lists of producers and distributors of video products, equipment vendors, and so on.

1985

Thorn/EMI HBO Video sells 427,000 copies of *Rambo* to video rental dealers at a wholesale price of $52 each, for a gross profit of $22 million.

Disney's *Pinocchio*, released at a $79.95 sale price, sells 150,000 copies; the price is lowered to $29.95 and sells another 250,000 copies.

By the mid-1980s, MCA and other companies start to produce titles exclusively for video release. *Jane Fonda's Workout* video, released by Karl Video, sells over one million copies. Vestron releases *Making Michael Jackson's "Thriller"*, selling almost one million copies at $30 each.

Using Copyrighted Videocassettes in Classrooms and Libraries is authored by Dr. Jerome Miller.

The January 1985 issue of *Variety* reports that prerecorded video sales dip and then soar in cities which have just been cabled (provided with cable TV service) . . . people buy a VCR when they get cable TV with the intent of recording but find it easier and more convenient to rent videos.

June 1985   Don Julien authors the article "Pioneering New Services: Videocassettes," in *Wilson Library Bulletin*, marking the first time video in libraries received a multipage article in a major library serial.

Two companies, Professional Media Service Corporation and Eastin-Phelan Corporation, offer a unique videocassette leasing plan for libraries similar to Brodart's McNaughton Plan for books.

Labeled the "Year of the Nonfiction Video" at the annual Video Software Dealer's Association (VSDA), *Esquire* unveils the *Esquire Success* series—*Career Strategies, Persuasive Speaking, The Short-Order Gourmet,* and *The Wine Advisor.*

The average price of a VCR is $353.

Baker & Taylor buys Sound Video Unlimited in order to venture into the library and video rental store wholesale business.

PLA AV Committee publishes *Policy Questions for Audiovisual Services in Public Libraries.*

John W. Ellison edits the standard text for media librarians, *Media Librarianship.*

1986   The VSDA reports that there are 20,000 video rental stores across the United States.

Paramount sells 1.2 million units of *Beverly Hills Cop* at a wholesale price of $20 each ($29.95 for retail sell-through market), grossing $24 million while other companies continue the $79.95 price.

February 1986   ALA publishes "Library Use of Copyrighted Videotapes and Computer Software," a special pull-out section appearing in *American Libraries.* This is the first time the American Library Association (ALA) announces a stand on the volatile copyright issue for electronic and video media, and is presented in concise, easily understandable language.

The Video Librarian, a serial published by Randy Pitman, appears. This landmark publication combines video industry and library news with video reviews.

| 1987 | Films Incorporated and the Motion Picture Licensing Corporation (MPLC) offer ''blanket,'' site-related, public performance licenses for MPAA studios' ''home-use only'' videocassettes. |

Leonard Maltin's TV Movies & Video Guide published.

Fast Forward: Hollywood, the Japanese, and the Onslaught of the VCR, by James Lardner, is published.

The Special Interest Video Association (SIVA) is established for the purpose of promoting the interests of special interest video.

Halliwell's Film & Video Guide is expanded to include feature videos.

February 1987
V—The Mail-Order Magazine of Videocassettes premieres. Designed to be marketed to video store customers and directly to consumers, this publication marks the first time direct marketing of special interest video is tried.

Dr. Charles W. Vlcek authors the book *Copyright Policy Development.*

ALA and the National Education Association jointly publish *The Copyright Primer for Libraries and Educators* by Mary Hutchings Reed.

October 1987
The Federal Appeals Court continues an injunction against Home Box Office (HBO) from selling or renting video copies of the Academy Award-winning film (and 1986 top box office grossing film, at $12.9 million) *Platoon*, in connection with a suit by Vestron, Inc. challenging distribution of that title. This marks the first time that a video company is involved in assisting with the finance of a movie production based on the assumption of future video distribution rights.

1987–1988
ALA and the Carnegie Foundation establish the Carnegie grant, providing $560,000 to ''enhance the role of videocassettes in libraries.'' Six hundred VCRs are provided for applying Carnegie libraries. Also, the first recommended monograph for videos, *Video for Libraries: Special Interest Video for Small and Medium-sized Public Libraries*, by Sally Mason and James Scholtz, is published.

A ''video-awareness'' newsletter called *Fast Forward* is inserted into PLA's serial publication *Public Libraries* as part of the Carnegie Project.

Billboard magazine premieres its top special interest videocassette sales charts with the March 28, 1987 issue—health and fitness; business and education; recreational sports; hobbies and crafts.

Also, as part of the Carnegie Project, two training videocassettes are produced by the Library Video Network to show librarians how to use the new video medium.

The availability of low-cost home video has caused some problems for producers and distributors within the educational market. Home Vision (initially created in 1985 as part of Public Media, Inc.) and Brighton Video (Wombat) create subsidary companies offering special interest "home-use only" products.

EFLA (Educational Film Library Association) changes its name to the American Film and Video Association (AFVA).

April 1988   Brad Carty's column, "The Video Shopper," appears in the *Wilson Library Bulletin.* Its purpose is to highlight new video titles, both features and nonfiction.

June 1988   Randy Pitman premieres his new "Av Frontier" column in the *Wilson Library Bulletin.* Its purpose is to keep librarians abreast of current developments and trends in the video business as it pertains to libraries.

Librarian's Video Review, published by Clearview Media, with James Scholtz as contributing editor, appears. A comprehensive review source of "home-use only" videos.

The CPB/Annenberg distributes its *Voices & Visions* series, providing documentaries and readings of famous American poets and their works.

The Association for Information Media and Equipment (AIME) produces an informational video for librarians on video copyright entitled *Copyright: What Every School, College and Public Library Should Know.* AIME also establishes a copyright Hotline 800 number.

1988   The John D. and Catherine T. MacArthur Foundation announce a $4.5 million Library Video Classics Project designed to offer 20 prime-time PBS programs to libraries at a 90 percent discount ($6,000).

Variety's Complete Video Directory, published by R.R. Bowker and listing "home-use only" features and special interest titles, appears.

The Heartland Institute publishes a study entitled "The Private Video Library: A Bright Beginning, An Uncertain Future," by Dr. William B. Irvine. This study challenges the notion that video lending by public libraries serves an educational purpose, questioning whether the provision of entertainment (feature films) is a proper and necessary function of a public library. Irvine felt the video store owner's livelihood was being threatened by the growing number of public libraries offering videos to patrons.

The ALA Yearbook described 1988 as a "watershed year" for video. VCR penetration reached 60 percent, with 80 percent of public libraries serving over 25,000 population possessing a circulating video collection.

Sally Mason becomes director of ALA's Video and Special Projects agency.

As the concluding project of a market survey on video in libraries initiated by Knowledge Industry, Martha Dewing edits the book *Home Video in Libraries: How Libraries Buy and Circulate Prerecorded Home Video.*

PBS Video premieres its low-cost video catalog, "Check It Out," with prices ranging from $29.95 to $99.

Films Incorporated produces a low-cost video catalog, "Library Video Connection."

The Anglo-American Cataloguing Rules is published in a revised, second edition. This edition expands the chapters on audiovisual formats, particularly in regard to video.

Distribution takes another step toward consolidation as Video Trend, based in Chicago, and Major Video Concepts, headquartered in Indianapolis, merge. In addition, Video Products Distributors of California and Sight & Sound, St. Louis, MO, agree to merge into a new company called Home Entertainment Distributors, Inc.

Video rentals move into supermarkets in a big way. The Movie Exchange opens its 200th location in Giant Food Markets, Pottstown, PA with over 2,000 movies available for rental.

Rackjobbers infiltrate the video rental markets. The Handleman Company agrees to rack West Coast Video/National Video with sell-through product.

1989   James C. Scholtz's book, *Developing and Maintaining Video Collections in Libraries*, is published by ABC-CLIO.

Gale Publishing takes over publication of the *Video Source Book,* expanding and improving its coverage and comprehensive indexes.

ALA and the Carnegie Foundation unite again for a Quality Video for Youth Project, publishing a newsletter, *Children's Video in Libraries*, appearing in issues of the *Journal of Youth Services.* The program also establishes a set of quality children's titles that can be purchased for $1000.

The Rockefeller Foundation organizes a video task force and conducts a national survey to assess the viability of four categories of special interest video in libraries—American, foreign, and independent features; social and political documentaries; fine arts/ performance programs; and video art and experimental films.

Randy Pitman initiates a new column in *Library Journal*, "Video Movies," that reviews current nonblockbuster video features of interest to libraries.

June 28, 1989   "Access for Children and Young People to Videotapes and Other Nonprint Formats: An Interpretation of the Library Bill of Rights," adopted by ALA.

Under the National Film Preservation Act of 1988, Librarian of Congress James H. Billington announces the first twenty-five films to be included in the National Film Registry. Up to twenty-five films will be added each year for the next five years and possibly beyond.

May 1989   Gale publishes the *Audio Video Review Digest.* Originally intended to take the place of *Media Review Digest*, this publication, designed as a quarterly review locator for libraries, looked promising and was enthusiastically received but was mysteriously abandoned in 1990.

Carolyn Frost authors *Media Access and Organization*, the premiere book for librarians interested in cataloging audio visual materials, including videocassettes.

1990   Freedom to View Statement updated and approved by AFVA in 1989 and endorsed by ALA, January 10, 1990.

Bowker changes name of *Variety's Complete Home Video Directory* to *Bowker's Complete Video Directory*, expanding its coverage to include both "home-use only" and public performance features and special interest with a comprehensive set of indexes.

PBS Video and Pacific Arts Video, through a joint agreement using the "PBS Home Video" label, embark on a consumer retailing venture to sell programs previously available only to the educational market. PBS also creates two new agencies: the Adult Learning Service to market via satellite to colleges and universities and the Primary/Secondary School Service to license off-air recording rights.

The Video Interest Group is established at ALA's annual summer meeting.

The Consortium of College and University Media Centers issues a Video Management Survey to its members, the data to be compiled and presented at the 1990 spring conference.

The Association of Research Libraries (ACRL) publishes *Audiovisual Policies in ARL Libraries* (SPEC Kit #162), by Kristine Brancolini.

The first issue of the video review serial, *The Video Rating Guide*, is published.

1991   The Video Interest Group becomes an official ALA Round Table.

Dixon Public Library (IL) wins the first annual award, sponsored by Baker & Taylor Video, for the best use of video in a public library.

July 1, 1991	The first Carnegie Medal (Andrew Carnegie Excellence in Children's Video Award) winner for excellence in children's video is announced in conjunction with the Caldecott Book Awards. The winner is *Ralph S. Mouse* (Churchill Film and Video).
August 1991	ALA closes the Video and Special Projects agency.

ABC-CLIO publishes a comprehensive library video marketing report as the result of a national survey. This report will be updated on an annual basis and provide important information for producers and distributors interested in selling to the library market.

Funded by the MacArthur Foundation, National Video Resources' (NVR) Independent Distributor Assistance Program (IDAP) grants offer awards of up to $15,000 to both nonprofit and for-profit distributors of independent film and video, seeking to explore new marketing strategies and/or improve their long-term distribution capabilities in the institutional and home video markets.

Senator Robert Kastenmeier crafts an out-of-Congress copyright agreement for public performance of "home-use only" video titles with the MPAA. This agreement allows nursing homes who are members of either the American Health Care Association or the American Association for the Aging to show "home-use only" videos to groups as long as an admission charge is not levied.

Home Video Express creates a new avenue for libraries to acquire videocassettes with its Library Video Express program where patrons purchase videos and the library, in return, amasses accrued credits toward the purchase of its videos.

The postmaster general investigates alleged misuse of postage rates by PBS Video, a not-for-profit agency. Some companies fear that PBS Video is offering unfair and illegal competition to for-profit companies.

The Video Annual 1991, edited by Jean T. Kreamer, premieres. This annual publication proves to be invaluable for selectors of video and acquisitions librarians.

ABC-CLIO publishes James Scholtz's book *Video Policies and Procedures for Libraries.*

1992	The Minnesota Scholarly Press publishes the third edition of Nancy Olson's highly praised book *Cataloging of Audiovisual Materials: A Manual Based on AACR 2.*
June 19, 1992	Commtron integrates operations with Ingram Library Services Inc. As a unit, this company will now account for 33 to 35 percent of the wholesale market share.

June 26, 1992   Congress enacts legislation to provide "automatic" copyright re-
                   newals for certain pre-1978 films. Films first released from 1964
                   through 1977 with copyright notices will enjoy this protection;
                   the law does not change the status of films during this period
                   released without the copyright notices. This law has ramifications
                   on films currently in the public domain by allowing them to return
                   to protective copyright status. "The vast [public domain] market
                   has long operated as a safety valve, ensuring continued public
                   access to thousands of films that would otherwise have disap-
                   peared completely."[3] Libraries possessing public domain video-
                   cassettes from places like Sinister Cinema and Video Sig need
                   not worry about violating copyright by lending their existing ti-
                   tles—only in duplication or public exhibition of those titles.

August 1992   PBS announces that it will "reserve the right to condition its
                   program funding commitments on the availability to PBS of in-
                   stitutional home video and/or home video rights."[4] Alarmed video
                   publishers and distributors, producers, educators, and media arts
                   organizations organize the Coalition for Public Television Pro-
                   gram Access and Diversity to oppose the move because it threat-
                   ens to adversely effect program diversity as well as mandating
                   distributor rights even when PBS is not the preferred distributor.

December 1992   Fast food giant McDonald's strikes an unprecedented deal with
                   Orion Home Video, offering the Academy Award-winning picture
                   Dances with Wolves on videocassette for $7.99. The action cuts
                   deep into the retailer sell-through market because the tape had not
                   been discounted to them, still selling for $99.95. The Video Soft-
                   ware Dealer's Association (VSDA) becomes infuriated and threat-
                   ens legal action.

                   Published since 1956, *Landers Film & Video Reviews* ceases pub-
                   lication with the Winter 1992 issue.

April 1993   The American Film & Video Association (AFVA) undergoes a
                   major reorganization, cancelling its annual festival and disbanding
                   the information service because of recognized changes in industry
                   (vendor) and membership support. AFVA unofficially disbands
                   and ceases all publication efforts including *Sightlines* and *AFVA
                   Evaluations*. This creates a fundamental rift in product marketing/
                   distribution for independent filmmakers.

                   A Bob Alexander & Associates retailer video survey reveals as
                   many as 12,000 previously uncounted video retail stores in ethnic
                   and rural enclaves, possibly accounting for $4 billion of a $17
                   billion market (previously thought to be only $12–$13 billion).
                   Previously thought to be an arena of 25–27,000 stores, this boosts
                   the number substantially, to almost 40,000 stores. Producers feel
                   that shipments of blockbuster titles would not be affected by this
                   increase, but titles delivering fewer than 100,000 units would def-

initely benefit. The problem the industry has now is in identifying and selling product to these stores.[5]

July 1993

Warner Home Video announces an unprecedented returns policy to retailers, beginning with the Academy Award winner *Unforgiven*. Moving away from the traditional 90-day return authorization, Warner will be accepting returns of unsold rental cassettes from distributors 30 days after the street date. Other producers such as MCA/Universal are predicted to follow suit. Kirk Kirkpatrick, Vice President of Waxworks/Videoworks, feels that this manuever indicates that the industry now recognizes that retail demand for a rental title "is virtually over" 2–3 weeks after it reaches the stores and is ready for the lower-priced, sell-through stage.[6]

October 1993

Disney tests direct sales in its release of *Aladdin*, expected to be home video's first 30-million unit seller, worth over $450 million wholesale. Disney hopes that this distribution plan will give them more control over retail pricing, previously lost to wholesalers who drastically cut prices. In 1992, Disney was able to establish a new industry sell-through record, moving 21 million copies of *Beauty and the Beast*.[7]

April 1994

PBS Video chooses Turner Home Entertainment to market its programs to the consumer market. The Turner-PBS contract is designed to overcome a major problem that plagued its predecessor, Pacific Arts Video. Rather than negotiating for contract rights on a per-title basis after broadcast airing, Turner-PBS will have a $20 million acquisition fund from which to draw.[8]

NOTES

1. Ron MacIntyre, "A Gathering of 25—Libraries & Film," *Sightlines* 25 (Spring 1992): 11.

2. Some of this information was excerpted and verified from the following article: Tony Cohen, "Video Rewind: 1975–1989," *Video Software Magazine* 5 (December 1989): 26–29.

3. William Pitman Priest, "Life With Video: At Play in the Fields of Law," *Film Comment* 28 (September/October 1992): 7.

4. Larry Adelman, "PBS Grabs Video Rights," *Sightlines* 25 (Fall 1992): 18.

5. Seth Goldstein, "Lost Vid Retailers Unearthed," *Billboard* 105 (April 24, 1993): 8, 70.

6. Seth Goldstein, "Warner Home Video Offering Distribs Earlier Return Option," *Billboard* 105 (July 10, 1993): 1, 78.

7. Jim McCullaugh, "'Aladdin' to Test Disney Pipeline," *Billboard* 105 (May 8, 1993): 1, 78.

8. Seth Goldstein, "Picture This," *Billboard* 106 (April 23, 1994): 77, 83.

2

Video in Libraries—
Trends Which Affect
Distribution

DISCOVERING TRENDS

Following in the footsteps of Chapter 1's video chronology, Chapter 2 will explore the many historical and current trends which influence video production, distribution, and resultant pricing within the home video, educational, and independent markets. In the recent past, home video pricing, while volatile, has been contained within its own industry—neither effecting nor being affected by the other markets. Today, while this fact remains true regarding feature films, such is not the case within the special interest niche of home video. In many cases, the same product found in the educational/independent market can also be found in the special interest and home video markets, but at much lower prices. Thus, this chapter will speak to those price discrepancies. In light of the above comments and, in attempting to clarify certain factors affecting each market, those markets will be discussed in a segmented fashion. Each market will be defined, with specific distribution methods (when applicable) detailed. The history and pricing rationale of feature films released on video will be discussed separately. In a following section, pricing, as it relates to special interest, educational, and independent videos, will be discussed as a single issue using a comparison style because of their interrelatedness. As with book publishing, the costs of production and distribution are not fully understood by librarians. Throughout this chapter, these production costs will be illuminated, culminating in a comprehensive discussion of production costs within the independent market segment.

A BOOK DISTRIBUTION ANALOGY

As a segue to video distribution and as a point of comparison, let us examine some surprising statistics of the book distribution market from *Book Publishing: A Basic Introduction*, John P. Dessauer's foremost book on the subject.[1]

The publisher side: In the current marketplace there are 22,500 publishers publishing over 751,000 in-print titles, with over 50,000 new titles published each year. The average hardcover trade book can be expected to sell only about 10,000 copies, while a mass-market paperback could sell around 100,000 copies.

The consumer side: In the United States, there are some 78,000 public schools lying within 15,749 school districts with 21,764 private schools, 1,887 colleges and universities, 1,179 community colleges, 10,210 special libraries, 8,884 main public libraries, and 18,719 bookstores. Thus the sales universe is composed of about 140,643 institutions. Out of these 8,884 public libraries, 23 percent have annual book budgets of $25,000 or more and 27 percent have book budgets between $1,000 and $5,000.

Sales/Distribution: The complexity of book production and its subsequent sales/delivery to these disparate markets has always been a problem. Sales of books to this entire market has accounted for an industry revenue of $13 billion. Libraries, schools, and other institutions account for about 40 percent of that total market, ranging from a high of 23 percent of the university press titles, 21 percent of the professional market, and 11 percent of the trade market. It is a safe assumption that neither university presses nor the professional market could exist if it were not for library purchases. Sixty-seven percent of book sales are channeled through wholesalers and jobbers, taking as much as a 50 percent discount on overall sales from the producer while giving the consumer anywhere from a 20 percent short discount to a 33.3 percent discount.

The point of mentioning these book market statistics is to show that even the book market suffers from production and distribution woes and that it should not be looked upon as a panacea from which to model video distribution. Also, as the text furthers the discussion concerning the video market, it may be appropriate to review these statistics to gain a certain perspective on the issue.

THE BEGINNINGS OF THE VIDEO MARKET

Videocassette collection size, development, and circulation in libraries have grown steadily for the last decade, due in part to the exponential dollar volume and demand in the consumer market. The leap from 16mm film collections to videocassettes can best be described as quantum. Film was far easier to select because the range of subjects and titles was substantially limited and distribution was primarily orchestrated through a few well-known, reputable vendors such as CRM Films, Time-Life Films, Encyclopaedia Britannica, MTI/Coronet, and Phoenix/BFA. Film was expensive to purchase and maintain, took substantial storage space, and required special physical shelving, as well as requiring some specialized circulation, maintenance, and repair routines and expensive, complicated playback equipment. Distribution techniques were fairly well-defined, relying on a small army of independent and company sales representatives who made contact with a few thousand schools, libraries, and universities, usually at the state, regional, and large, central level. This system perpetuated a small, close-knit clique of sales representatives and their customers. Film production was an expensive proposition. There existed only a small body of independent filmmakers; however, many of these independents relied on the major companies for advertising, marketing, and distribution of their product. Photoduplication costs to make duplicates from masters were fairly hefty but consistent. Therefore, all companies had similar pricing structures, albeit on the high side. All films came with nontheatrical public performance rights because there was no question that it was a ''group show'' medium. Many films, especially full-length features, were only offered on a short-term rental or lease basis, and companies like Clem Williams, Swank, and Films Incorporated developed a substantial film rental business. Because of these drawbacks, 16mm film was not usually in demand or obtainable for the general public or for smaller libraries. As a result, only larger public libraries such as New York's Donnell Library, regional and system centers, college/university film centers, and school systems could afford film collections.

In 1975, Time-Life was one of the first companies to open the doors on the Sony U-matic format. At that time video was priced along a similar equation to film, and not viewed as a threat to the film format. Beta and VHS video came along in the late 1970s and early 1980s, giving rise to two district markets: the educational market (historically, the traditional film market) and the consumer, ''home-use only'' market. The latter market significantly changed the distribution scene, as well as eroding the pricing hierarchy previously set by the educational market. Even though these two markets sold the same format, although not necessarily the same title, the disparity in pricing between these markets was obvious. The home market's prices ranged from $9.95 to $89.95, while the educational market's prices ranged from $150 to $1,000. As special interest video grew and small niche interest broadened, so did home video. As a result of this growth coupled with the attractive prices and increasing availability, libraries and other institutions began purchasing home video in place of the much more expensive educational product. Thus, the erosion of clearly defined lines of pricing, distribution, and product began, severely hitting the educational film and video industry. It culminated in the mergers and buyouts of established film companies with multiple parties holding distribution rights for the same program, now available in video, but previously released on film several years before. By the time the half-inch VHS format took hold of the market around 1985, the home video industry was well-established. In order to make video more affordable, vendors realized they had to sell more product; however, the educational distribution market was set up to deal with the larger centers which were, in declining budgetary times, definitely not a growing market. Thus, a "building level" sales concept evolved—one of contacting individual building level personnel rather than just the regional center. Potentially, video gave vendors the opportunity to move into the building level markets, but the costs of direct marketing—sales representative calls and contacts, catalog mailings, direct mail flyers, and previewing—was prohibitive, especially considering the poor initial response by libraries. Also, educational vendors really did not know who to contact at the building level and, once contact was made, how to go about doing business. Most of the educational vendors did not see the consumer market as a threat and were not "forward-thinking" enough to view this fledgling market as having an adverse effect upon sales. As a result, educational market video prices were still out of reach of the average building level budget, but with consumer demand skyrocketing, librarians were forced into buying the lower-priced consumer product, and thus built collections without undertaking responsible collection management or investigating alternative methods of acquisitions. The ALA provided no guidance, standards, or core lists for libraries, and library schools did not offer any formal training for the general librarian. Therefore, many librarians took the easy way out. Bending to, and relying upon, patron demand to guide the selection process, many libraries purchased easily-obtainable features and blockbuster titles, available through highly visible distributors and jobbers like Sound Video Unlimited (now Baker & Taylor Video) and Ingram and Commtron (now Ingram Library Services, Inc.). Many librarians, responding to the overwhelming demand for videos, ordered titles from dealer/distributors because book jobbers had a poor selection of titles available at substantially higher prices.

In an effort to show how libraries fit into the overall scheme of the diverse videocassette market, seven discrete pieces of information, taken from the 1990 and 1992 National Library Surveys from ABC-CLIO and presented as a partial profile of all U.S. libraries with videocassette collections, are excerpted in the following statistics:

- 58 percent of libraries with videocassette collections held classic features, while 39 percent held current feature titles.
- Annual budgets ranged from $200 to over $35,000, with the average falling to $3,477 (public libraries); $630 (schools); $6,145 (academic); and $1,706 (special), for a total average of $2,620.
- 10 to 14 percent of libraries had per-title spending limits, with price ceilings ranging from $95 to $232, with an average of $128.
- The average per-title cost was very low overall, ranging from $36 to $53, with an average of $40.
- The video budget represented between 5 and 10 percent of the overall materials budget

of the library, with circulation ranging from 1.3 percent to 11.4 percent of total library materials annual circulation.

• Packaging and price are both very important to libraries. Over half of the libraries survey in the MacArthur Foundation survey reported a general price limit of $100 or less.

• Collections tended to reflect the sources for information available to the librarian. Many librarians choose videos from mainstream marketing vehicles such as glitzy jobber catalogs, direct mail, and flyers. Even though review sources for videos are now readily available, librarians do not use them to a great degree. However, those collections built on the basis of reviews are recognized to have more subject/genre breadth and depth than their narrow-focused, mainstream, consumer video counterparts.[2] The rank order for the most effective selection resources was as follows: (1) producer and distributor catalogs; (2) patron requests; (3) referrals from colleagues; and (4) producer and distributor promotional brochures.[3]

THE PLAYERS—THE CONSUMER MARKET, THE EDUCATIONAL MARKET, AND THE INDEPENDENTS

Prior to 1980, and even up to 1985, the video industry had three distinctly defined markets which did not interact with one another and, to a certain extent, distrusted one other. These three markets were the consumer market (home video), the educational market, and the independent market. The educational and independent markets comprised the remnants of traditional film companies which survived the transition from film to video. The home video market was born out of this transition fire, phoenix-like, targeting the individual consumer rather than the educational and institutional markets, and seeking a "grassroots" marketing program through rental and sell-through. At first, home video represented no real threat to the other markets because its product, full-length features, did not encroach on the educational or independent's turf. But as exponential growth continued and niches developed, a branch of the home video market, called special interest video, emerged causing much grief to the traditional markets because of disparate pricing and marketing problems. Then, beginning in 1987, an aberration of the educational/consumer markets developed. Special interest niche producer/distributors such as Karl Lorimar, International Video Network (IVN), Finley Holiday, Questar, Ambrose Video Publishing, and Pacific Arts Video formed the nucleus of a quasi-educational market which touted subject/nonfiction videos, some with public performance rights, offered at attractive, home video prices. The following pages will define these markets through a discussion of product distribution, production, and pricing.

The Consumer (Home Video) Market

Definition. The consumer video market is analogous with that ubiquitous phrase, "home-use only" video (aka home video), which expressly refers to rights granted to the copyright holder through United States Copyright law. Of particular interest to librarians and teachers, these rights take form in contractual law as public performance (also called nontheatrical exhibition) and "home-use only." As such, videocassettes with the labeling "for home-use only," as well as those with no labeling and/or ambiguous labeling, should be viewed only by individuals in a home setting. Group showing is strictly illegal. Home video has also taken on a pluralistic meaning—that of all feature and special interest videos available in retail stores and video outlets.

Feature Videos—Definition and Tiers. For the purposes of this book, a feature video will be defined as a full-length (i.e., more than 60 minutes running time), fictional work with a story plot, either live-action or animated. Feature films can almost always be pigeonholed into various genres such as drama, science fiction, fantasy, and action/adventure. Within the feature film industry, there are four recognized levels, essentially defining a title's distribution or "popularity" level: "AAA," a blockbuster title like *Batman Returns*; "A," a popular theatrical release subsequently released on video, such as *Sneakers* and *Howard's End*; "AB," a limited theatrical release or movie with lackluster theatrical performance, such as *Universal Soldier*; "B" and "C," titles with no theatrical release, such as a made-for-television special like *Sarah Plain and Tall*; or a special, made-for-video presentation like *Deep Cover*. Revenues from these "AAA" and "A" features as video products can be predicted by their box-office acceptance; however, some producers have tried to buck the trend, lowering prices on "AB," "B," and "C" titles in hopes of enticing video retailers and consumers to buy them. Features, even obscure titles, differ from other forms of video because they benefit from millions of dollars spent on advertising, and thus have a wider base of title awareness, if not popularity. Today, even a modest direct-to-sell-through title can move a minimum of several million units. Theatrical success usually translates well into home video success, but the "revolution" has created a new marketing dynamic: a film no longer has to do $100 million in box-office revenue to seriously contend for home video sell-through status. In 1992, for example, MCA/Univeral Pictures set a sell-through precedent by releasing *Beethoven*, which grossed less than $50 million at the box office.[4] That same video title ended up selling over 3.1 million units domestically at $24.95 each, or almost $78 million.

Distribution and Pricing. Until now, this text has used the words vendor and distributor interchangeably, but there is a distinct difference. Analogous to the book publishing industry with its printers, publishers, dealers, and jobbers, the video industry has its own hierarchical levels of manufacture and distribution, complete with its own unique nomenclature. In the book *Understanding the Business of Library Acquisitions*, contributor Charles Forrest notes that the motion picture entertainment industry encompasses three steps of production, distribution, and exhibition. Production is the creation of a work, being analogous to the manufacturing of a product. For the purposes of this discussion, a vendor is any person, organization, and/or business that sells videocassettes at wholesale or retail. The last step in the distribution chain is exhibition—a motion picture being shown for an admission price in theatrical release, rented in video stores and libraries, and sold in video stores and other retail consumer businesses.[5]

Distribution is the merchandising and sale of product across various markets on a regional and/or national basis. Home video unit prices (i.e., individual cassette prices) are so closely tied to distribution that it is difficult to separate the two concepts. From 1985 to the present, home video distribution has undergone considerable change and upheaval. Today, with the individual consumer as the primary target audience, home video is available through traditional retail markets such as book stores and supermarkets and other "nonspecialty" stores, as well as video rental stores as "sell-through" product. Libraries and schools purchase home video because of three factors: (1) much of the educational/independent product is unknown because of the lack of building level distribution of flyers and catalogs and the use of reviews by librarians for purchase; (2) prices remain high for educational and independent videos; and (3) consumer (i.e., patron) demand is so high that librarians feel obligated to invest in library video collections.

Historically, however, the distribution system was not always set up in that manner. Originally organized to sell product to video rental stores on a regional level, wholesalers like Metro, Commtron, and Star were loosely organized, designed mainly to generate quick sales of features for the rental market. These companies received competition from companies experienced in book store sales, such as Baker & Taylor and Ingram. Also, "remainder houses," like Publishers Central Bureau, quickly got into the act, creating a direct marketing channel to the consumer, as well as to institutions.[6] At the start of the video revolution, the film companies, wanting to retain control of video distribution, undertook the task of selling product through their offices. They soon found the process to be too costly and time-consuming, thus giving rise to the video wholesaler (aka jobber) and distribution industry. The arrival of the video superstore chains such as Blockbuster, Tower, and Erol's were soon outstocking the "mom and pop" shops. These chain stores seized the majority of the rental pie and, with their buying clout, commanded a new, more efficient method of distribution. New territories were being carved out and distribution consolidated after the buyout of Sound Video Unlimited and VTR by Baker & Taylor, the acquisition of Metro Video by Ingram, and the partnership of Major Video Concepts and Video Trend. Today, very few production companies handle sell-through, relying on these national and regional jobbers. These well-known and respected book jobbers, like Baker & Taylor Video and Ingram Library Services, who were now diversifying into videocassettes, placed themselves squarely into the chain of video distribution to libraries and book/video stores because of their existing markets, volume pricing, and available discounts. Soon, these companies were offering "one-stop shopping" for books, audiocassettes, compact discs, and videocassettes, as well as providing extra service amenities like automated ordering, preprocessing, cataloging, and large discounts and processing supplies.

Home video distribution is strictly a high-numbers game, with consumer outlets ranging from video stores to supermarkets. Emerging from a run of bankruptcies in 1989–1990, the number of video stores stabilized in 1991 with a total of 29,000 video rental stores along with 60,000 nonspecialty stores stocking video product for sale and/or rental. In 1992, total consumer spending for sell-through and rentals was $3,864,000 and $7,328,000 respectively.[7] During 1991, the home video market (feature market and special interest market) reached rental revenue totals in excess of $10.2 billion, and video sell-through (prerecorded videocassette sales) of $4.6 billion, outpacing the $8.9 billion book industry.[8] Combined rental and sell-through figures for 1992 were $14.89 billion,[9] with video sales (sell-through) accounting for $4.7 billion or better.[10] Chart 2.1 illustrates video distribution by type of retailer during 1990. Gary Hunt, Technicolor Video Services marketing and sales senior vice president, feels that the industry should emerge from its rut on the strength of sell-through, predicting a 37 percent jump to $19.3 billion by the year 2000.[11]

Individual title prices are figured on a formula of production/distribution costs plus expected profits divided by number of titles expected to be sold, as well as what the market will bear. In 1982, the sell-through market was a fledgling secondary market, with the rental market being the prominent profit maker. So when Paramount broke new ground in the sell-through market by breaking the $89.95 price barrier through its offering of *Star Trek II: The Wrath of Khan* at $39.95, the home video industry held its breath.[12] However, it worked very well and eventually, two-tiered pricing became standard operating procedure, with low and high-ends falling at $29.95 and $89.95, respectively. Assisting to lower sell-through video prices, commercial sponsorship of major movies released on video became prominent with the release of *Top Gun* in January of 1987. Over the past five years, the average cost of a consumer video title has dropped about 21 percent, from $19.53 to $15.46.[13]

Secondary "AB" and "B" titles also flourished in this new sell-through market. A "B" title shipping 40,000 units and under would be priced from $24.95 to $29.95 for sell-through, while a top grossing "AAA" title like *The Silence of the Lambs*, selling 300,000 to 500,000 copies, would sell for $79 to $99 in its initial rental release and then drop to a lower sell-through price of $15 to $20 to gain added sales. Larry Price, vice president of Ingram Library Services, Inc., calls this phenomenon "the paperbacking of video."[14] Commenting on the volatile nature of the consumer video industry, Randy Pitman, editor of the *Video Librarian*, notes that

From its inception video has been a "fast" business [hitting] the market by the score each . . . week, [shooting] to the top of the rental charts in four to five weeks, and then when initial interest died, [collecting] dust on video store shelves. The video store own-

Chart 2.1
Video Distribution by Type of Retailer

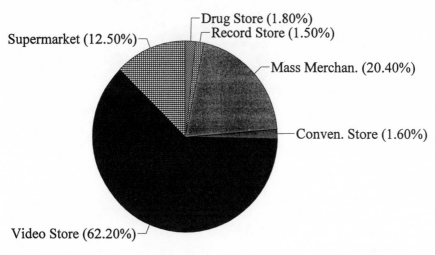

Drug Store (1.80%)
Record Store (1.50%)
Supermarket (12.50%)
Mass Merchan. (20.40%)
Conven. Store (1.60%)
Video Store (62.20%)

Source: Video Magazine Store research.

er's survival depended on buying the right number of copies to fulfill the public's demand, yet not be stuck with multiple copies of a title once interest had subsided.[15]

Chart 2.2 shows the percentage groupings within various retail selling price ranges within the home video marketplace for 1991, and Chart 2.3 illustrates 1991 video sales broken down into broad genre types (note that features are broken down into five categories).

Features—Movie Theaters and Video Distribution Avenues. In 1991, a typical blockbuster video title (an ''AAA'' title) which grossed over $100 million during its theatrical run sold more than seven copies per video retailer, while films which took in less than $5 million during its theatrical run usually shipped fewer than two copies (see Table 2.1, for further analysis).[16] Using this formula to determine the number of copies purchased in video rental stores for movies such as *Batman Returns*, as well as an unprecedented nine of 1992's top ten movies which grossed over $100 million in theatrical revenues, made 1992 a banner year. This segment will show how motion pictures released in video are affected by their respective theatrical releases and box office performance. A producer of movies, educational films, documentaries, or short subjects has the following distribution channels, used alone or in combination, available: foreign television; domestic television (commercial or public); pay-per-view (e.g., RequestChannel) or cable television; theatrical release, foreign or domestic; nontheatrical release, including colleges and libraries; and videocassette (and/or other formats) through vendors in the educational, independent, and/or·consumer markets.

Fifty years ago, Paramount, RKO, Warner Brothers, 20th Century Fox, and MGM all owned, or were owned by, major theater circuits throughout the United

Chart 2.2
Percentage of Unit Sales by Retail Price

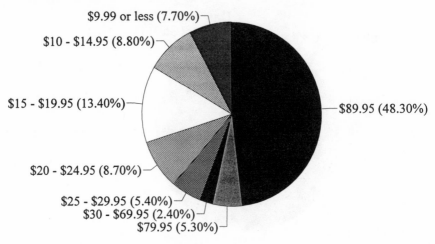

Source: *Video Magazine Store* research.

States. Such vertical integration guaranteed the studios exhibition for all their releases. Government statistics showed that in 1945 the five major studios had financial interest in 3,137 of the nation's 18,076 theaters (17.4 percent), which accounted for about 45 percent of the total box office revenues for that year.[17] In 1948, the Supreme Court, deeming that this monopoly was not fair to independent theater owners, passed the antitrust Consent Decree, which required film companies to divest themselves of theater ownership. But on October 21, 1981, the ban was lifted and, following Columbia's purchase of 31 percent of New York's eleven-screen Walter Reade circuit, a breathless succession of similar transactions followed involving such names as MCA/Cineplex Odeon, Gulf + Western/Mann Theaters, and Tri-Star Pictures/Loews Theatres. In 1988, it was estimated that seven major studios controlled 9,000 of the 24,000 theaters (37.5 percent) in the United States, accounting for 85 percent of total box office revenues.[18] Controlling production, distribution, and exhibition ultimately benefits a studio because they can exert control over a film's release strategy and influence advertising and demand. In July 1988, Vestron Video purchased about 50 video rental outlet stores in Cincinnati, Ohio and Manhattan. Richard Cohen, senior vice president of Walt Disney Home Video, feels that the nation's video retailers should not worry, citing that "The video retail base is so fragmented that in order to really make an impact you'd have to buy several hundred stores."[19] The many advantages for video companies owing retail stores include test sites for advertising campaigns, point-of-purchase (P.O.P.) displays and possible elimination of the middleman (the video distributor), enabling the company to sell direct to its own retailers.

Contrasted against the educational and independents' higher-priced video pos-

Chart 2.3
Percentage of Video Sales—Genres (Types)

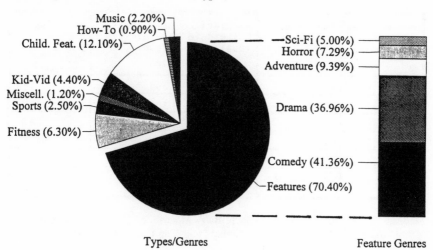

Types/Genres   Feature Genres

Source: Video Magazine Store research.

sessing nontheatrical public performance rights, home-use only, consumer video represents the low-priced end of the video spectrum. From 1979 on, after Andre Blay's Magnetic Video successfully licensed 50 major movies from Twentieth Century Fox in 1977, the major Hollywood studios and their subsidiary companies comprised the majority of the consumer market, relying mostly upon the blockbuster (''AAA'' and ''AB'' titles) theatrical release, box-office hits available on video and sold to video rental stores. Video rental stores were looked upon as the primary market, but today consumer sell-through is increasing its market share. In the beginning, the Motion Picture Association of America (MPAA) felt that videocassette rentals would destroy the movie industry. With rental prices being cheaper than the price of taking the family out to a movie theater, the movie industry would be decimated. However, around 1984, those same companies saw that they were mistaken. The number of video stores in the United States had soared to 15,000 and, although they received no royalties on a per-rental basis, they saw that the rental market was not necessarily a reflection of box-office popularity. Thus, ''B'' and ''C'' titles flooded the market—theatrical releases that had bombed and those with limited, regional releases found avid audiences in the rental market. During the late 1980s, home video decisively raced past the theatrical side of the business. In 1989, the $5 billion box office for combined theatrical releases seemed rather small in comparison to home video sales to consumers, estimated between $9 and $11 billion.[20] According to Robert Cohen, senior vice president of Buena Vista Home Video, ''video held an adversarial relationship with theatrical in 1980. Ten years later, video is the decisionmaker . . . [in 1987], contributing over 50 percent of

Table 2.1
1991 Box Office Analysis

Box Office Receipts (millions)	Number of Titles	Total Video Units Sold (000)	Ave. Units Sold/Title (000)	Ave. Numb. Copies Purch. by Video Stores
Over $100	6	2.415	402.5	7.8
$50 - 99.9	9	2.752	305.8	5.9
$25 - 49.9	23	4.917	213.8	4.2
$10 - 24.9	36	5.507	153	3.0
$5 - 9.9	35	3.836	109.6	2.1
Less than $4.9	61	4.894	80.2	1.6

Sources: Video Magazine Store research; Barry Monush, ed., *1991 Television & Video Almanac*, 36th ed. (New York: Quigley Publishing Co., 1991), p. 621.

studio revenues."[21] Prism Entertainment and LIVE Distribution seem to agree with this "B" movie release concept. The average "AAA" movie costs $40 to $80 million to produce, compared to the $1.5 million of a "B" movie. Prism ships 25,000 to 50,000 units to video stores across the United States at a wholesale price of about $50 each, thus yielding revenues of at least $1.25 to $2.5 million per title.[22] Experimenting with a "right price" concept, LIVE Home Distribution released a "B" title, *Waxworks 2*, and it became one of the top ten titles with respect to return on investment.[23] In the early days of video, so-called "blockbusters" were released well after the same feature had appeared at the box office. Today, video stores often see video release simultaneously or just after theatrical release. However, markets are prone to over-expansion, and video is no exception. A 16 percent decline in rental-priced videotapes ordered by video stores occurred in 1989, with much of that trend having to do with those stores ordering less of the burgeoning "B" titles.[24] Pay-per-view cable television movie channels are given windows of 30 to 90 days before the video release of a film and, in 1993, Tele-Communications and Carolco Pictures rewrote television history by exhibiting four movies on pay-per-view before their theatrical release.[25] Indeed, there is a wide variety of potential markets available to consumer video products. Recognizing the continued growth of sell-through video, George Feltenstein, vice president of MGM/UA Home Video, notes one of 1992's major events was the release of so much important product that went direct to sell-through, bypassing the higher-priced rental market. Moreover, the trend toward repriced catalog product, boxed sets, and both anniversary and special editions continued with greater fanfare than the year before.[26]

Special Interest Video

Definition. With the advent of *Jane Fonda's Workout* video from Karl Video, in 1982, the special interest video market was born. Companies like Vestron, Karl-Lorimar, Pacific Arts Video, MPI Home Video, and Kartes Video (KVC) started to produce a broad range of subject videos targeted toward specific groups, such as snow skiers, gardeners, quilters, exercise enthusiasts, and so on. The Special Interest Video Association (SIVA) defines special interest video to be all home video except feature films (U.S. and foreign), television titles (made-for-TV, variety shows, TV series), kidvid, concerts (musical and comedy), and adult video. While special interest videos broadly encompass everything but feature films, they are more specifically defined as "those features and non-features appealing to special interest audiences . . . including children's and educational titles."[27] This market is known by various names, such as self-help, nontheatrical, and alternative video. These programs were unique because many were "made for video" rather than television programs or theatrical releases just transferred to the video format. Table 2.2 lists the various genres within the special interest video industry, according to the Special Interest Video Association (SIVA).

Distribution. The sell-through concept took hold and video sales threatened to overtake rentals. As previously mentioned, the helter-skelter home video distribution patterns worked well for quick sales of highly visible features but broke down completely for the low-volume, relatively unknown but diverse special interest market. Instead of deep (multiple-copy) title purchases, single copies of many titles were required, delivered on a timely basis.

In contrast to the "fast" home video retail market, selling video to libraries is a slow business. One of the most notable differences in distribution is the lead time and waiting time involved in sales transactions. In home video, like theatrical releases, sales timing is crucial. Normally, new programs are released monthly, followed by a six-week selling period which also includes a pre-order date and a street/ship date. It is expected that, during the first month of release, the largest volume of any title is expected to be sold; therefore, distributors/ wholesalers servicing the market must warehouse sizable amounts of inventory. Also, in the retail market, the effects of a promotion or advertising campaign can be seen within one to three months. Direct mail ads work extremely well. Responses from libraries and other institutions typically arrive three months to one year after a promotion.[28]

Home video wholesale and retail distributors did not fully understand that the library market was completely different from the retail business with divergent wants, needs, attitudes, and decision making and buying/paying cycles. The arrival of special interest video ushered in a new breed of video distributor, or "middleman." With institutions as their primary markets, these distributors offered a smaller, preselected collection screened from the 7,000 to 10,000 available titles and marketed them via attractive catalogs, complete with full-color

Table 2.2
Special Interest Video Genres

* **Documentaries:** General * Art * Biography * History * Legal
* Medicine & Health * Military * Performing Arts * Politics &
Government * Religion * Science & Technology * Sociology

* **How-To:** General * Animals & Pets * Auto Repair & Maintenance
* Aviation * Boating * Child Care & Parenting * Computers &
Computer Technology * Cooking * Exercise, Fitness & Health *
Fashion & Beauty * Foreign Language Instruction * Gardening
* Health Care * Hobbies & Crafts * Home Repair & Improvement
* Legal * Mathematics * Money Management * Music & Musical
Instruments * Personal Growth * Sex * Sports & Recreation

* **Dance**
* **Nature & Nature Study**
* **Opera**
* **Sports:** Biography * Highlights & Matches
* **Travel and Travel Guides**
* **Wildlife and Wilderness**

Source: "Special Interest Genres," *Variety's Special*, I (September 28, 1989), p. 1.

pictures and annotations that read like reviews. These distributors, called "catalogers" because of their method of sales, became extremely popular with institutions. However, they offered product at retail or sometimes well over retail
price, and back orders were common because they stocked limited quantities of
titles or ordered "on demand" from wholesalers. Examples of catalogers are
The Video School House, Videotakes, Zenger Video (aka Social Studies School
Service), Library Video Company, Greenleaf Video, U.S.A. Information Service, and Instructional Video, Inc.[29] As a result, feature videos and special interest titles wound up in virtually every mail-order catalog and a booming
cottage, mail order video industry developed. "Remainder houses," such as
Publishers Central Bureau and Hotho Books, also offered videocassettes in their
catalogs. Holding aloft hefty price discounts as purchase incentives, it soon
became apparent that most titles ordered through remainder houses had to be
back ordered and took months to arrive. Customer service in many of these
companies was sadly lacking—no one knew anything about video or understood
library needs. Today, as special interest video has grown at the consumer level,
large wholesalers such as Baker & Taylor Video and Ingram Library Services
are offering the same product at substantially reduced prices, and these catalogers are finding it difficult to compete.

Many catalogers have expanded to the consumer level, and today there is
a plethora of retail catalog distributors like The Mind's Eye, Critic's Choice,
Signals, and Time/Warner Viewer's Edge. Video is everywhere—from 800-
numbers on cable television advertising *The Trials of Life* and *Where There's
a Will There's an A* to specialty catalogers like Signals and Sybervision offering
programs ranging from British television programs like *The Six Wives of Henry*

VIII and *Brideshead Revisited* to muscle-memory sports videos. Observing this rapid cornucopia of growth, Randy Pitman notes that

The number of "how to" videos [has steadily] grown. Every major area of human endeavor has been transferred to video. Exercise tapes, sports tapes, cooking tapes, tapes on hobbies, crafts, and the arts abound. But so do specialized programs on beekeeping, building a bike wheel, exercise for senior citizens, playing bluegrass fiddle, trekking in the Himalayas, preparing your last will and testament, passing the postal exam, and training your cat to do tricks. Wherever Melvil Dewey saw fit to place a decimal number, programming on video is likely to be available.[30]

While one can find a plethora of special interest titles and features, prices vary widely, and the unsuspecting librarian can wind up paying as much as two hundred percent more for the same title if they do not shop around. Many videocassettes do not carry sole distribution rights and are offered by multiple vendors at widely disparate prices. Companies such as HomeVision offer two-tiered pricing—one price for "home-use only" and another for public performance rights; however, these same public performance videos can be purchased at discount prices through wholesalers like Baker & Taylor Video. Also, Pitman recognizes that major wholesalers, as a general rule, do not carry specialty programs unless they have either a proven track record or a recognizable star.[31] However, an examination of Table 2.6 indicates that almost 54 percent of special interest videocassettes listed in *Variety's Home Video Directory* (now titled *Bowker's Complete Home Video Directory*) retail for under $40, while approximately 30 percent can be purchased for under $30. Today, the consumer video market is diverse—it includes not only "mom and pop" video rental stores, some of which provide sell-through product from rackjobbers, but large rental "chain" stores as well. Mail-order catalogs and telemarketing are also methods of reaching the consumer, as is advertising on cable television with easy ordering through 800 telephone numbers. Mail order video clubs are another method of advertising/marketing.

According to ABC-CLIO advertisements, libraries account for $250 million of the total $4.6 billion sales figure; therefore, by extrapolation, it can be determined that libraries comprise about 5.4 percent of the total consumer video market. While libraries do not seem to exert the substantial purchasing leverage upon the consumer video market as they do in the book industry (approximately 40 percent), it is nonetheless valuable to examine the following comparative charts and tables showing the relationships between library and video store collection composition, popularity/circulation, and industry genre production. Tables 2.3–2.6 provide a diverse picture of the popularity of feature genres and special interest video in video rental stores and libraries based on circulation (rentals), sales, survey popularity, and industry manufacturing (production and unit sales). This information is helpful, not only for predicting possible popularity, but also in assessing the difficulty of obtaining reviews and product re-

Table 2.3
U.S. Factory Unit Sales of Video by Genre, 1987 and 1993 (Projected)

Genre	Unit Sales 1987	% of Total	Unit Sales 1993	% of Total
Features	74,500,000	65.0%	135,200,000	65.0%
Children's	21,275,000	18.5%	45,760,000	22.0%
Music	2,300,000	2.0%	5,200,000	2.5%
Sports	2,300,000	2.0%	3,120,000	1.5%
How-to	1,150,000	1.0%	3,120,000	1.5%
Exercise	2,300,000	2.0	3,120,000	1.5%
Other	6,325,000	5.5%	6,240,000	3.0%

Source: Video Marketing Newletter (August 29, 1988), p. 5.

lated to industry production and availability. Please note that these tables contain information about both feature and special interest videos. Also note that these statistics have been gathered over a period of six years (1987–1992) and serve to emphasize certain points made in the text more than to reflect up-to-the-minute data. The statistics and data gathered by the video industry have changed substantially over those six years, and much of the data is no longer collected.

The Educational Market

Definition. Unlike the consumer video industry, it is difficult to define the educational market in isolation from methods of distribution, production, and pricing. It is in fact these three methods that distinguish the educational market from the consumer market. Traditionally, both the target sales audience and the public performance issues have served to separate and distinguish between the educational and home video markets. Thus, the educational market comprised those mainstream producers and distributors who were, prior to the video revolution, selling 16mm films to schools, libraries, colleges and universities, and other institutions, offering product that included public performance rights (group showing rights). Today, however, there are many quasi-educational producers/distributors targeting both the institutional and consumer markets, as well as educational markets with "home video" subsidiary companies. Some educational distributors have also teamed up with home video companies to produce product lines. Many times, this home video product comes with public performance rights as well. One company, Listening Library, serves as a prime example of this group. Established in 1957 to serve the needs of the educational market as a producer of unabridged, book-based audio, Listening Library expanded to include home video in its 1983 direct-mail catalog. In 1988, video accounted for about 15 percent of Listening Library's total sales. Of that 15 percent, 70 percent was sold to schools, 20 percent to public libraries, and the remaining 10 percent to individuals and other institutions.[32] Primarily including home video features in its catalog, Listening Library confused the public performance issue

Table 2.4
Rental/Sales of Prerecorded Videocassettes (From VSDA; Video Stores by Genre and Subject [1990] Compared with Available Market Composition)

Genre	Rentals	Sales	Prod. 1989
Movies	86.2%	40%	----
Actn/Advent.	25.9	13	3014
Comedy	31.8	13	2989
Classics	1.7	4	----
Drama	19.0	7	3904
Horror/Sci-Fi	5.8	2	1338
Foreign	----	---	2854
Sports	----	---	1848
Westerns	----	---	1155
Mystery	----	---	852
Musicals	----	---	420
Other	.6	---	569
Child/Family	10.5	44	3452
Non. animated	4.4	9	----
animated	6.1	35	2087
Exer./How-to	---	2	----
Music Video	.7	---	713
Document.	1.0	2	----
Other	.9	6	----

Sources: Variety's Special, Data Base Report I (March 15, 1989), p. 5; *Home Video: State of the Industry—1990* (New York: Fairfield Research, Inc.).

by listing its own product side-by-side with distributed "home-use only" product without including a disclaimer concerning "educational school use."

Distribution. The distribution of 16mm films was set up in a formal and structured orchestration involving personal contact, review/preview, and purchase. During the 1970s, the erosion of that structured environment began with mergers and buyouts among established film distributors. In the days of film, the producer was the sole distributor or was directly under contract with the distributor. As video usurped the market, structured distribution vanished with virtually unknown, second, third, and fourth parties gaining distribution rights to products originally held by well-known film distributors. Up until about 1985, educational distributors like MTI/Coronet, Churchill Films, Lucerne, and Encyclopaedia Britannica had a sales business composed of 80 to 90 percent film sales and 10 to 20 percent video. In 1992, it has turned around completely, to 90 percent video and 10 percent film. Today, the educational market is much more diverse and complex. Quasi-educational producers/distributors like Pacific Arts Video, MPI Home Video, Atlas Video, and V.I.E.W. Video have emerged, hoping to sell product to both institutions and a special niche consumer market.

In writing about the changing video distribution market, Peter Schillaci notes that

Traditional educational distributors have taken a number of initiatives [to combat the sale of home video to institutions]: releasing their [16mm] collections on video at low-

Table 2.5
Total Library Video Collection Makeup and Highest Circulation Ranking

Popularity of Videocassettes in Libraries by Genre and Subject

Genre	Pub. Lib. % coll.		Ranking by Highest Circ.
Current Movies	20%	(48.3%)	39%
Classic Movies	18		58
Children's	35	(33.5)	63
How-to	14	(7.5)	45
Educational	43	(8.6)	78
Exercise	4.2		
Performing Arts	10	(3.7)	42
Other	33		17
Music Videos	3.6		
Literature	20		57
Geog./History	16		59
Pure Science	14		50
Social Science	16		52
Language	9		30
Religion/Phil.	13		35
Pract. Science	14		39

numbers in ( ) indicate 1988 survey results.

Note: Genre/subject totals equal more than 100% because of cross-over responses in other categories. Highest circulation ranking is expressed as a percentage of total responses, **not** as a percentage of total circulation.

Source: Taken from The Survey Center, *Summary Report and Data Tables—1990 National Library Video Survey* (Santa Barbara, CA: ABC-Clio, 1990), p. 59.

cost; incorporating available home video programs [both features and special interest] into their catalogs; and entering the home video market through subsidiary companies or cooperative ventures.[33]

Recently, in an unprecedented movement, traditional educational film companies such as Films Incorporated and AIMS Media have either generated a low-cost video catalog or created subsidiary "home video" companies, such as Home Vision and Apollo Video. Films for the Humanities & Sciences has created a new home video entity, Evergreen Video, and includes home video titles in its catalog. Ambrose Video Publishing sells to both the consumer and educational markets using a two-tiered pricing system similar to Films Incorporated, one for "home-use only," the other for public performance. Many of these titles are marketed via telemarketing and through 800-number television advertisements by Time-Life Video. In 1989, Barr Films purchased Kartes Video, a special interest home video company based in Indianapolis, and successfully operated KVC Video until 1991. In 1987, Coronet/MTI Film & Video launched an unsuccessful attempt to become a "home video" distributor to the educational market by offering a collection of over 2,000 feature and special interest titles. Increased market penetration means increased advertising and overhead;

Table 2.6
Data Base Report—Relative Composition of Subject Videos

Overall Composition

Genre	% Composition
How-To	18.64%
Nature	4.76
Sports	29.77
History	5.67
Travel	6.66
Exercise	5.75
Personal Growth	6.16
Perform. Arts.	3.12
Document.	21.99
Hobbies & Craft	3.34

Note: Rental percentages indicate actual percent of 100%. Title numbers indicate actual numbers of titles counted by genre in Variety's Compete Video Directory. This is the last date such records were kept.

Source: Variety's Special I (September 28, 1989), p. 2.

therefore, many producers are forming partnerships with distributors and/or creating subsidiary consumer video companies. As a further example of the unprecedented growing integration of product between existing educational distributors and home video, the educational vendor Weston Woods, known for its quality animated adaptations of children's literature, in 1989 formed a subsidiary consumer video company called C.C. (Children's CircleR) Home Video to market selected groupings of their titles (originally selling for $150 and up) at $29.95. Recently, in an attempt to increase market penetration, C.C. Home Video reached a deal with Wood Knapp Video to distribute their videos to retail stores at a price of $14.95 per title.[34] The National Geographic Society has formed a similar partnership with Vestron Video (now distributed by LIVE Distributing). Wombat Films formed a subsidiary company, Brighton Video, to distribute its special interest, "home-use only" line. In 1991, the educational film giant Alschulz Companies purchased Wombat Films and Video, and in 1993, MPI Home Video acquired some of their product, distributing it to the home video market. Also in 1990, PBS Video sold the use of its label, PBS Home Video, to Pacific Arts Video for the coordinated development of a consumer line of PBS product, previously only available to the educational market.

Sales of educational 16mm films was traditionally handled through producer/distributor regional sales representatives. Gus Collins, long-time company and independent film sales representative, remembers the film market from the late 1950s to the present and describes the change:

Educational film companies aligned themselves with equipment distribution companies to sell product. Later, they relied upon an internal sales staff, branching off to regional, independent sales reps as a method to increase visibility and market penetration. Just as in the early days of library book marketing, before the emergence of jobbers like Baker & Taylor and Ingram, educational film sales reps would visit local libraries, showing their wares on a cyclical/call basis. While the role of independent sales reps has diminished, largely being replaced by a small staff of company sales staff who use the telephone rather than site visits, today's educational video marketing strategy has not changed significantly.[35]

The advent of video coincided with a sliding economy and a dramatic decrease in public funds. Even though video promised an increased sales population (number of institutions) potential, the educational market mindset had difficulty in justifying lower, per-title prices based on potential sales. As a result, prices stayed on the high side, equated with similar film product, and the potential sales audience was never fully realized.

Home video changed the marketing game significantly with "full-line" wholesalers like Baker & Taylor Video offering product from many companies at substantial discounts. In 1991, a video wholesaler, Professional Media Services, turned the tables on the industry. Previously marketing primarily "home-use only" videos to libraries, they started to offer the products of 32 educational video companies like AIMS Media, Coronet/MTI, Bullfrog Films, Guidance Associates, and The Media Guild. While Baker & Taylor Video has not adopted this marketing strategy, they do obtain much specialty product and indicate public performance rights when available.

The Independent Market

Definition. In 1990, funded by a Rockefeller Foundation project, National Video Resources undertook an assessment of the state of video buying and proposed suggestions for independent marketers. A report conducted by the Harvard Business School, entitled "Creative Marketing Strategy Field Study," summarized their findings within the public library, university, and school (K–12) video markets. The report's focus was independent alternative video, which it defined as "American and foreign independent features, social and political features, art programming and video arts and experimental film."[36] Independent AV consultant Sally Mason-Robinson defines independent video as

Both fiction features and documentaries, not produced by major studios or television networks. They include social documents with a point of view, animated films, personal statements by filmmakers, films based on quality children's books, portraits of artists, literary adaptations of short stories, satires, and many others. Many are too specialized for network television, many don't fit neatly into thirty- and sixty-minute programming slots, and some are too controversial for nervous programmers. In fact, it is this very specialization that makes them perfect for libraries.[37]

In short, the independent videographer/filmmaker is somewhat analogous to the vanity presses in the book world.

Distribution. In short, the independent market is comprised of a potpourri of small, fragmented, specialized videomakers, often working out of a basement or small facility, involved in all levels of production from scriptwriting to camera work. Today, almost anyone with a video camera can be an "independent filmmaker/videographer" (hereafter referred to as independents). There is not much difference between the special interest home video market and the independent market. Only price and distribution methods offer distinctions between the two markets and, as such, the two cannot be separated. Consider the independent filmmaker Ken Burns, whose landmark series *The Civil War* won many accolades in 1991. As an independent, he sought and received production funding from various foundations, businesses, and groups. Distribution and institutional video production rights were picked up by PBS Video and home video, and special interest rights picked up by Pacific Arts Video with distribution through Time-Life and other retail markets. Distributed by PBS Video with public performance rights, the multi-volume *Civil War* series sold for $450 and was discounted as low as $125. The home video version sold for $149.95. This two-target distribution effectively expanded the market and lowered the price for everyone. As it is with many videos today, *The Civil War* is an independent program that has effectively made the crossover into home video and expanded the market.

As with the *Civil War* series, product distribution in the independent market is up to the producer. Oftentimes the producer concurrently seeks distribution channels along with video duplication rights. Occassionally, television airing of a program initiates increased audience awareness and demand, which may act as an incentive for video distribution companies to buy the rights to that title. PBS Video's decision to unilaterally usurp "first choice" video distribution rights to all programs acquired for PBS television airing is only one way to acquire product. Various national and international film and video festivals are held throughout the United States, such as the American Film & Video Festival, National Educational Film Festival, and the Birmingham International Educational Film Festival.[38] Video distribution companies come to these festivals in the hopes of acquiring video rights.

Some independent filmmakers, such as award-winner John Matthews (of *Stanley and the Dinosaurs* and *Ralph S. Mouse*), work exclusively for one company (in this case, Churchill Film and Video). However, most independent videographers do not align themselves with one video distribution company, choosing instead autonomy and individual expression. These independents must then find distributors for their product or distribute them on their own. Product distribution and marketing is expensive and time-consuming, involving the printing of flyers and catalogs, identifying potential markets, getting names, mailing out those flyers and catalogs, telemarketing and follow-up, sending in product for review and for festivals/awards, and arranging for duplication. These intensive, self-contained marketing activities consume valuable time which might be better spent in the creative process, rather than being done by inexperienced and fledgling marketers. Tom Drews, Special Interest Video Association (SIVA) member and president of Quality Books, comments on independents marketing to libraries:

The logistics of selling to libraries is often more difficult than the acceptance of the product itself. Direct mail is one approach, but the response rate is generally lower . . . and there is a very good chance the mail piece will never be routed to the appropriate individual. Catalog inclusion may be another approach, but the title can get lost among the . . . other titles. The most successful response rate a video publisher will receive is by making a direct sales call on the [library]. The next obstacle is distribution logistics. Most libraries will order only a single copy . . . unit costs soar quickly when promotional costs, fulfillment costs and overhead [enter] into the equation of reaching a single library and subsequently receiving and shipping one copy of a video. Librarians are very reluctant to buy from an unknown source; there is no knowledge of product quality and no guarantee that the product will be received, [and] many direct mail solicitations require payment with the order [rather than accepting purchase orders].[39]

It is clear that distribution in the independent market is a extremely precarious activity, as well as an exclusively entreprenuerial activity. The number of bankruptcies per year per film companies have little to do with the companies' product or creative talent, but rather their understanding of the business end. Examples of independents who successfully market their own products are Davenport Films, Kaw Valley Film & Video, Flower Films, James Agee Film Project, and Berlet Films.

To make matters worse, many educational videos are being sold simultaneously, either by multiple distributors at radically disparate prices, or as a "home use only" version sold by one vendor and as an educational version, with public performance rights, by another. In 1981, Bullfrog Films, an educational producer/distributor of niche environmental films and videocassettes, was one of the first educational distributors to drop its prices down from the $200–$300 range to $100 per half-hour. Bullfrog normally sells about 300 or fewer units per title. This new pricing scheme did not work, because increased sales to offset a narrower profit margin never materialized.[40] Bullfrog's president, John Hoskyn-Abrahall, admits to feeling the pressure on distributors to reduce prices, especially considering the home video, special interest market. However, he also feels that independent producers will be the ultimate victims, stating that "The major public libraries which used to be a major market only buy operas and gardening videos."[41] While there are a plethora of cheaper special interest videos than before, that very demand that is exhausting production and driving down prices in the mass market is killing educational and independent markets.

ECONOMICS 101—MARKET COMPARISONS IN PRODUCTION AND PRICING

As a rule, libraries do not create new markets—they only react to them. Educational film producers and distributors were similarly slow to react to the changing market concerning the evolution of the consumer video market, as well as a realization of institutions' preference of the video format over film. The story of educational video pricing and the continuing conflict and resultant comparisons with the cost of home use video reads like a modern soap opera. Before a discussion of pricing and comparisons between home video and educational video are drawn, the history of film pricing, as well as production economics, must be shown.

Until about 50 years ago, almost all films were only available through rentals for a fixed fee, based on expected revenue from a theatrical market. A preeminent and long-time figure in the film world, Weston Woods' producer, Morton Schindel, feels that the rationale for film pricing grew from an established book production/pricing precedent:

A book that cost a dollar to print generally sold for five dollars—a multiple of five times its manufacturing price . . . the cost of printing ten minutes of [16mm] film was about $20, including the reel and can, so a film came to be priced at five times that amount [or] $100.[42]

Schindel also indicates that another factor directly influencing pricing is the estimated number of copies that can be sold. Research during the mid-1950s indicated that the best-selling film title was *The Red Balloon*, selling a total of around 700 copies. In those days, the production cost of a film was generally amortized over the sale of about 300 copies.[43] Today, film production costs, including film lab development expenses, have increased (quadrupled since 1970, according to Les Blank)[44] but film prices have remained virtually unchanged, staying at 1960s prices. Currently, individual film title prices range from $200 to $1,500 and up, and long-term leases (five-year plus) are still available, especially for full-length features.

The video revolution brought pricing to its knees. Schindel recalls Weston Woods' 1980 venture into video by filling an order for the Baltimore County School System for one hundred titles at a price of $50 each—that was the beginning of "low cost video."[45] Actually, Time-Life was the first to offer a substantial video title list, basing the selling price on a percentage of the film price rather than considering it as a new format and pricing accordingly. They even revamped their name to reflect the importance of the format, Time-Life Video. Reminiscent of Time-Life's pricing rationale based on the original 16mm film price, Filmakers Library follows a similar pricing structure: If a 30-minute film sells for $525 in 16mm film, the video should sell for $525 minus the differential in duplication costs. The film costs $120 to duplicate while the video costs about $5, resulting in a $115 differential. Thus, the $525 program would sell for $410. This pricing structure seems very archaic when the high costs of film lab developing are compared with low costs of slave duplicating and of the blank videocassettes themselves.[46] To librarians, price, especially between a title from an educational vendor and one from a home video producer, is a volatile issue. Today, price seems to be discussed as a singular, isolated issue, with the vendor mostly at fault. While the vendor does indeed maintain control over pricing, certain economic/distribution truths ultimately play a large part in price determination. The pricing of videocassettes, both in the consumer and educational markets, not only effects whether or not a title is purchased over another but also affects and influences vendor choices, selection, collection development and, ultimately, long-term circulation.

As previously stated, individual title price of any item is a direct result of measuring the cost of production plus reasonable profit gains (as incentives to sustain future productions) against the number of copies of that title which can be expected to be sold. No matter what market we are talking about, the formula is the same. The determination of any title's market potential is the easy part; the difficult and costly task is in attempting to increase that title's sales market. This section will explain the dynamics of production and price, offering market comparisons where appropriate.

The home video industry has a market potential of over sixty million households, while the educational/independent markets have a potentially small base of between 105,000 to 200,000 schools and libraries.[47] While selling to a larger market helps drive down the per unit price, even special interest consumer video producers can only expect to sell between 50,000 and 100,000 units of a given title. Sales between 300 and 1,000 units mean success for an educational producer compared to sales exceeding 400,000 for a home video feature. In the past, educational vendors sold primarily to the larger academic and public libraries, school systems, and districts, avoiding the building level markets because of the increased marketing costs. Therein lies the single major difference between a $15.95 video and a $300 video—the market base and the number of copies sold.

Educational producers often hold up public performance rights as the carrot for higher prices. However, many of the so-called home videos possess public performance rights from prices ranging from $9.95 to $125. It is somewhat perplexing that public libraries, over all other types, purchase videos with public performance rights but, in the same breath, state that those rights were of little importance regarding their initial selection.[48]

The home video industry recognizes the importance of marketing, specifically the role of expanding the market base, and increasing penetration by targeting niche groups of consumers. They also are uniquely aware of the laws of supply and demand, as well as the role of price in dictating sell-through success. While the giants such as LIVE Home Distributing and Disney dominate the video world, there is still room for smaller companies. An example of a smaller company is Kidvidz, competing through alternative marketing methods, such as book fairs and book clubs, focusing on institutional markets like schools, libraries, hospitals, and direct mail, and handling their own distribution. Jane Murphy, a partner in Kidvidz, feels that innovation and perseverance pay off and that "by putting a higher price on the product for the institutional markets, it becomes less costly to [succeed in those markets]."[49]

Contrasting the consumer video industry with the educational market, the former has a virtually unlimited potential market with the individual consumer as the target coupled with the realization that selling one million or more units of one title at $29.95 is easily possible. The educational market as a whole feels that their traditional institutional market base is not expanding (and in some areas is contracting). While they see that building-level market penetration is the key to future success, educational vendors are grappling with the economics of advertising and selling to this larger but extremely more segregated and diverse market. Peter Edwards, president of Atlas Video, feels that the potential market is the major factor in pricing videos. At the most, there is a potential customer base of 200,000 schools and libraries in the United States, compared with over sixty million VCR households in the consumer market.[50] Andrew Schlessinger, president of Library Video Company, sees the potential market for educational videos as follows: 3,500 colleges, 15,000 public libraries (main and branches), 10,000 junior high schools, 25,000 high schools, and 50,000 elementary schools.[51]

According to the *Bowker Annual Library & Book Trade Almanac 1991*, the average cost of videocassettes reviewed in *Choice, School Library Journal,* and *Booklist* was $169.21, down from highs in 1988 and 1985 of $262.08 and $333.94, respectively.[52] ABC-CLIO's *1990 National Library Video Survey* indicated that the majority of videos purchased by libraries fell in the $15–$35 range, with an average of $39.60 per title.[53] A new movie released on consumer video may appear at $19.95 or $89.95, while the majority of special interest titles fall between $19.95 and $59.95.[54] The average per-title cost was $39.60. The average running time of videocassettes purchased in 1989 was almost 30 minutes, with a per minute cost of $5.67.[55] *The Video Marketing Newsletter* correctly predicted a 1994 drop in the average price of feature videos from $40.67 to $25.52. Exercise videos dropped from $25.78 to $17.69; children's from $16.43 to $14.07; and how-to from $26.43 to $19.90.[56] As a comparison of prices related to the above statement, Table 2.7 shows the dispersion of special interest home video prices. It is interesting to compare these prices with those for feature videos presented in Chart 2.3.

Today, several major educational vendors are offering low-priced video product, as well as opening up consumer video arms. Weston Woods owns C.C. (Children's CircleR) Studios; Films Incorporated has HomeVision and Public Media, Inc.; and Lucerne and National Geographic have made deals with LIVE Distributing and Tristar/Columbia, respectively, for home video product distribution. Some companies such as Ambrose Video Publishing have successfully

Table 2.7
Special Interest Video Pricing by Percentage

Genre	Over $79	Under $20	Under $30	Under $40
Document.	5.6%	27.5%	28.4%	54.6%
How-to	5.4%	13.0%	32.2%	54.8%
Sports	1.6%	13.2%	27.6%	44.9%
All Other	2.3%	5.6%	29.1%	60.3%
Average (all SI genres)	3.2%	14.8%	29.3%	53.6%

Source: Variety's Special I (September 28, 1989): 2.

marketed their products simultaneously to both the consumer and institutional (educational) markets through direct mail and cable television advertising. PBS Video has sold the use of their label "PBS Home Video" to Pacific Arts Video for the consumer market. Disputes over "who could sell what product to whom" in the educational video arena have caused some problems with the PBS Video–Pacific Arts Video agreement. Also, Pacific Arts apparently misjudged the size and demand of the niche consumer sell-through group, causing some frustration on the corporate level about the success of selling subject videos of this type directly to consumers. These marketing changes have caused prices in the entire video industry to level out, but their wake has also caused considerable frustration for librarians involved in selection and acquisitions in dealing with pricing differences and public performance rights, and dealing with a wide range of distributors selling video at widely disparate prices. Librarians are asking questions to educational vendors like, "Why is there such a huge disparity in prices between consumer video and educational video?" and "Why is this video so low [priced], and this one so expensive?"

While we have established that the potential educational market of some 200,000 in the United States is a drop in the bucket compared to the vast ocean of the consumer market, the laws of supply and demand and recouping of costs still apply. Videos struck from 16mm films shot and released in the 1960s and 1970s still carry high prices. Certainly, those titles have recouped their initial production costs, so why the high price?

Jim Churchill, Marketing Director for Churchill Films, sheds some light on the subject of relative unit cost in the educational market. Depending on production techniques, running time [length], use of well-known performers and directors, and so on, the production costs of an educational film may run between $30,000 and $125,000. The ALA puts the number of public libraries currently possessing video collections at about 9,000, or 60 percent of 15,000. However, Quality Education Data indicates that there are only 930 main and 1,323 branch public libraries with video collections—2,253 in all. Using a $50,000 production cost as an example, Churchill's extrapolations reveal that unit sales of 477 at $300 per video would break even. Comparatively, if the title sold for $50, sales of 2,858 would be needed to break even.[57] If only half of the 9,000 libraries (4,500) were to purchase a Churchill video at $300, the revenue would total $1,350,000, and $225,000 at the $50 price. Atlas Video's Peter Edwards and John Pardos of Twin Tower Enterprises feel that they must sell 18,000 or 100,000 units of a title in one year, respectively, at $19.95 and $14.95 in order to break even.[58] Both Edwards and Pardos realize the futility of marketing only to the educational market. Edwards markets his products primarily through bookstores, catalogs, and wholesalers. His outlets include Waldenbooks, Book-of-the-Month Club, Reader's Digest, and the Signals and Wireless catalogs.[59] While recognizing that institutional penetration is the key to increased sales and lower prices, Churchill does not want to become a "warehousing/distribution/mass mailing organization," feeling that attempting to increase penetration to reach the 2,858 is not their goal. As much as 35 percent of the per unit sales price is gross profit, paying for lab costs, free previewing, sales costs, and other costs of doing business, including making more films.[60] Frank Visco, President of Lucerne Film & Video, and Bill Ambrose, President of Ambrose Video Publishing, feel that the time has come for the educational market to acknowledge and work with the consumer video industry.[61] Defining his company as a "boutique video publisher," Ambrose feels that by selling his product to both consumers and institutions, even though the system uses two-tiered pricing, his company can offer quality product at lower prices for both groups than would be otherwise available through marketing to one group alone. He also feels that the vendor's practice of dangling the carrot of public performance in front of the purchaser as a defense for charging a higher price is no longer valid.[62] Ambrose Video Publishing is somewhat unique in that the company does not produce its own product. Product is acquired by purchasing the distribution rights of programs which have already been produced or by underwriting the cost of production in turn for video distribution rights. Video production has a narrow range of profitability, and Ambrose believes that the industry should be considered a "portfolio business," with a few titles outperforming the rest to level out a company's retail price structure. The cost of acquiring product, such as the heralded *Trials of Life* series, may range from $15,000 to $100,000. However, the costs involved in marketing that same series, such as catalog printing, advertising, and packaging can range from $30,000 to $250,000. Sales "reps" can make anywhere from 10 to 30 percent of the sales price, depending on how willing they are to discount a price to get/keep a customer. Within this narrow range of profitability, Ambrose tries for a five-year return on investments. He feels that the key for the 1990s in educational markets will be market penetration.[63]

In terms of production costs, the independent filmmaker has a much tougher row to hoe. They are intricately involved in the process of fundraising, and foundations, government, and endowments like the National Endowment for the

Humanities, entrepreneurs, and friends and family play important catalytic roles in pioneering independent productions. If and when funding is found, there is no guaranteed market, and only the very lucky ones get their programs aired on PBS, the Arts & Entertainment network (A&E), or some other cable channel. Most independents are not versed in the aspects of marketing and view video as an outlet for their art—leaving the selling for someone else as a secondary result of the program's existence.[64]

Many independents are sold by single-source educational distributors rather than by the larger video jobbers, or are marketed directly to "targeted" institutional audiences by the independents themselves. Pricing in the independent market is one of the most misunderstood aspects to librarians. Often, the latest feature can be purchased for $24.95. Why should a library with a limited budget pay $200 and up for a documentary of which no one has heard? A feature film has had the advantage of sell-through market penetration with unlimited sales potential, while even a runaway best-seller in the independent market will never sell more than a few hundred copies.[65] Hollywood's recent blockbuster features, like *Dances with Wolves*, *GoodFellas*, and *Reversal of Fortune* moved over 655,000, 340,000, and 158,000 units, respectively, upon release (from release until August 1992).[66] The 1990 television hit *Lonesome Dove* has recorded over 850,000 unit sales since August of 1991. *Lonesome Dove*'s distributor, Cabin Fever, feels that this is a result of substantial price decreases, from an initial $99.95 suggested list price down to $39.95 in SP (standard play) mode, to only $19.95 in EP (extended play) mode. By contrast, since release in 1986, the special interest title *Jane Fonda's Workout* has only sold over one million units, but can be considered a "whopping" success in the special interest market. However, as an average, a consumer special interest title can be expected to sell anywhere from 7,400 to 12,000 units during its lifetime. Only a select few special interest videos sell upwards of 27,500 to 50,000 units for the life of the tape, with even fewer reaching the 100,000 mark. At the extreme end, producers of educational videocassettes may often sell only 300 to 1,000 units of any titles throughout that title's life. Linda Gottesman of Filmakers Library, Inc. feels that price should be based on the perceived/expected type of use and number of people who will use a title during its life. She uses the analogy of a book being used only by one person and a class using the same book, purchasing multiple copies. Price to Gottesman, then, is like an insurance policy against possible misuse. Price for a public library might be based on the expectation of use (and misuse) by a large number of people.[67] Although related specifically to the low-end priced special interest market, represented by the SIVA, Tables 2.8 and 2.9 provide some basic information concerning production/distribution costs and profits of independent video.

Two-tiered Pricing. Tiered pricing is the practice of producers offering a video at one price to a certain clientele and a different price to another clientele. Often a distinction in clientele is made between an individual versus an institution or organization/business. Other times the distinction is made pertaining to the fore-

Table 2.8

Division of Program Revenues for the Typical $29.95 Videocassette

```
30% will go to the retailer,
25% to marketing and distribution,
13% to the wholesaler,
12% to royalty payments,
2% to co-op advertising,

leaving 18% profit, or about $6.28. In the case of a $19.98 retail
price, the profit is only $2.68 per unit sold.
```

Source: "Some Statistics for Thought ... and Comment," *SIVA News* II (June 1989): 3.

casted use; for example, home use or public performance. More often than not, schools and colleges are regarded as educational institutions but, generally, public libraries do not fall within the educational category. Essentially, Films Incorporated has a two-tiered pricing system based on public performance rights or home use. However, Films Incorporated calls this marketing "cross-selling," because the three divisions, Films Incorporated, Public Media Incorporated, and HomeVision sometimes sell the same product to different clientele. But, particularly with the *Wonderworks Family Movie* series, their marketing scheme fails to hold true. A library may buy directly from Films Incorporated, either purchasing product with public performance rights, for an extra $10 per title, or the "home-use only" version for suggested retail. In many cases, the public performance version is already available from a wholesale "jobber," like Baker & Taylor Video, at discounts varying from 10 to 35 percent off retail price. Bullfrog's John Hoskyn-Abrahall has "mixed feelings" about the multi-tier price structure, "fearing it will breed resentment for major institutions." However, both Linda Gottesman of Filmakers Library and Gary Crowdus of The Cinema Guild are intrigued by tiered pricing. Crowdus is contemplating a three-tiered pricing structure based on public performance rights for institutions and individuals, a lower price for use without public performance rights for institutions, and a "bargain basement" price for home video. Gottesman feels that there is a precedent for tiered pricing to institutions in periodical subscriptions, and argues that "universities and large public libraries can and should pay more because of the increased use they will get from the videos.[68] Les Blank, owner of the independent film production company Flower Films and Video, has instituted such a three-tiered pricing structure for his videos. Starting with an initial per title price of $350, he has dropped his prices for colleges and universities to $150 and $250 for half-hour and one hour videos, respectively. Public libraries, high schools, community colleges, and special interest groups are offered the same product at $99.95 (including public performance rights). Blank has also expanded into the home video market by offering the same product, without public performance rights, for $49.95 to $59.95 each.[69]

Table 2.9
Book Publishing versus Niche Video Publishing
(special interest/independent)

A comparison of the economics of home video [special interest]
publishing versus nonfiction adult book publishing:

	Books	Video
Retail price	$20-25	$15-40
Discount to distributor	43-50%	38-45%
Net to publisher	$10-15	$9-24
Royalties	$10-15%(retail)	$10-20%
Advance	$5,000-$400,000	$5,000-$100,000
Cost of goods sold	$1.50-$2.50	$4.00-$6.00
Advertising	$50,000-$100,000	$10,000-$50,000
Returns (unsold units)	100%	10-50%
Contribution to overhead	4-24%	9-30%
Average operating profit	14%	12%

Source: "Some Statistics for Thought . . . and Comment," *SIVA News* II (June 1989):
   3.

FINDING ANSWERS—SO WHAT DOES IT ALL MEAN?

There is a tendency for new video buyers to equate video prices with those
of books, and thus, they never purchase the high-priced educational or independent titles, despite collection needs. Comparison pricing is not practiced
enough—meaning that the selector seeks alternative, lower-priced avenues for
acquiring the same title. Alternative avenues may take many forms including,
but not limited to, off-air taping, purchasing the program without public performance rights, and seeking other vendors. Pat Lora, columnist for *Wilson
Library Bulletin*'s "AV Frontier," cites some interesting statistics: "Although
[sixty] percent of the 16,000 public libraries have video collections, the number
of libraries buying independent video remains at the pre-video-era figure of
approximately 400 libraries."[70] Reflecting on these findings, Lora feels that libraries with 16mm film collections have simply transferred their broadly based,
balanced collection-building practices to the video format, rather than expanding
the collection because of lower prices and more available product.[71]

The threat of high video prices with no libraries willing to purchase them is
real and threatens to kill the already starving educational and independent markets. This fragmentation of the video market is clearly evident in the Spring
1993 dissolution of the American Film and Video Association (AFVA). Once
a stalwart buoy in the media ocean, the AFVA has lost its member and industry/
vendor support. A Harvard report comments on the changes in video sales and
marketing by stating

Buyers in the institutional market perceive[ed] low-cost commercial video as a viable
substitute for educational and cultural video. . . . Large vendors with established ties to

libraries have entered this market . . . threatening competition to small independents, whose prices are often much higher and who lack the distribution scale and efficiencies of these large enterprises.[72]

In the previous segments, pricing has been discussed in terms of market potential and the recouping of production costs. While the selector chooses the titles and in some instances also the vendor, many times the price paid for the title and the vendor purchased from will be at the discretion of the acquisitions personnel. It is difficult to formulate a consistent methodology for buying any medium when the price split is so disparate—on the home video end the price split may be between $10 and $90, and between $50 and $1,500 on the educational/independent ends. There is no analogous situation for hardcover books; novels do not come in rental or sell-through versions directed toward the educational or consumer market. By contrast, however, hardcover books carry a fairly consistent average price while videocassettes have widely disparate prices.

Recent surveys initiated by ABC-CLIO on the videocassette business in libraries indicated that only 11 percent of responding libraries had a limit on how much could be spent in any one video category, but 19 percent had single title limits with an average limit of $128 per title.[73] Based on a 1–6 scale of importance (6 being the highest), subject and intended audience ranked above price, with scores of 5.60, 5.10, and 5.06 respectively—all ranking slightly above quality and availability.[74] Librarians have always been highly commended for their ability to stretch budgets. Sometimes, however, these penny-pinching tactics severely restrict selection and collection development when they artificially limit purchases above a certain dollar amount. Commenting in a *Library Journal* article, Mark Pendergrast noted that

There are more and cheaper videos available than ever before. . . . The bad new is: only videos appealing to a mass market may survive in the capitalist shakeout of the next few years. The equivalent scenario for books would be one in which mass market paperbacks put all other books out of business.[75]

Educational video producers often complain about the economics of selling their products versus selling consumer, "home-use only" video, stating that variety is at risk, putting in its place "formula programs." If educational vendors go out of business, the video market will be devoid of a certain subject breadth, freshness, freedom of expression, and alternate viewpoints that have traditionally been supported by libraries. Gene Feldman, president of Wombat Film & Video (now owned by the Alschult Company), echoes these sentiments by stating, "The rush to low-cost video will destroy distinguished films aimed at a limited market . . . libraries should be treasure houses, not warehouses. People should go there to look at jewels with long-term value."[76] These jewels are the essence of the "demand versus quality/need" controversy which today pervades librarianship no matter what format is discussed, boiling down to two issues: dwindling budgets pitted against increasing available product and the blurring of lines as to the mission and purposes of any library. In addressing both the demand versus quality/need issue and the rationale for purchasing home-use only video instead of the more expensive educational/independent titles, Pat Lora, audiovisual head for the Toledo-Lucus Public Library in Ohio, feels that in buying low-cost video, one "gets [one-hundred] pennies for every dollar spent, but [in the end] does not have any titles that are worth more than one penny."[77] The aforementioned quotes alone serve to exemplify the lack of thought behind librarians placing ceiling restrictions on "per title prices" or "per minute running time" while simultaneously serving to open discussion for Chapter 3's topics of vendor types and copyright.

Currently, the independent and educational markets feed off one another—the mainstream independent programs being picked up and distributed by educational vendors via film festival entries and informal lines of communication with independent producers. Independent productions and libraries are extremely compatible for several reasons. Most video stores do not carry them, theaters do not show them, and television airs only a small percentage of them. However, problems in distribution make it difficult for librarians to identify, verify, and purchase these programs. Educational and independent vendors must find ways to break into the building level market, thus expanding their market potential.

As previously mentioned, educational vendors are slowing widening their horizons in that direction by developing coordinated marketing plans with consumer video producers, offering the same title with either public performance or home-use only rights. However, this new distribution effort has also made purchasing more complex. Now, librarians must assess use (home-use or public performance), do comparison shopping, and seek out the distributor offering the best price for that use. Librarians must also act in a positive fashion to change the pricing situation by revamping policies which reflect artificial price barriers, seeking out eclectic and broad-based review sources such as *The Video Rating Guide for Libraries*, *Sightlines*, and *Booklist*, and developing a new, long-term understanding of video in libraries other than just for short-term entertainment. Video prices must not be equated with prices of hardcover books. This does not mean that librarians should acquiesce and pay exorbitant prices for those titles; rather, it means that they should buy based on demand, need, overall collection value, and use. Dr. Jean Kreamer's findings that producer and distributor catalogs, patron requests, colleague referrals, and promotional brochures all ranked above reviews as the most effective [i.e., most used] resources in selecting video is most distrubing.[78] Now that expanded, broad-based video review sources are available to librarians, they should be used. Librarians should make concerted efforts to collect educational and independent vendor catalogs and make contact with vendor representatives. Prices are always negotiable, and communication is the key. It is clear than if price changes in the marketplace are to occur, both the vendors and the librarians will have to learn more about each other, be sensitive to the issues, and be willing to experiment with the current distribution network, widening attitudes and changing selling/purchasing behaviors in the process.

SUMMARY

This chapter has defined the three diverse but integrated prerecorded video-cassette markets—consumer (home video), educational, and independent—and provided a detailed synopsis of each market environment, complete with production, pricing, and marketing information. But what does all this information mean to the video acquisitions librarian? As the librarian hones his/her skills, this information will prove invaluable in making initial vendor contacts and conducting discount price negotiations, as well as making the wisest choices for vendor selection based upon perceived library needs/use.

NOTES

1. John P. Dessauer, *Book Publishing: A Basic Introduction*, new expanded ed. (New York: Continuum Publishing Co., 1989), pp. 148, 149.

2. The Survey Center, *Summary Report and Data Tables—1990 National Library Video Survey* (Santa Barbara, CA: ABC-CLIO, 1990), p. 8.

3. Jean T. Kreamer, "Statistical Survey 1992," unpublished, done for ABC-CLIO, 1992, p. 12.

4. Jim McCullaugh, "Vid Retailers Value Hollywood Emphasis on Family Films," *Billboard* 105 (May 29, 1993): 104.

5. Charles Forrest, "The Nonprint Trades," in Karen A. Schmidt, ed., *Understanding the Business of Library Acquisitions* (Chicago, ALA, 1990), p. 225.

6. Peter P. Schillaci, "Speciality Video Sources: Balancing Your Library Collection or Buying by the Pound?" *Sightlines* 20 (Summer/Fall 1987): 7.

7. Barry Monush, ed., *Television & Video Almanac*, 36th ed. (New York: Quigley Publishing Co., 1991), p. 610.

8. "On Home Video, Hope for Upturn," *Chicago Tribune*, May 26, 1992, sec. D, p. 13.

9. Seth Goldstein, "Duplicators Dub Sell-Thu Tops," *Billboard* 104 (December 12, 1992): V1.

10. Jim McCullaugh, "The Year That Was: Finishing Better Than It Started," *Billboard* 105 (January 9, 1993): V2.

11. Goldstein, "Duplicators Dub," p. V1.

12. Tony Cohen, "Video Rewind—1975–1989," *Video Software Magazine* 5 (December 1989): 28.

13. Goldstein, "Duplicators Dub," p. V1.

14. Larry Price, "Q & A: What Price Video?" *Sorting It Out: An Ingram Newsletter for Librarians* 10 (July 1992): 2.

15. Randy Pitman, "A Tale of Two Cultures: The Video Business and Libraries," *Wilson Library Bulletin* 62 (May 1988): 28.

16. Monush, *Television and Video Almanac,* p. 605.

17. Max J. Alvarez, "When Studios Own Theaters," *Video Software Dealer* 4 (December 1988): 36.

18. Ibid.

19. Ibid., p. 40.

20. Jack Schember, "Don't Yearn for the Good Old Days," *Video Software Magazine* 5 (February 1990): 12.

21. Ibid.

22. McCullaugh, "The Year That Was," p. V2.

23. Ibid.

24. Monush, *Television and Video Almanac*, p. 605.

25. Don Jeffrey and Seth Goldstein, "Video Retailers Troubled by TCI, Carolco PPV Venture," *Billboard* 105 (May 8, 1993): 1.

26. McCullaugh, "The Year That Was," p. V2.

27. Peter P. Schillaci, "Specialty Video Sources," p. 7.

28. Lois Kramer, "A Large Publisher's View of Video in Libraries," in Martha Dewing, ed., *Home Video in Libraries: How Libraries Buy and Circulate Prerecorded Home Video* (Boston: G.K. Hall & Co., 1988), p. 29.

29. Schillaci, "Speciality Video Sources," p. 7.

30. Pitman, "A Tale of Two Cultures," p. 40.

31. Ibid., p. 30.

32. Timothy Ditlow, "A Distributor's View of Video in Libraries," in Martha Dewing, ed., *Home Video in Libraries: How Libraries Buy and Circulate Prerecorded Home Video* (Boston: G.K. Hall, 1988), p. 42.

33. Peter S. Schillaci, "Speciality Video Sources," p. 8.

34. Loretta MacAlpine, "Wood Knapp to Boost CC Studios," *Video Insider* 9 (April 7, 1992): 1.

35. Interview with Gus Collins, Ambrose Video Publishing Sales Representative, March 12, 1992.

36. Pat Lora, "AV Frontier—Harvard Report Challenges ALA, and ALA Pulls the Plug on Video," *Wilson Library Bulletin* 65 (September 1991): 70.

37. Sally Mason-Robinson, "AV Frontier—A Declaration for Independents," *Wilson Library Bulletin* 65 (December 1991): 68.

38. See list of festivals in Irene Wood, comp., "Festivals and Awards," in Jean Thibodeaux Kreamer, ed., *The Video Annual 1991* (Santa Barbara, CA: ABC-CLIO, 1991): 75–95.

39. Tom Drews, "Selling SI Videos to Libraries," *SIVA News* II (June 1989): 3.

40. Mark Pendergrast, "A Window on the Video Price Wars," *Library Journal* 115 (May 15, 1990): 37.

41. Ibid., p. 35.

42. James Scholtz, Les Blank, and Morton Schindel, "Video Pricing: Three Perspectives," *Sightlines* 25 (Fall 1992): 16.

43. Ibid.

44. Ibid., p. 15.

45. Ibid.

46. Pendergrast, "A Window on the Video Price Wars," p. 37.

47. Ibid., p. 34.

48. Kreamer, "Statistical Survey 1992," p. 7.

49. Tomm Carrol, "Sports and Kidvid," *Video Software Magazine* 5 (March 1990): 32.

50. Pendergrast, "A Window on the Video Price Wars," p. 34.

51. Ibid., p. 36.

52. "Table 8/U.S. NonPrint Media: Average Prices and Price Indexes, 1984–1989," *Bowker Annual Library & Book Trade Almanac 1991* (New York: R.R. Bowker, 1991), p. 516.

53. The Survey Center, *1990 National Library Video Survey Summary Report and Data Tables* (Santa Barbara, CA: ABC-CLIO, June 1990), p. 46.

54. "Table 8—U.S. Nonprint Media," p. 519.

55. Ibid.

56. "Children's, Music Programming to Nearly Double in Dollar Volume by 1993," *Video Marketing Newletter* (August 29, 1988), p. 5.

57. Jim Churchill, "What's a Fella to Do? The Dilemma Facing Small, Independent Producers/Distributors of Video to Libraries," *Public Libraries* 26 (Winter 1987): Fast Forward section, p. 2.

58. Pendergrast, "A Window on the Video Price Wars," p. 34.

59. Ibid., p. 35.

60. Churchill, "What's a Fella to Do?" p. 2.

61. Personal interviews with Frank Visco, president, Lucerne Film & Video, and Bill Ambrose, president, Ambrose Video Publishing, Atlanta, GA (June 28, 1991).

62. Personal interview with Bill Ambrose, Chicago, IL (March 23, 1992).

63. Ibid.

64. Ibid.

65. Mason-Robinson, "AV Frontier," p. 69.

66. Bob Strauss, "What's an Oscar Worth to Video?" *Video Software Magazine* 7 (March 1992): 12.

67. Linda Gottesman, conversation at National Film & Video Market, Phoenix, AZ (October 22, 1993).

68. Pendergrast, "A Window on the Video Price Wars," p. 37.

69. Scholtz, Blank, and Schindel, "Video Pricing," p. 15.

70. Lora, "AV Frontier—Harvard Report," p. 70.

71. Ibid.

72. Ibid., p. 71.

73. The Survey Center, *Summary Report and Data Tables*, p. 8.

74. Ibid.

75. Ibid., p. 35.

76. Ibid., p. 37.

77. Pat Lora, presentation at PLA's Very Best Workshop (Chicago, IL), May 15, 1992.

78. Kreamer, "Statistical Survey 1992," p. 11.

3

Distribution Routes and Vendors Defined

The selection and acquisition of nonprint materials is generally considered to be more difficult, complex, and time-consuming than for print materials. This is due in part to the ways in which the prerecorded videocassette distribution market is set up, with its three distinct categories of home video, special interest video, and educational video. Even when purchasing from large wholesale jobbers like Baker & Taylor Video, Ingram Video Services, or Professional Media Services, there is quite a lot of product that is currently unavailable. A diverse portfolio of various types of vendors is needed, and this diversity is precisely what causes many problems in acquisitions. Selecting videocassettes is largely analogous to purchasing serial/journal subscriptions. A large jobber like Faxon or Ebsco can be utilized for many titles; but a great number of title subscriptions must be purchased directly from the publishers. This method requires additional staff time to process orders assuring no duplication, special order handling due to each publisher's different ordering methods, and different payment schedules and methods. In a 1990 *Library Trends* article, librarian Charles Osburn identified five barriers toward acquiring any library item, three of which serve as an appropriate introduction to this chapter:

- selecting from vendor catalogs because of convenience;
- selecting from certain vendors because of dislike of others [use of jobbers rather than distributors, producers, and independents because of added paperwork]; and

• difficulty in acquiring certain materials [and verifying their existence and vendor avail-
ability][1]

Vendor choice can have a great positive or negative impact on a materials
budget. Usually, vendor choice is made serendipitously—whatever catalog
comes across the selector's desk having that title in it is the one from which it
is ordered. However, in most cases there may be many vendors available for
that same title. Vendor choice should be made carefully after considering factors
such as price, discount, fill-rate, back-order status, ability to deal with library
order/payment methods, order convenience, geographic location/proximity, good
customer service, and special, value-added services. Vendor choices made in
such an educated fashion may save the library hundreds of dollars, effectively
translated into many more items available to be purchased with the same funds.
This chapter will assist librarians in making a more educated vendor choice. It
will categorize vendors by type, primarily focusing on services offered, and
detail the advantages and disadvantages of dealing with each type.

SEEKING TO CATAGORIZE VENDORS BY TYPE

Books can be divided into two distinct categories based on their content genre:
nonfiction and fiction. Likewise, videocassettes can be divided into two similar
content genres, called features and nonfiction video, sometimes referred to as
"educational" and/or special interest video (referring to their niche market). In
Buying Books, author Audrey Eaglen further separates book publishers by size
and type: alternative; small; independent and vanity publishing; reprinters; association publications; and government publications. Basically, book and video
vendors/publishers are categorized according to three factors: the nature of their
producers (publishers) and the types of materials they specialize in; the books'
intended audience or market; or the method of their distribution to that audience.[2] Based on these criteria, the Association of American Publishers (AAP)
categorizes book publishers into ten types: trade; religious; professional; mass
market paperbacks; university press; elementary/secondary textbooks; college
textbooks; subscription reference books; mail order publications; and book
clubs.[3] In the book world, the publisher may sometimes act as the distributor.
Similarly, in the video marketplace, the producer may distribute product in much
the same manner as a book publisher. Using a similar categorization technique
based on the aforementioned factors, the video distribution industry can be segmented into the following groups:

Home-use only

1. Blockbuster features (A titles)

2. B, C, and D features—these are features which have enjoyed theatrical release and
   failed, have had only limited (regional theatrical) release, or have had no theatrical
   release.

3. Previewed video market. Analogous to the second-hand and out-of-print (aka moratorium titles) book trade, the used video market sells blockbuster features "AAA," "A," AB," and "B and C" titles, as well as moratorium titles, on 60-, 45- and 30-day windows at a fraction of their list/discounted price. These prices even beat early sell-through discounting.

4. Special interest—these are nonfiction, subject-oriented videos produced for the home-use only, consumer market. Many titles are produced with a specific niche population in mind (aerobics, fitness, bicycling, etc.), hence the phrase "special interest."

   A. Subscription video magazines

   B. Video clubs—Columbia House is a good example. Join up and get five videos for free, after which one must buy seven videos within the next year at member (list) prices.

Educational (noncommercial public performance)

1. Features

2. Specific subject—curriculum related

University productions

Vanity productions (self-funded productions)

Independent producers

Government and industry productions/producers

Public domain/out-of-copyright productions—sold by individuals and/or companies, usually not advertised

As in the book trade, the type of video often offers clues for choosing the best acquisition route.

Vendors Defined

In the book world, there are seven somewhat hierarchical levels within the creative publishing arena: author; printer; publisher; wholesale distributor/jobber; retail bookseller and dealer; cataloger; and remainder houses. To librarians, the traditional roles, functions, and definitions of each level are well known and well defined. However, while the video industry has its own analogous creative elements including, but not limited to, the producer, distributor, distributor/jobber, retail video outlet, cataloger, nonspecialty stores, and remainder houses, they are not well defined and often overlap. This chapter will assist in defining the roles of the five vendor avenues available to librarians for purchase of video product: producer, distributor, jobber, cataloger, and video retail store. For the purposes of this book, a vendor is any company, individual, or organization that sells videocassettes, either wholesale or retail.

Producers. While a book is most often the culmination of one person's (the author's) effort, a video is usually the result of many people's efforts—from the people responsible for funding the production (executive producers) to the cameramen, grips, directors, and performers. The term "producer" is perhaps the most clearly defined of all the vendor types, being the person or persons responsible for the creation of the work and its realization as a video product. Also, the producer usually holds the copyright to a production and, as a result, dictates contractual distribution, sales, duplication and mastering, and public performance and other rights. These rights are analogous to the author's contractual rights regarding movie rights, dramatic rights, reading rights (an audio book, abridged/unabridged), paperback, and other separate rights within the book publishing field.

A book is usually published by a publishing company but may be printed by another company. In the same sense, a video may be produced by one company, actually duplicated for sales distribution by another company, and then distributed and subdistributed by still other vendors. Similar to a book produced in both hardcover and paperback, a full-length, theatrically released feature may be released on film by one vendor but on home video by another vendor, and by yet another vendor to the educational market. This tri-level distribution is the result of distribution contracts and licenses which confuse not only librarians, but producers and lawyers as well. A video company such as HBO or Ambrose Video Publishing may even help subsidize production or serve as co-executive producer of a film in exchange for a limited-time exclusive distribution of the product on video. As with books, videos may be sold directly by the producer, such as Disney, Warner, MCA, and RCA/Columbia or independents like Bullfrog, Filmakers Library, and Davenport Films. Some examples of producers who market their own titles are WQED (Pittsburgh), Encounter Productions, Kaw Valley Films and Video, Davenport Films, Filmakers Library, and Churchill Films and Video. Some producers such as Berlet, Flower Film and Video, and the James Agee Film Project handle all the marketing themselves, distributing mail flyers, performing telemarketing, and sometimes employing the use of an in-house sales team or independent sales representatives. Other producers, while simultaneously distributing their own titles, allow different companies to subdistribute for them, thus increasing their market coverage. Producers usually do not keep a supply of their titles on hand because duplication and storage is expensive. Instead, duplication is done on a "demand-sales" basis. Often title prices are negotiable, even though they appear set in catalogs. Sales representatives, normally receiving from 5 to 20 percent commissions on sales, have the power to juggle prices and reduce their commissions, resulting in drastically reduced prices. Public performance rights can often be obtained directly through the producer at no extra cost. However, marketing and advertising costs are extremely high, especially when dealing with "building level purchases." Therefore, both book and video companies look toward other vendors to distribute their product. These companies, comprised of catalogers, distributors, and jobbers, take the burden of marketing away from the company and exponentially extend the marketing reach of the producer/publisher, resulting in more potential sales, while extracting a "commission" for titles sold.

Distributors. These companies handle the expensive marketing of videocassettes for one or more producers (often a producer may work exclusively for one distributor). Usually, distributors have a vested interest in their products, selling one "brand" over another instead of offering a potpourri of titles. Often a distributor will specialize in a specific genre or subject field, or only distribute one or more producers' catalogs. Some distributors only sell to a specialized market such as libraries, schools, and universities. For example, Henwood specializes in classic and foreign films, while Filmic Archives specializes in old National Film Board of Canada titles plus classic American documentaries and classic feature films. Some companies are both producer and distributor, such as Barr Films & Video, producing their own titles and distributing them, as well as distributing titles from Centre Productions. Another example is the Altschul Group Corporation, a large conglomerate that has purchased smaller video production/distribution companies such as Journal, Perennial, Wombat, and Beacon and now distributes their titles. Marketing involves organization, production, and mailing of catalogs; handling reviews and customer previews; identifying markets and sales plans for those markets; keeping an active sales force or alternative contact vehicle; pricing, duplication, title packing, shipment and billing; as well as sales tracking and reports. Product sales is usually accomplished through sales representatives, either making in-person calls to locations or telephone sales/telemarketing. These salespeople are knowledgeable about the product and catalogs and can negotiate discount prices, often as much as 40 to 50 percent off the catalog price. Composed primarily of the traditional educational film vendors, most distributors serve schools, academic libraries, and public libraries rather than the consumer retail market.

Wholesale or Retail Distributor/Jobber. Actually, these terms are misnomers in the video market, widely misunderstood and misused. Wholesale and retail usually refer to both the customer and volume of business done by that customer. Retail stores primarily serve the individual consumer, purchasing on a single title basis. Wholesale usually involves volume purchases with a deep discount, often from 10 to 40 percent. Video wholesalers almost exclusively deal with organizations rather than individuals. However, per title price and volume discount are the keys to watch for when deciding if a company is a wholesaler or a retailer. Some educational distributors like U.S.A. Information Service and Zenger Video are actually retail catalogers for institutional sales rather than wholesale distributors.

In a 1990 *Library Journal* article, Joanne Salce, commenting on the differences between a wholesale jobber and a "distributor," noted that a wholesaler is a company that acquires a vast assortment of titles, selling them to a varied customer base. A wholesaler will not produce any of its own programming, nor will it license programming for sale under its own name. On the other hand, distributors deal with large numbers of videos, but also acquire programming from independent producers and produce programming in-house. Distributors can also license titles and sell them under their own name. Examples of such companies are Films Incorporated, Coronet/MTI/LCA, Live Home Distributing,

The Cinema Guild, and The Maier Group.[4] However, jobbers such as Professional Media Services (PMS) are radically changing the distribution scene by offering product access to many independent video producers' catalogs. PMS does not stock these specialty products and orders on a "demand only" basis, offering only the standard distributor discount. Baker & Taylor Video now tries to negotiate public performance rights when acquiring product and also tries to acquire specialty titles from independents and other sources, but does not demand "distribution exclusivity" for those titles. A new type of vendor, known as a quasi-distributor, is a joint project of the Video Forum, sponsored through National Video Resources (an initiative of the Rockefeller Foundation), and the John D. & Catherine T. MacArthur Foundation Library Video Project. This project produces several catalogs, with each issue devoted to a specific, focused topic. Various vendors are represented and the project has made special discount arrangements for those titles. With projects and offshoot derivations like the one just described, the lines between producer, distributor, and jobber are not as well-defined.

Jobber. A jobber, often termed a "wholesaler," offers a wide range of titles (most often proporting that they can get anything currently produced/available on video) from various sources, including direct from producers, distributors, and even other jobbers. Jobbers are, in essence, a "one-stop shop." For the most part, jobbers' terms of sale are more attractive than those of a producer, cataloger, or distributor because they purchase in large quantities and pass those discounts—often 15 to 40 percent—on to their customers. Jobbers such as Baker & Taylor Video and Ingram/Commtron offer large price discounts, broad title access and selection, and special services such as computer ordering and title/subject searches. Other jobbers, like Professional Media Services and Brodart, offer cataloging and processing options, as well as other special "value added" services like processing and storage supply sales. Jobbers usually have inventory on hand; many distributors do not, choosing instead to duplicate product as required. Most jobbers deal primarily in high volume, multiple copy purchases of "home video only" videos, selling to bookstores, video rental stores, and rack jobbers in department and specialty stores (the sell-through market). Schools and libraries are a secondary market; however, they possess widely variant needs and have extremely different methods of doing business. Often titles possessing public performance rights are desired; single copies of a wide variety of titles instead of multiple copies of the *Billboard* Top 25 rentals/sales are purchased; or nonfiction (special interest) titles are emphasized instead of features. Ordering is most often done through purchase orders, with payment following receipt of the titles and invoicing within 30 to 60 days. Most jobbers sell at wholesale of their retail clientele and volume business. Other jobbers offer net (no discount) or small discounts, largely dependent on a wide range of factors such as dollar volume spent per order and specific titles ordered.

Carl Mann, vice president of marketing at Baker & Taylor Video, presents a unique view concerning video distribution that is helpful in defining vendors.

Baker & Taylor, by definition of this book, is a wholesale "jobber." A wholesaler relies on volume on both ends of the spectrum—in purchasing product from producers and distributors and in selling that product to the library, educational, and retail markets. Therefore, the jobber's entire world focuses around the "margin of sales" or volume related to price rather than specifically per title sales price. Mann makes it clear that Baker & Taylor is not a rack jobber such as Handleman (Troy, Michigan). He feels that a definition of vendor by type revolves around service functions supplied by that vendor rather than markets sold to or pricing structures. The service functions he feels are important are as follows:

1. Convenience—Analogous to a "7-Eleven," this refers to the ease of product acquisition by the purchaser. An example of convenience is having an 800-number for ordering and customer service.

2. Lot Size—inventory of titles, specifically the depth (multiple copies of those titles warehoused).

3. Delivery time—time from the inception of the order to that order's fulfillment and subsequent delivery to the customer.

4. Product variety—again relating to inventory, specifically the breadth (number of titles offered).

5. Provision of credit—offering a variety of ways for the buyer to pay for product such as C.O.D. (cash on delivery), purchase orders, net 30 days, and so on.

6. Maintenance of product quality—within two areas, the physical quality of the videocassette concerning defective merchandise and the subjective quality, meaning inventorying product possessing positive evaluations and reviews. Baker & Taylor's magazine, *Video Alert,* quotes reviews when possible.

7. Availability of information about product—providing product information related to all videographic information needed for ordering (and possibly cataloging). Possible information included: ISBN, catalog number, manufacturer number, copyright date, title, series title, performers, running time, and price (retail and extended price). The provision of information on various formats such as paper catalogs, monthly magazines, telephone customer service, special lists, and microfiche fulfills this requirement.

8. Stability of supply—relates to lot size in that product will be available to fulfill orders with a minimum of back orders. Specifically, Baker & Taylor does not insist on product exclusivity to sell; many other distributors and jobbers may offer the same product. Distribution agreements are done on a license basis.

9. Availability of personal service—relates to customer service, possibly in terms of convenient geographic location to the customer, telemarketing, number of branch offices, and field representatives.

10. Risk reduction—ensuring customer satisfaction with product, allowing a reasonable returns/exchange policy or offering previews.

11. Value-added services—electronic ordering, availability of cataloging/processing,

availability of various supplies such as video cases, labels, and so on. Price is not a value-added service.

Cataloger. A cataloger is a relatively new breed of retailer, often operating under the guise of a retail distributor. With strict attention paid to marketing, catalogers such as Library Video Company, Zenger Video, and Rudolph Johnson offer slick, eclectic-title catalogs. Some catalogs, done in full color with descriptive annotations and out-of-context review comments, are exquisite marketing devices designed to give the impression of selection tools. Prices may be up to 50 percent higher than the same title purchased through a jobber. Some catalogers such as Instructional Video, Inc. and the Video School House sell primarily to the educational market. Other catalogers like WaldenBooks, Critic's Corner, and S.I. Video target the consumer market. Still other specialty sources, like the Signals and Mind's Eye catalogs, offer some hard-to-find, special interest videos, selling to both the consumer and educational markets. Most catalogers do not maintain an inventory; that is, upon receiving an order, the cataloger in turn purchases those titles from a wholesale vendor. As a result, back orders, delayed shipments, and no-ships are quite common. Title knowledge and customer service are sometimes lacking, although much better than from most jobbers. Educational catalogers usually have much better title knowledge than their consumer counterparts. Consumer catalogers usually require order prepayment, while educational catalogers will accept purchase orders and invoice the purchasing party. As with jobbers, catalogers' specific per-title prices and discounts are not negotiable.

Video Retail/Rental Store. The video retail store can be a "mom and pop" video rental store, a video rental chain, or a conglomerate department, supermarket, pharmacy, or other store where one of its purposes is the sale of video, commonly called sell-through. These stores are true retail, selling to individuals on a per title basis. These stores acquire product from distributors and wholesale jobbers and mark product up from 5 to 60 percent. Often, however, stores such as these will have sales and specials that bring titles equal to, or even below, wholesale price.

METHODS OF ACQUIRING VIDEOCASSETTES

Thanks to the proliferation of video review publications, today's emphasis on acquiring videos has largely shifted from a concern about the lack of adequate reviewing tools for selection to dealing with the following questions concerning acquisitions: From whom does one purchase videos? Should one rely on a single vendor for all acquisitions or try for a more diverse portfolio from several vendors? What are the advantages and disadvantages of dealing with a few, or many, vendors at once? When and how should one choose one vendor over another for a specific product? Can one save money and reduce order paperwork at the same time?

In dealing with any vendor there are certain advantages and disadvantages (i.e., ''pros and cons'') which must be carefully weighed and evaluated before a decision to do business with that vendor should be made. A decision to deal with one vendor over another should be made with knowledge about that type of vendor, the vendor's specific strengths and weaknesses, plus information about how that vendor does business and if that method will suit the library's needs, as well as the method used for acquiring product. This section will discuss the evaluative ''pros and cons'' one should look for in evaluating vendors while concurrently detailing the following alternative acquisitions methods:

1. Title-by-title purchase from vendor (includes ''free'' videos)

2. Long-term leases (usually 5-year, renewable) and rentals

3. Duplication (from a master copy)

4. Off-air taping (rights for life of tape or other negotiated rights)

5. Gifts

6. Title-by-title purchase—used (previewed) videocassettes

7. Rotating collections—video circuits and leased collections

8. Co-op purchases, discount purchases—title-by-title or group purchase packages

9. Placed collections—entire collections, sometimes only specific subjects placed in a library, either for a fee or for free

Title-by-title purchasing is the most common method. In a typical library scenario, individual multiple-order forms are made out and batched by vendor, from which purchase orders are completed and sent off, either by mail or electronically. As described in Chapter 5 (on Copyright), the First-sale Doctrine covers this type of sale as long as the physical cassette is being sold, rather than just leasing the intellectual property contained within that cassette. Long-term leased videocassettes, such as all titles purchased from Direct Cinema, Ltd. and the University of Illinois' extended lease plan, are not covered by that doctrine. Accompanying lease licenses/contracts must be examined very carefully upon title receipt so that both parties are fully aware of their future responsibilities, both monetarily and rights-wise. Examination of catalog-contained contracts before purchase or contacting the vendor is essential. Gift acquisitions are also done on a title-by-title basis. The most important aspect of these types of videocassettes added to the collection is to ascertain, as reliably as possible, if they are legally sold copies. Any and all producer/distributor video labels should be accurate and securely adhered and visible; case tampering or alteration should not be present and the FBI copyright warning label should be clearly visible. Overseas acquisitions may present an equipment compatibility problem. Compatibility means playability. Videocassettes produced in the United States, Mexico, and Canada are recorded in an electronical standard known as NTSC, based on our alternating current of 60 cycles per second. The rest of the world uses two different standards, neither of which are compatible with the other—PALS and SEACAM. Overseas vendors should be able to provide the purchaser with a version recorded in the NTSC standard, or at the very least, offer a one-time duplication right allowing transfer from an alternate standard to NTSC. This transfer can be done commercially or in-house through a special videocassette record/play deck.

Duplication rights are usually not specified in company catalog-contained contracts. These rights are usually specially negotiated through sales representatives and require special pricing. The price for a title licensed for public performance and duplication rights should be no more than 20 to 25 percent more than the same title with public performance rights only. Companies such as Barr Film & Video, Altschul, and PBS Video routinely license titles for unlimited duplication rights. In all cases, the master should remain pristine, never circulating; it should only be used in an archival setting, ready for duplication at any time. In the best-case scenario, the number of title duplicates should not remain static, but be dynamic, related directly to the seasonal/patron demand. Using masters with duplication rights can be an excellent way for libraries with branches, as well as school districts and universities with multiple sites, to acquire titles expediently and at substantial per-title cost savings. However, professional duplicating/editing equipment, knowledgeable staff, and adequate time for duplication and processing are needed to make duplication work.

Many programs can be obtained free of charge and/or at substantially reduced prices when taped off-air. In 1992, Modern Talking Pictures offered over 150 programs from a publishers series on cultural diversity via off-air satellite reception. Programs from Whittle's Channel One, the Learning Channel, and the Mind Extension University can routinely be obtained free via off-air taping. As with duplication, the only cost incurred by the library is the initial cost of blank tapes. An organized system of taping including knowledgeable staff and sophisticated equipment, ensuring high-quality reception, must also be available.

Because of price increases in blockbuster features from the high end ($79.95 to $99.95) and the elimination of the middle price bracket ($49.95 to $70), previewed videocassettes have become an exceptional way for libraries to increase their buying power. Historically started to help siphon off video stores' excess inventory, previewed video vendors have expanded from "video underworld" dealers to accepted, reputable distributors. Previewed video vendors can save libraries thousands of dollars when used to their best advantage. When deciding whether to order a video from a previewed vendor or new vendor, the librarian should ask the following questions:

1. How soon do I want/need the title and can I wait that long?

2. Are there any indications that the title will be re-released at a lower sell-through price than I can currently get now from a previewed vendor?

3. Am I willing to accept the current lower purchase price from a previewed vendor so

that I can acquire the title immediately to satisfy the demand rather than waiting for a lower sell-through price later?

In evaluating previewed video vendors, librarians should look at title price structure from date of release, as well as types and number of titles offered. Prices should be delineated on a chart by type of video (i.e., "AAA," "AB," moratorium, etc.), as well as by the number of months after release date. Librarians should follow these rules of thumb when deciding whether to purchase from a previewed vendor or buy new product. Generally speaking, purchase new "AAA," "A," or "AB" titles now available at sell-through prices below $18.00 from other vendors who offer a 15 to 40 percent discount, especially if your acquisition can be delayed six months to one year from release date. Purchase "B" titles from other vendors if the price is below $21.00 from six to twelve months after release. Previewed vendors may be the only place to get moratorium titles such as the Disney releases. Prices for these titles range from $9.95 to $99 and up. Many previewed video vendors also sell new videos at list prices. Therefore, it is very important for the vendor to have a standard method of communication allowing purchasers to specify whether they wish to buy a previewed title (and at what month window and price) or if they wish to purchase a new title. A library may be given an option on the order form to purchase a new title at list or at a slightly discounted price if a previewed title is not available. The vendor should have a cancellation period and a reporting procedure for those cancellations that is acceptable to the library. The library should also have the option of cancelling outstanding orders after a specified length of time. When a vendor follows a month-release price chart, the price is a general indication of the desires of the purchaser. However, it is important that the library acquisitions staff understand the importance of specifying all specific conditions of purchase (such as 6–9 months after release at $21.95) on the order form or purchase order, otherwise the library will be at the mercy of the previewed vendor for determining price and availability.

Previewed vendor sales personnel should be knowledgeable in the way libraries do business and be accommodating regarding the purchase order, 30 to 60 day payment schedule. Back order delays are difficult to track with previewed vendors because the library may have placed certain conditions on titles or ordered titles that have not yet been released on video. Intact video packaging, the playable condition of videos upon arrival, the company's return policy, and any "quality" checks the company might follow should be acceptable to the library before ordering from that vendor. Libraries that purchase significant numbers of previewed videos should consider investing in a videocassette cleaning/inspection machine. Currently there are two vendors who manufacture commercial quality, dry-process machines that use a cleaning tissue: Research Technology International (RTI) (4700 Chase, Lincolnwood, IL 60646; (708) 677-3000/(800) 323-7520), manufacturing the VT2100 and the TapeChek 400 series; and Paulmar Industries (391 Lake St., P.O. Box 638, Antioch, IL 60002;

(708) 395-2080) manufacturing the V/Scan 500C. The RTI machines are unmatched in quality, durability, and reliability, and both their service and sales
departments are staffed by extremely knowledgeable people. Consumer quality
cleaning-only machines are available from a variety of video store distributing
sources including the following: Video Store Services, 6115 Monroe Ct., Morton
Grove, IL 60053; (800) 325-6867; and The Video Store Shopper, 8100 Remmet
Ave., Canoga Park, CA 91304; (800) 325-6867.

Placed collections include rotating collections and large "sets" of titles provided free-of-charge or sold to libraries. Modern Talking Pictures provides a
free corporate library of several hundred videocassettes. Libraries must agree to
keep track of circulation, returning titles which do not circulate a certain number
of times over a given time period. Title selection is usually done as a block—
all or nothing, never title-by-title. Corporate-sponsored collections may specify
certain processing restrictions such as no permanent library ownership stamps
being placed on the cassettes. The acquisitions librarian must be aware of all
special requirements to facilitate the media's easy transition to the processing
stage. In a similar fashion, rotating collections may have to be deleted from the
database, catalog cards prepared or added to the card catalog, packing lists
checked against title contents, library ownership stamps applied, or any number
of other small tasks.

Co-ops and other coordinated purchasing plans also may require some special
consideration. Except when dealing with large jobbers, volume purchases usually translate into lower per-title prices; therefore, when any institutions can form
a group buy with one company, it can mean considerable budget savings to
every library involved. Often these group buys use a special order form and
require prepayment; sometimes they require payment to another library or
agency, rather than to the producer/distributor. In all cases, the purchasing librarian should know the ordering and payment routine and time frame (dead-
lines), the invoicing and order receipt method, the returns and damages policy
and procedures, performance rights license inclusion, original per-title price versus group-purchase, discounted price, as well as any other special requirements
that might impact upon the acquisitions department routines.

Choosing Vendors

As previously mentioned, the traditional channels for videocassettes include
the producer (manufacturer), wholesale and retail distributor, jobber or "wholesaler," and retail video outlet (chain or local). Dealing with one over the other
for a particular purchase may have several advantages, only one of which may
result in a savings of budget monies (per-title price). The questions the librarian
must ask when deciding upon a vendor are as follows: Why am I buying this
product from this vendor? What services am I receiving from this vendor that
I want and need and cannot get from another vendor? Are the price discounts

and other terms of sale offered by that vendor enough to offset any burdens of additional order paperwork, price negotiations, or other factors?

Producer. A producer is the entity who actually produced the program and, in most cases, possesses the copyright and public performance rights. Likened to purchasing serials directly from the publisher, direct buying from producers can save money but often results in added paperwork because of many individual purchase orders rather than a bulk order from a distributor or jobber. In dealing with producers, librarians must be prepared to haggle over prices, and can often negotiate lower prices and special deals. Producers know their product inside and out, but often have independent sales representatives selling their product. The commission is therefore an important part of the sale, often amounting to 10 to 25 percent of the sale. Volume sales are important to the sales representative; often the librarian can save substantial amounts of money by buying more than one title or multiple copies rather than just buying one copy of one title. Librarians should always know with whom they are dealing so they can negotiate successfully. Under no circumstances should a librarian purchase product from a producer without contacting the producer/sales representative and trying to negotiate first. Producers have catalogs and mail flyers of varying quality—some are glossy with pictures and a title/subject index and some are just title lists. Prices often reflect nontheatrical public performance rights (which will be discussed in Chapter 5). If public performance rights are not desired, it is extremely important that the librarian perform a title search using various video sourcebooks and computer databases for the same title, home-use only equivalent, because sometimes the producer may not know of its existence. Always ask the producer if they can supply the name of the company that distributes a home-use only version of the program(s) in question.

Distributors. Distributors are usually organized to do business on a regional or national basis. Some distributors are producers as well; others just sell other producers' products. Distributor catalogs offer a wide variety of titles from many producers. Some distributors specialize in certain types of video titles such as specialty (nonfiction) titles or features, while others offer a mixture of both types. An example of a small educational/institutional distributor is Film Ideas (Chicago, Illinois). Instructional Video, U.S.A. Information Service, Select Video Publishing, and Johnson Rudolph are examples of retail distributors that deal strictly with organizations and institutions. Most often, the video titles are "home-use only" because distributors do not usually negotiate public performance rights. Also, set discount prices are available, but usually not negotiable. Most distributors do not have title exclusivity, meaning that titles are available through more than one vendor. Therefore, it pays to shop around. Today, many distributors offer more intense customer service—distributor newsletters and product hotlines abound. Wholesale distributors usually have lower prices and sell to retailers and retail distributors, who in turn sell for a marked-up profit. Librarians would be wise to purchase materials from a wholesale distributor because the dollar savings can be substantial.

Jobber. A jobber is a large wholesale distributor who offers a large product line, usually at substantial discounts based on volume purchased. Jobbers usually stock their titles in-house; therefore, many back-order problems can be eliminated by purchasing from them. A jobber possesses the buying power to offer a tremendous variety of producer and distributor titles. Jobbers usually do not negotiate public performance rights (except in the case of Baker & Taylor Video); therefore, all titles can assume to be for home-use only. Generally, a wholesale vendor can supply products at discounts above most retail vendors, but shopping around for the best deal makes good fiscal sense. Ocassionally a title may be exclusively available through only one source.

Vendors should be chosen for the following reasons:

1. Giving the best price or standard volume discount (this includes total price, with shipping and handling). Many vendors offer free shipping and handling over a certain dollar amount.

2. Giving timely and pleasant service—knowing the product, offering individual customer service, providing billing/invoice procedures and forms that are understandable and adaptable to library methods.

3. Geographical proximity or easy access via an 800 number.

4. Offering a full title line in terms of title variety and depth and possessing an attractive, easily usable catalog and/or special newsletter.

5. Possesses methods of handling back orders and returns in a timely, accurate, and acceptable manner.

6. Ordering and vendor reporting on invoices, back orders, and cancellations must be easy, title specific, and timely.

7. Payment methods and durations should also coincide with the library's needs.

8. Any value-added services should be conveniently available, separate from regular invoicing procedure, and valuable to the library—not just used as an incentive (perk) to get an order.

Many jobbers and distributors give two discounts—a net title discount plus another based on volume orders. Librarians should check into this option and "batch" volume orders together. Batched orders from several libraries might be orchestrated by some innovative librarians, which will result in substantial discounts. Also, producers and distributors may offer "two-tiered" pricing, where a distinction between home and institutional use is made on a price basis.

TELEMARKETERS AND 800-NUMBERS

Appearing relatively recently on the marketing scene are a wide variety of video telemarketing companies and television advertised 800-numbers. Both of these purchasing avenues are reliable sources of titles, but the librarian must be aware of some caveats. Telemarketers exist to sell a product by quota. As such quick sales rather than customer service are high on their priority list. They usually are reading from a practiced script and know virtually nothing about the product they are selling. Telemarketers will not know anything "extra" about a title, or if it is available elsewhere; they will not know if the title is part of a series or who the producer is. A typical telemarketing company specializing in how-to sports videos is Video Action Sports, Inc., 200 Suburban Rd., Suite E, San Luis Obispo, CA 93401; (805) 543-4812. Usually the telemarketer will contact the librarian and initiate an order on preview or approval subsequent to payment or return within a set time (normally 15 to 30 days). The telemarketing company should be able to deal with purchase orders. The librarian should ask if the invoice will accompany the order, and if it will have the telemarketing company's name/address on it or some other, unidentified address. Sales tax should not be charged and late payment or late return charges, if any, should be specified. The return name/address and company policy for any returns must be clearly indicated. A method for reporting any damages, incorrect title inclusion, incorrect billing, and partial retention of titles sent should also be discussed in the initial telephone conversation. If accompanying manuals, booklets, audiocassettes, or other material is included with the videocassettes, the librarian should inquire how replacements might be ordered. The library requesting product in this manner must be able to deal with using the invoice as a purchase order from which to pay by, as well as being able to pay within the short time periods stated on the invoice. In most cases, titles sold by telemarketers are available through other sources at much cheaper prices. The telemarketers are hoping that the convenience of ordering over the telephone will clinch the sale. Often, dealing with telemarketing companies can be an accounting and logistical hassle and the library will end up paying much more for the same title acquired elsewhere.

Similar to telemarketing companies are television advertised 800 numbers. These advertisements often state "not sold or available in stores." However, many of these titles are available from wholesale/retail distributors and jobbers in the library market. Most of the time, 800-numbers transact business only through credit cards such as VISA, Mastercard, or Discover—rarely will they accept institutional purchase orders, money orders, or even C.O.D. Therefore, the library must be able to accommodate orders through one of the following methods: have a credit card and be able to charge materials on that card; be able to reimburse a staff member ordering a title through the use of a personal credit card; or have a substantial petty cash fund to use for these types of purchases. Upon contacting the 800-number, the acquisitions librarian should ask the company representative if they will sell to a library and if they will accept a purchase order. Often, the company representative will refer them to another company where a purchase order accompanied by prepayment will be accepted. The company representative should supply the company name, address, phone number, contact person, and exact prepayment price. The questions asked of the telemarketer also apply when ordering from an 800-number. In all cases, it behooves the librarian to first check other sources for title availability, ordering from telemarketers and 800-numbers only as a last resort. Today, video 800-numbers appear everywhere, from subject and general-interest magazines to QVC (the shopping channel) and almost all other cable channels. Consumer video marketers are using the power of saturation television advertising to reach new markets and "niche" groups never before available. The future will only see an increase in this type of marketing activity. Librarians who do not take advantage of this acquisitions avenue will be depriving their constituency of some high-demand titles and missing some high-quality titles. A simplified, somewhat flexible ordering structure with no artificial barriers should be in place so that both the selector and the acquisitions librarian can be free to order titles from a wide variety of vendors using many different purchasing tactics.

DEALING WITH VENDORS

Illustrated in Figures 3.1 and 3.2 are actual "Term and Conditions" contracts from two different producer/distributor companies, PBS Video and Ambrose Video Publishing, Inc. Normally, these contracts appear in the back of the company catalogs opposite the order pages. In most instances, copies of such agreements are included along with the packing slips and/or invoices. Before purchasing anything from any vendor, the librarian should know the limits of purchasing from that vendor, including the following information: the rights—public performance, duplication, cable transmission, limited instructional television fixed service and so on; payment date (30, 60, 90 days) and late charges policy; manner in which delivery is made (United Parcel Service [UPS], U.S. Postal Service, freight transport, or other); return and replacement policies; warranties and remedies (defects—also having to do with replacements). When dealing with company sales representatives, it is a good idea to establish these facts in the initial conversation. If modifications and/or additional limits (such as duplication rights or closed circuit transmission rights) are negotiated, they should appear in writing on the purchase order as well as on the invoice.

Mark Richie, Director of the Burlington County AVA Center in Mt. Holly, New Jersey, offers two approaches for dealing with vendors: (1) the many suppliers approach; and (2) the few suppliers approach. These approaches have been expanded below, detailing their respective disadvantages and advantages:

Many Suppliers Approach

Advantages:

• Highly specific titles from a broad range of sources;

• Can get exactly the titles wanted;

• Can get the "best" and/or lowest price.

Figure 3.1
PBS Video Agreement

AGREEMENT

PBS VIDEO is a department of the Public Broadcasting Service

Agreement between the Public Broadcasting Service, operating through PBS VIDEO (hereinafter "PBS") and the customer ("Customer") named on the PBS VIDEO Invoice between PBS and Customer ("Invoice"), wherein PBS grants Customer and Customer accepts from PBS the limited license to exhibit the program(s) identified on the Invoice (hereinafter the "Program" or "Programs") in accordance with the following terms and conditions. Customer agrees to these terms and conditions by accepting delivery of any videocassette of the Program(s) from PBS VIDEO. Customer acknowledges that the Programs may not be utilized in any manner other than as specified herein and in no event shall the Programs be exhibited before an audience where admission is charged for the viewing of the Programs. Customer shall not sublicense, sublease or part with the possession of the Programs secured by Customer hereunder. Nothing herein shall derogate from any rights of PBS or any other copyright proprietor(s) of the Programs under the United States Copyright Law.

1. RIGHTS.

a. In-room Use. For the Program price identified in the current PBS VIDEO Resource Catalog, Catalog Supplement, direct mail brochures or newsletters, Customer has the right to exhibit the Programs to a limited number of viewers where all viewers, monitor(s) and playback units are in the same room (in-room use"). Such exhibition shall be in accordance with the Arrangement indicated on the Invoice and during the period applicable thereto. Customer acknowledges that the Programs may not be duplicated, broadcast, transmitted by cable, transmitted on any open circuit system, or otherwise transmitted, unless otherwise specified herein or agreed to by PBS in writing.

b. Limited Instructional Television Fixed Service ("Limited ITFS") and Closed Circuit Television ("CCTV"). Unless otherwise specified in the current PBS VIDEO Resource Catalog, Catalog Supplement, direct mail brochures or newsletters, the Program price includes the right to transmit or exhibit the Programs over ITFS and CCTV limited to transmission within a building, single campus or cluster of buildings, where those rights are available.

c. Basic Cable ("CATV") and Instructional Television Fixed Service ("ITFS"). For some of the Programs where necessary rights are available and for an additional fee, PBS may authorize Customer to transmit the Program on Basic Cable channels, Closed-loop Cable channels and/or ITFS for transmission beyond a single building, campus or cluster of buildings. Such authorization is covered by special arrangement. Customer must contact PBS prior to submitting an order for any Programs requesting CCTV or ITFS transmission rights. "Basic Cable channels" means cable channels provided to cable subscribers for which no additional charge is made to the subscriber other than the basic subscriber fee.

2. ARRANGEMENTS.

a. Purchase. "Purchase" shall mean the release of the Programs by PBS to Customer for use during the life of the materials. Under this Agreement, a tape will be shipped or mailed to Customer.

b. Off Air License. "Off Air License" shall mean the right of Customer to license and retain a tape of the Program from the broadcast transmission as it is being aired by Customer's local public television station for use during a specified period as stated on the Invoice. Under this Agreement, materials for such taping shall be supplied by the Customer.

c. Term License. "Term License" shall mean the release of the Program for use by Customer during a specified period beginning on

the "Date Required" and ending on the "Return Date" or in the Special Comments section as indicated on the Invoice (hereinafter "Loan Term"). Under this Arrangement, a tape will be shipped or mailed to Customer and other materials for use by Customer. The Programs must be returned by the Return Date, unless renewed in another PBS VIDEO agreement.

d. Life License. "Life License" shall mean the release of the Programs for duplication by Customer for use during the life of the materials. Under this Arrangement, a tape will be shipped or mailed to Customer and other materials for duplication shall be supplied by Customer. No duplication of copies beyond the number listed on the Invoice is permitted unless prior written approval is obtained from PBS.

3. PAYMENTS, DEPOSITS, SERVICE FEES, LATE CHARGES.

Customer shall pay to PBS at the address noted on the Invoice the following sums in the manner and at the times specified, time being of the essence for all such payments.

a. The price for the Programs as set forth in the current PBS VIDEO Resource Catalog, Catalog Supplement, direct mail brochures or newsletters, including applicable discounts or special quantity purchase pricing, and:

b. Any and all taxes, fees, or other like charges billed against PBS and imposed, levied, or assessed upon the delivery, possession, exhibition, or use of any Program, upon the grant or exercise of any rights hereunder, or upon the sum payable by Customer to PBS pursuant hereto, if any; and

c. All other charges specified in the Invoice, or in the current PBS VIDEO Resource Catalog, Catalog Supplement, direct mail brochures or newsletters, including but not limited to late charges, charges for damage to videocassettes, cancellation fees, duplication fees, and rush order service charges.

PBS will verify with Customer any order received indicating that an improper price was used. Invoices are payable within thirty (30) days of receipt of invoice by Customer.

Should cancellation of an order become necessary, service fees may be charged against Customers who fail to cancel orders before shipment of the Programs from PBS. PBS may impose on Customer a late charge for any Preview or Purchase Programs returned to PBS after the "Return Date." However, in no case will the late charges or cancellation fees exceed the purchase price for the Program. Service fees and late charges are payable within thirty (30) days of receipt of invoice by Customer.

4. TERM OF AGREEMENT.

The term of this Agreement with regard to each of the Programs shall commence as of the date each Program is delivered to Customer and shall continue for the applicable Agreement period pursuant to Paragraph 2 above.

5. DELIVERY.

PBS will use reasonable efforts to mail or ship the Programs to Customer in the time normally required for the Programs to reach Customer by the "Date Required." The Program shall be deemed in satisfactory condition for exhibition (and/or transmission) unless Customer immediately after inspection thereof, notifies PBS to the contrary specifying the nature of the defect. PBS shall not be in breach of this Agreement for failure to deliver any of the Programs by the "Date Required" and shall not be liable for incidental or consequential damages.

6. RETURN.

Customer will be responsible for the full purchase price plus applicable shipping and handling fees of any return of Programs Purchased or made

available from PBS if returned after sixty (60) days from the "Date Required" as shown on the Invoice. Return shipment insurance shall be for the amount of $50 for each videocassette. Customer should obtain return receipt from shipper to verify proof of shipment. Failure by the Customer to return Programs for canceled orders will result in the Customer being invoiced for the full catalog price of each Program not returned.

7. REPLACEMENT.

Customers previewing the Programs shall pay to PBS the purchase cost of any Program(s) lost, stolen destroyed, or injured other than through normal wear and tear or not returned by Customer. Such payment shall not transfer title to or any interest in the Programs to Customer or to any other party. Customer shall immediately notify PBS in writing of the loss, theft, injury or destruction of any of the Programs.

8. DELETIONS.

Customer shall transmit each of the Programs in its entirety only. Customers shall not cut or alter the Programs or otherwise tamper therewith and in no event shall the Programs be transmitted without the complete copyright notices and/or credits contained therein.

9. WARRANTIES AND REMEDIES.

PBS warrants the Programs to be free from defects in material and workmanship at the time of delivery. In the event of PBS's breach of such warranty, or Customer's dissatisfaction with program content, Customer's exclusive remedies shall be that PBS will replace the defective or unwanted Programs, exchange the defective or unwanted programs for different programs that are equal in purchase price, or receive a full refund for the purchase priced of the defective or unwanted Programs, provided Customer notifies PBS of said defect or dissatisfaction within sixty (60) days of receipt and returns the defective or unwanted Programs to PBS. The terms and conditions of this Agreement apply to any Programs furnished as a replacement. NO OTHER WARRANTY EXPRESSED OR IMPLIED, INCLUDING THE WARRANTY OF MERCHANTABILITY, SHALL APPLY TO ANY PROGRAM HEREUNDER. PBS shall have no other liability, and Customer shall have no other remedy, except as specifically provided in this Paragraph; and in no event shall PBS be liable for any consequential damages.

10. RESERVATION OF RIGHTS.

Legal title to the Programs shall at all times remain in PBS and all rights therein are reserved to PBS. The term "purchase" as used herein means only the right to license for use and reuse the Programs by Customer without limitation as to the number of uses or reuses, but without any change in ownership or title and otherwise subject to the terms and conditions of this Agreement.

11. DEFAULTS.

If Customer defaults hereunder:

a. PBS, in addition to other remedies, may repossess any Program previously delivered hereunder; and/or

b. PBS may refuse to make further orders from Customer and may refuse to made further shipment of Programs to Customer; and/or

c. Customer agrees to pay PBS's costs and expenses of collection and/or repossession including maximum fees permitted by law.

PBS VIDEO

Public Broadcasting Service
1320 Braddock Place
Alexandria, VA 22314-1698

Source: 1994 PBS Video Catalog.

Figure 3.2
Ambrose Video Terms and Conditions Contract

TERMS
AND CONDITIONS

AGREEMENT between AMBROSE VIDEO PUBLISHING, INC. (Hereinafter called "Ambrose") and the Party (hereinafter called "Customer") named on the order form (hereinafter called "Schedule").

1. License: Ambrose grants Customer and Customer accepts from Ambrose the limited license under copyright to exhibit one or more of the films, video and/or sound filmstrip programs or both ordered or rented by Customer (hereinafter called "Programs"), but only for exhibition to non-paying private audiences during the period set forth and in accordance with the specific terms of said order or rental; and Ambrose hereby licenses to Customer and Customer licenses from Ambrose each Program in 16mm film, sound filmstrip or that video system type ordered or rented.

CUSTOMER ACKNOWLEDGES THAT THE PROGRAMS MAY NOT BE DUPLICATED, BROADCAST, TRANSMITTED BY CABLE OR OTHERWISE TRANSMITTED, ON ANY MULTI-RECEIVER OPEN OR CLOSED CIRCUIT SYSTEM, OR DISPLAYED BEFORE THE PUBLIC, WHETHER OR NOT ADMISSION IS CHARGED. CUSTOMER SHALL EXHIBIT THE PROGRAMS ONLY AS HEREIN SPECIFIED AND USE THE PROGRAMS FOR NO OTHER PURPOSE. Customer shall not sublicense, sublease or part with possession of any Program received by Customer hereunder. Performing rights to music contained in any Program are not granted herein. Nothing herein shall derogate from any rights of Ambrose or any other copyright proprietor of any Program under the United States Copyright Law. ✱

2. Price: Customer shall pay to Ambrose for the right to exhibit the Program under the conditions set forth herein the amount required for the order or rental and as set forth in Paragraph 3 hereof immediately upon invoicing by Ambrose.

3. Payments: Customer shall pay to Ambrose the following sums in the manner and at the times herein specified, time being of the essence with respect to all such payments.

(a) The price for each Program together with the delivery charge therefore, and

(b) Any and all taxes, fees or other like charges billed against Ambrose and imposed, levied or based upon this license agreement, the delivery, possession, exhibition or use of any Program, or upon the grant or exercise of any rights hereunder, or upon the sums payable by Customer to Ambrose pursuant hereto, and

(c) All other charges specified elsewhere in this agreement in the manner there set forth.

4. Advertising: Customer shall not advertise the Program hereunder in any public media and any advertising undertaken shall recite only the title of the Program and the performers, if any, and shall prominently set forth that the Program is an Ambrose Video Publishing, Inc. presentation.

5. Term: The term of this license with regard to each Program shall commence as of the date each Program is delivered for shipment to or mailed to the Customer and shall continue for the term of the order or rental. If Customer is renting the Programs, Customer agrees to return the Programs to Ambrose on or before the date "to be returned by" set forth on the Program's label when mailed or delivered to Customer.

6. Reservation of Rights: Legal title of the Programs and the containers, cassettes or reels on which the Programs are delivered shall at all times remain in Ambrose and all rights therein are reserved to Ambrose and thus any use of the term "Purchase" shall be deemed

to mean only the right and license to use and reuse the Programs hereunder, without limitation as to the number of uses or reuses, but without any change in ownership or title and otherwise subject to and upon the terms and conditions hereof.

7. Delivery: With respect to rentals, Ambrose shall at Customer's expense deliver a positive film print or a video cassette or video tape or other video tape system type of each Program, as specified by the Customer, to Customer (by delivery of same to the post office or other delivery service) in time normally required for such Program to reach Customer for Customer's first scheduled performance. Such Program shall be deemed in satisfactory condition for exhibition unless Customer, immediately after inspection thereof, notifies Ambrose to the contrary specifying the nature of any such defect. Ambrose shall not be in breach of this agreement for failure to deliver any Program by any requested date, and shall not be liable for incidental or consequential damages. Ambrose shall have the right to deliver any Program C.O.D.

8. Return: With respect to rentals, Customer shall immediately after the expiration of the rental term, return each rented Program prepaid with its reel(s) and/or cassette(s) in the containers provided to Ambrose at the return address set forth on the container label by parcel post, special delivery, insured, in the same condition as when received, reasonable wear and tear due to proper use expected. Color 16mm prints shall be insured for $300.00 and video cassettes, tapes or other video systems shall be insured for $200.00 or if less than the foregoing amounts, the maximum permitted insurable allowance to the United States Post Office. Black and white 16mm prints shall be insured for $150.00 and black and white video cassettes, tapes or other video systems for $100.00. For each day's delay in depositing any Program for return with the Post Office as herein set forth, Customer shall pay to Ambrose 25% of the price paid or payable to Ambrose as the rental price thereof hereunder.

9. Customers renting Programs hereunder, shall use the films or video system ordered hereunder only on the appropriate projection equipment or playback system as approved by Ambrose for use with said film or video system as set forth in the catalog in which these terms and conditions appear.

10. Replacement: Customers renting Programs hereunder shall pay Ambrose the replacement cost of any 16mm prints, reels or containers or video system tape lost, stolen, destroyed or injured other than through normal wear and tear resulting from use on the correct projection device or playback system in the interval between delivery to Customer and return thereof by Customer. Such payment shall not transfer title to or any interest in any program to Customer nor to any other party. Customer shall immediately notify Ambrose in writing of loss, theft, injury or destruction of any Program.

11. Cuts: Customer shall exhibit each Program only in its entirety and shall not copy duplicate, sublicense or sublease or part with possession thereof. Customer shall not cut or alter any Program or otherwise tamper therewith (except with regard to 16mm film, Customer may make necessary repairs thereto); and in no event shall any Program be performed or exhibited without complete copyright notices and credits contained therein.

12. Prevention of Performance: If Ambrose shall be unable to deliver or prevented from delivering any Program by reason of governmental action, regulation or order, or by reason of fire, flood, hurricane, labor dispute, riot, war, catastrophe, or the unavailability of

the Program in the film or video system ordered, or without limiting the foregoing, any cause beyond the control of Ambrose, this license shall be terminated as to such Program without liability to either party.

13. Default: If Customer defaults hereunder:

(a) Ambrose in addition to other remedies may repossess any Program previously delivered hereunder:

(b) Ambrose may refuse to take further orders from Customer and may refuse to make further shipments of Programs to Customer.

(c) Customer agrees to pay Ambrose costs and expenses of collection and/or repossession, including maximum attorney fees permitted by law.

14. Termination: In the event that:

(a) Customer defaults in the timely payment of any sums hereunder, and such default continues for a period of five days, or

(b) Customer advertises the program contrary to the provisions of Paragraph 4, or

(c) Customer defaults with respect to any of the other provisions hereof and fails to cure such violation of default within three (3) days after written notice thereof from Ambrose, or

(d) Customer becomes insolvent, or files a petition in bankruptcy, or is adjudicated bankrupt, or executes an assignment for the benefit of creditors, or an involuntary petition in bankruptcy is filed against Customer, or a receiver or trustee is appointed for any of Customer's property, then, in any one or more of such events, Ambrose may in its discretion at any time thereafter, terminate the license herein granted and all rights to Customer thereunder. Such remedy shall be in addition to and without prejudice to any right or remedy in law or equity or provided for elsewhere in this agreement of account of any violation or breach. Immediately upon termination of the license herein granted, Customer shall, at its expense, deliver any and all the Programs previously delivered to it, together with the reels, cassettes and containers pertaining thereto, to Ambrose and shall pay to Ambrose all moneys payable to Ambrose hereunder.

15. Warranties and Remedies: Ambrose warrants each Program to be free from defects in material or workmanship at the time of delivery. In the event of Ambrose's breach of such warranty Customer's exclusive remedy shall be that Ambrose will replace the defective Program provided Customer returns said defective Program to Ambrose in the United States. The terms and conditions of this agreement shall apply to any Program furnished as a replacement. NO OTHER WARRANTY, EXPRESSED OR IMPLIED, INCLUDING THE WARRANTIES OR MERCHANTABILITY SHALL APPLY TO ANY PROGRAM HEREUNDER.

16. Assignment: The agreement shall not be assignable by Customer.

17. Interpretation: This agreement is complete and embraces the entire understanding between the parties. No change or modification hereof shall be binding upon Ambrose unless in writing and signed by an authorized representative of Ambrose. This agreement is made in New York and shall be construed under and in accordance with the laws of the State of New York. A waiver by Ambrose of any breach or default by the Customer shall not be construed as a waiver of any other breach or default by such Customer.

Paragraph headings are for convenience and shall not in any way affect the intent of any provisions or be given any legal effect.

✱Public Performance rights come with all video programs purchased from AVP for school and library use. Admission may not be charged at a public performance.

Source: Ambrose Video Publishing, Inc. 1993 Catalog.

Disadvantages:

• Order processing requires much in-house staff time, resulting in a much higher total per-unit cost;

• Many separate purchase orders (P.O.s) and invoices create more opportunities for product receipt problems as illustrated in the following, real-life example:

Separate orders to 30 vendors for a total of 500 video titles over a fiscal year created heavy demands on staff time needed to correct the resultant problems:

—keeping track of 30 P.O.s, 30 invoices, 30+ packing slips

—12 deliveries with the wrong titles

—18 deliveries with back orders

—6 deliveries with duplicate titles

—14 deliveries with invoices not matching the packing slips.

Note that the totals equal more than 30 due to multiple problems in a single order. The remedy for this problem is to reduce the number of vendors ordered from at any one time which will result in fewer product receipt errors, freeing up staff time and reducing the total per-unit/title cost.

Few Suppliers Approach

Advantages:

• Fewer P.O.s to prepare, fewer invoices, fewer packing slips;

• Library will develop a business rapport with each vendor, allowing business to transpire smoothly on both ends;

• Reduce the chance of errors on both the vendor and library end because order and reporting methods, payment, and return policies will be well-known;

• Ability to negotiate deals based on volume sales;

• Low unit cost associated with staff order preparation time.

Disadvantages:

• May not receive the "best" or lowest price;

• Could be sacrificing title availability for lower per-title cost.[5]

In actual practice, the best ground falls in the middle. With each order there is a beginning (sending the purchase order) and an end (receipt of the order and payment), but the order process is continuous, even passing through fiscal years. The main objectives of the acquisitions department are to get the title requested at the best price, in the least amount of time, using the most efficient manner available at the time. Pick one or two large jobbers and/or distributors, one or two previewed video dealers (for newly released, more expensive releases and out-of-print, moratorium titles), and one or two catalogers (for titles that cannot be obtained from the jobbers). The number of producers/distributors that any one library deals with should be dictated by the library selection goals/objectives for that year. Never purchase directly from any catalog using the order form. Always contact a company sales representative or find out the name of the independent representative serving the region. Negotiation, even when purchasing one title, is the key to more efficient and cost-effective buying. Buying from a small number of these vendors can result in substantial savings because volume sales deals can be struck. Duplication rights can be negotiated for seasonal and other high-demand titles. Using this approach will cut down on total per-volume cost, provide optimum savings and materials budget utilization, and provide titles in a more cost- and time-efficient manner.

The following is a comprehensive, but not necessarily exhaustive, list of video-cassette vendors—jobbers, distributors, catalogers, and used/previewed videos, nationwide. It does not list educational producers. This list should be used neither as a collection development source nor as a definitive, eclectic buyer's list. Rather, it is a nationwide sampling of reputable, currently available vendors enabling video acquisitions librarians to gain a head start for comparing title availability, title inclusion, public performance rights availability, and purchase price.

Catalogers

1. ARP Videos Inc., P.O. Box 4617, North Hollywood, CA 91617. (800) 843-3672.

2. Art Com/Contemporary Arts Press—Media Distribution Catalog, P.O. Box 193123, Rincon Center, San Francisco, CA 94119-3123. (415) 431-7524.

3. artsAmerica Inc., 12 Havemeyer Place, Greenwich, CT 06830. (800) 553-5268.

4. The Athletic Institute, 200 Castlewood Dr., North Palm Beach, FL 33408-5697. (800) 933-3335.

5. Bennett Video Group, 730 Washington St., Marina del Rey, CA 90292. (310) 821-3329.

6. Better Books Company, Dept. 867, P.O. Box 9770, Fort Worth, TX 76147-2770. (800) 433-5534.

7. Cambridge Career Products, P.O. Box 2153, Dept. CC10, Charleston, WV 25328-2153. (800) 468-4227.

8. Champions on Film, 745 State Circle, Box 1941, Ann Arbor, MI 48106. (800) 521-2832.

9. Creative Learning, Box 134, Saunderstown, RI 02874. (800) 542-2468.

10. Crest Video Marketing, 415 North Figueroa St., Wilmington, CA 90744. (800) 682-7378.

11. Critic's Choice Video, P.O. Box 549, Elk Grove Village, IL 60009-0549. (800) 367-7765.

12. Educational Record Center, Bldg. 400, Ste. 400, 1575 Northside Dr. NW, Atlanta, GA 30318-4298. (404) 352-8282.

13. Educators' Video, P.O Box 82, Park Ridge, IL 60068.

14. Emery Pratt Company, 1966 W. Main St., Owosso, MI 48867-1372. (800) 762-5683.

15. Flashback/Video, Inc., 40 Cedar St., Dobbs Ferry, NY 10522. (914) 693-8100.

16. Frederic H. Weiner, Inc., 1325 2nd Ave., New Hyde Park, NY 11040. (516) 437-9873; (800) 622-2675.

17. Henwood Cinema Video, 106 N. Kesnick Ave., Glenside, PA 19038. (215) 884-7533.

18. Hotho & Co., Dept. H75, P.O. Box 9738, Forth Worth, TX 76147-2738. (800) 433-5534.

19. Media Basics Video, Lighthouse Square, Guilford, CT 06437. (800) 542-2505.

20. Music for Little People, Box 1460, Redway, CA 95560. (800) 727-2233.

21. Nostalgia Family Video, P.O. Box 606, Baker City, OR 97814. (503) 523-9034.

22. Proud to Be . . . A Black Video Collection, One Kendal Square, Bld. 600, Ste. 125, Cambridge, MA 02139. (617) 868-8965.

23. Publishers Central Bureau, Dept. 494, One Champion Ave., Avenel, NJ 07001-2301.

24. RMI Media Productions, 2807 West 47th St., Shawnee Mission, KS 66205. (800) 821-5480.

25. Schoolmaster Video, 745 State Circle, P.O. Box 1941, Ann Arbor, MI 48106. (800) 521-2832.

26. Signals (WGBH Educational Foundation), 274 Fillmore Ave. E., Saint Paul, MN 55107. (800) 458-4535.

27. Special Interest Video, 100 Enterprise Place, P.O. Box 7022, Dover, DE 19903-7022. (800) 336-9660.

28. Theodore Front Musical Literature, Inc., 16122 Cohasset St., Van Nuys, CA 91406. (818) 994-1902.

29. The Video Catalog, 1000 Westgate Dr., Saint Paul, MN 55114. (800) 733-2232.

30. Viewfinders, Inc. (Uncommon Video!!), P.O. Box 1665, Evanston, IL 60204-1665. (800) 342-3342.

31. Vintage Video, P.O. Box 262, Fairburn, GA 30213. (404) 969-7342.

32. Waldenbooks by Mail (formerly Video F.I.N.D.S.), P.O. Box 9497, Dept. 605, New Haven, CT 06534-0497. (800) 443-7359.

33. Yes! Books & Videos, P.O. Box 10726, Arlington, VA 22210. (800) 937-0234.

Distributors

1. American School Publishers, P.O. Box 408, Hightstown, NJ 08520-9377. (800) 843-8855.

2. Apple Video, P.O. Box 345, Palatine, IL 60078-0345. (708) 359-1115.

3. C.A.I. Software, Inc., 168 Express Dr. South, Brentwood, NY 11717. (800) 247-7009.

4. Canterbury Distribution, 9925 Horn Rd., Sacramento, CA 95827. (800) 878-5084.

5. Chambers Record & Video Corp., 61 Bennington Ave., Freeport, NY 11520. (800) 892-9338.

6. Edu-Tech Corporation, 65 Bailey Road, Fairfield, CT 06430. (203) 374-4212; (800) 338-5463; FAX (203) 374-8050.

7. (EG) Edward Grant—Media for Schools and Libraries, 621 N. College, P.O. Box 1021, Bloomington, IN 47402. (812) 332-7373; FAX (same).

8. Facets Multimedia, Inc., 1517 W. Fullerton Ave., Chicago, IL 60614. (800) 331-6197.

9. Instructional Video, Inc., 727 "O" St., Lincoln, NE 68508. (800) 228-0164.

10. Johnson-Rudolph, 1027 Broadway, Bowling Green, KY 42104 (502) 781-1915.

11. Librarians' Video Service, 184 East Main St., Middletown, CT 06457-0468. (800) 828-4450.

12. Library Source—"How-to" Video Distributor, 0790 W. Tennessee Ave., Box 5852, Denver, CO 80217. (800) 456-5806.

13. Library Video Company, P.O. Box 110/Dept. M-23, Bala Cynwyd, PA 19004. (800) 843-3620.

14. Listening Library, One Park Ave., Old Greenwich, CT 06870-1727. (800) 243-4504.

15. Modern (formerly Modern Talking Pictures), 5000 Park St. North, St. Petersburg, FL 33709. (800) 243-6877.
    Modern provides a large collection of corporate videos for free, distributed as a set.

16. Playing Hard to Get, 580 Old Mine Office, Madrid, NM 87010. (505) 471-7814.

17. Priority Systems Company, 4189 Cleveland St., Calumet Township, Gary, IN 46408. (800) 325-6755; (219) 985-3303; FAX (219) 985-3313.
    Specializes in special interest videos. Also has a video finding service. Catalog is called the "Videobrary."

18. Rainbow Educational Video, 170 Keyland Court, Bohemia, NY 11716. (800) 331-4047.

19. SLM Distributing Company, 84 Bud Lane, Levittown, NY 11756. (516) 933-1146.

20. Social Studies School Service, 10200 Jefferson Blvd., Room 1811, P.O. Box 802, Culver City, CA 90232-0802. (800) 421-4246. (see Zenger Video, Inc.)

21. SVE (Society for Visual Education, Inc.), Department DE, 1345 Diversey Parkway, Chicago, IL 60614-1299. (800) 621-1900.

22. U.S.A. Information Service. 237 Saw Mill Rd., P.O. Box 11, West Haven, CT 06516. (203) 933-2551.
    Offers a selective list of titles especially for classroom use. Many of these titles are not readily available to the consumer in the retail/entertainment-dominated video marketplace. Subject areas of inclusion: history, science, geography, and the arts.

23. Video Yesteryear, Box C, Sandy Hook, CT 06482. (800) 243-0987.

24. Williamson Distributors, 1545 Gilmer Ave., Montgomery, AL 36104. (800) 283-4684.
    Profess to have largest database in operation representing over 8,000 publishers and producers and access to over 200,000 audio and video titles. Offer some videos with public performance rights, database searching assistance for titles/subjects, processing, and personalized service.

25. Zenger Video, 10200 Jefferson Blvd., Room VC8, Culver City, CA 90232-0802. (800) 421-4246. (aka Social School Services)

Jobber (Wholesaler)

1. Baker & Taylor, 501 S. Gladiolus, Momence, IL 60954. (800) 435-5111.
2. Brodart Video, 500 Arch St., Williamsport, PA 17705. (800) 233-8467.
3. Commtron/Ingram Library Services Inc., 1124 Heil Quaker Blvd., P.O. Box 3006, La Vergne, TN 37086-1986. (615) 793-5000; FAX (615) 793-3810.

   Now offers an automatic new release selection called "Video Hits Service." Marketed as a value-added service, it is available to libraries on three levels. Contact (800) 937-5300.
4. Professional Media Service Corp., 19122 S. Vermont Ave., Gardena, CA 90248. (800) 223-7672.

   PMS provides distributor-like access to many educational vendors such as AIMS Media, Barr Films, Phoenix/BFA Films, and others. They also provide comprehensive US-MARC custom cataloging and processing for a fee. Cataloging provided uses LC subject headings, LC, DDC, ANSR, or unclassed and is available in many formats including disk, tape, edit sheets, and catalog cards. Custom cataloging is done by completing a profile sheet for the library's specific needs. PMS has perhaps the most extensive videocassette database in the industry.
5. Schwartz Brothers, Inc. (Special Accounts Division), 4901 Forbes Boulevard, Lanham, MD 20706. (800) 638-0243 ext. 225; FAX (301) 731-0323.

   Monthly video catalog is called "The Helical Scan."

Previewed Videos

1. AAA/Priority Video, Inc., 500 Mill Rd., Bensalem, PA 19020. (800) 220-2200.
2. American Video Distributors (AVD), 708 Chestnut St., Clearwater, FL 34616. (800) 277-6454.
3. Distribution Video & Audio (DV&A), 1060 Kapp Drive, Clearwater, FL 34625. (800) 683-4147; (813) 447-4147; FAX (813) 441-3069.

   All titles checked against a 31-point quality list before being entered into inventory. Prices range from $37 to $7.95 and include new releases, children's, classics, and documentaries. All titles guaranteed.
4. Foss-Man Distributors, 147 Washington Ave., Little Ferry, NJ 07643. (800) 827-6134.
5. Major Video Concepts, Inc. (formerly Playback International Video), 13321 S.E. 26th St., Bellevue, WA 98005. (800) 284-5855.

   Discount tapes from $7 to $38. Recent releases and B titles with over 12,000 catalog titles in stock. Now mergered with Major Video Concepts, which is also a new tape video jobber.
6. Midwest Tape Exchange, 1750 West Laskey Rd., Toledo, OH 43613. (800) 875-2785; FAX (419) 471-1029.

   Discount used videos from $5 and up, available on 30-, 45-, and 60-day windows. All tapes are unconditionally guaranteed for playability and checked in-house with Research Technology Incorporated's (RTI) videotape inspection/cleaning machines.

They also sell new videos. Offers excellent, personalized service, free P.O.P materials, and low prices.

7. Movies 4 Sale, 500 N. Kimball Rd., Ste. 103, Southlake, TX 76092. (800) 883-0303.

8. Movies in Motion, 8752 W. 159th St., Orland Park, IL 60462 (800) 333-6553.

9. Roadrunner Video Enterprises, Inc., 819 South Floyd St., Louisville, KY 40203. (800) 728-6128.

   Four flyers per year containing previously viewed titles from their video rental library, comprised mostly of Top 25 video feature hits. Satisfaction guaranteed up to 30 days from order receipt. Also available are new titles and titles not in their flyers. Credit card, check and/or money orders only method of prepayment; no purchase orders accepted. Prices range from $9.94 to $19.95.

10. Stock Rotation Services. (800) SEL-LVHS.

11. Video King, 1094 Pleasant St., Worcester, MA 01602. (800) 348-1440.

Special

1. DVS Home Video, 125 Western Ave., Boston, MA 02134. (800) 333-1203.

   DVS sells described movies, designed for people who are blind or have low vision. Their 1993 catalog lists approximately 40 titles. A described movie includes an audible soundtrack placed over the existing soundtrack that provides a running description of the action, plot, scene, and characters. Titles such as *Honey, I Shrunk the Kids*, *Anne of Avonlea*, and *Three Men and a Baby* are available for $19.99 to $29.95.

2. Karol Video (Division of Karol Media), 350 No. Pennsylvania Ave., P.O. Box 7600, Wilkes-Barre, PA 18773-7600. (800) 526-4773.

   Essentially a retail video distributor for libraries, Karol Video offers some interesting services. Besides offering some unique titles not found elsewhere in the market in its monthly magazine, the *Cassette Gazette*, Karol offers some quality, special interest, "corporate-sponsored" videos for free.

3. Madera Cinevideo, 612 E. Yosemite Ave., Madera, CA 93638. (209) 661-6000; FAX (209) 674-3650.

   Distributes a wide variety of Spanish language videos including features and educational titles for both children and adults.

4. Pentrex, P.O. Box 94911, Pasadena, CA 91109. (818) 793-3400.

   An excellent source for videos on and about trains and travel.

5. Pickwick's Travel Video Catalogue. 11146 S.E. Diana Ave., Boring, OR 97009. (800) 333-3367; (503) 658-7476.

   An excellent source for worldwide travel videos.

6. Whole Toon Access. 1450 19th Ave. NW., P.O. Box 369, Issaquah, WA 98027. (206) 391-8747.

   A comprehensive cataloger source for cartoon, national, and international videos for children and adults. All available Disney titles, *Felix the Cat*, *The Flintstones*, *Mr. Magoo*, *Casper*, and the National Film Board of Canada titles are all here plus hundreds of others. Includes hard-to-find Japanese animation titles.

SUMMARY

This chapter has attempted to help librarians in their videocassette purchasing efforts by defining and categorizing vendors. The advantages and disadvantages of dealing with particular vendor types has also been outlined, along with specific methods to assure the best price, best service, and fastest delivery. A nationwide, select list of vendors has been provided in the hopes that readers will inquire about services and request catalogs/flyers from those vendors. Junk mail breeds more junk mail, but in the volatile world of videocassette vendors, knowing "who sells what?" and "at what price?" is vital.

It is recommended that receivers of this "junk mail" look specifically at all vendor order forms and "Term and Contract Condition" statements (particularly the producer/distributor catalogs), calling if necessary for clarification. An excellent, albeit somewhat dated overview source to help the reader get started is J. Michael Pemberton's *Policies of Audiovisual Producers and Distributors: A Handbook for Acquisitions Personnel*, 2nd ed. (Metuchen, NJ: The Scarecrow Press, Inc., 1989).

NOTES

1. Charles B. Osburn, "Impact of Collection Management Practices on Intellectual Freedom," *Library Trends* 39 (Summer/Fall 1990): 168–169.

2. Audrey Eaglen, *Buying Books: A How-To-Do-It Manual for Librarians* (New York: Neal-Schuman Publishers, Inc., 1989), p. 29.

3. Ibid.

4. Joanne Salce, "Video Distribution: The Maze Made Manageable," *Library Journal* 115 (July 1990): 42.

5. Mark Richie, in-person interview at National Film & Video Market, Mesa, AZ (October 22, 1993).

4

The Acquisitions Process

ACQUISITIONS—GOALS AND FUNCTIONS

Chapter 3 separated vendors by type, outlined the specific services provided by those types, and detailed various plans of action for optimum purchasing. Since purchasing policies and procedures in most libraries have historically worked sufficiently well, this chapter will not discuss the full range of acquisitions, but instead will concentrate only on those aspects peculiar to videocassette acquisition. Some general acquisitions concepts may be mentioned to give the reader landmarks so that specific refinements for dealing with videocassettes can be detailed. The reader wishing a more detailed discussion on general acquisitions routines, including accounting practices, would do well to consult the following three sources:

Eaglen, Audrey. *Buying Books* (New York: Neal-Schuman Publishers, Inc., 1989).
Grieder, Ted. *Acquisitions: Where, What, and How* (Westport, CT: Greenwood Press, 1978).
Schmidt, Karen A., ed. *Understanding the Business of Library Acquisitions.* Part 5—"Methods of Accounting and Business Practices" (Chicago: ALA, 1990).

In discussing library acquisitions, many texts use a broader definition which encompasses both collection development and selection in a hierarchical relationship, as well as the physical acquisition, processing, and cataloging of materials to ready them for circulation. While this conceptual definition may be suitable for larger public libraries, academic institutions, and special libraries that utilize many separate departments and subject bibliographers, the focus of acquisitions within this chapter is much narrower—that is, limited only to the actual tasks and functions involved in the purchase, acquisition, and record-keeping of videocassettes.

Collection development is the broadest activity, and includes all planning and policymaking for the systematic and rational building of a library collection. Collection development does not concern itself with individual titles; rather, it seeks to shape and mold the entire collection based on measurable [and obtainable] goals and objectives. Narrower in scope is selection, a single function within the broader collection development activity, which is concerned with selecting individual titles to fulfill patrons' needs and demands. Selection pits one item against another for inclusion into the collection, much like matching and fitting the pieces of a jigsaw puzzle together. Collection development sees the entire puzzle as a whole first, and looks to see if the picture on the puzzle is the same as the one on the box (i.e., specific acquisitions goals met). Then a process is begun to put the pieces together in a sequenced, efficient manner.

Acquisitions, in the narrower sense, refers to the single-purpose process of verifying, ordering, and paying for those needed materials. Purchasing materials in the modern-day library has become a dominant aspect of work. Although automation has expedited the process, library staff are still needed to make sure that the items are ordered, entered into the library's files, and purchased within the constraints of the library's budget. After purchase, these materials must be accessible, in terms of bibliographic access, to patrons—otherwise the purchase is meaningless. Because of this fact, acquisitions operations must also entail some precataloging and associated operations regardless of the type of catalog (i.e., computerized [PAC, OPAC] or catalog cards). Before the activities and functions of acquisitions can be detailed, it is essential that all library staff come to a mutual understanding of their specific goals and expectations related to various functions and tasks.

It is assumed that the ultimate goal of any library acquisitions department is to acquire the materials which have been requested through the selection process. Library acquisitions departments should not have a different range of goals which is dependent upon the media/format they are ordering; rather, the prioritization of those goals will be different based on internal (library) and external (availability) variables. Various goals include the following:

1. Materials are obtained as quickly as possible;

2. Materials are obtained as inexpensively as possible;

3. Materials are obtained with a high degree of accuracy;

4. Work processes and procedures are as simple as possible to keep the unit cost of securing materials as low as possible;

5. Monitoring and control of expenditures are maintained;

6. Necessary fund accounting is maintained and accurately reported;

7. Payments to vendors for materials received are made in a timely manner;

8. Vendor performance is monitored and evaluated on an ongoing basis;

9. Cordial and professional relations with vendors are maintained; and

10. Accurate and timely reporting on availability/nonavailability of materials are transmitted to those responsible for selection and collection development.[1]

Automation of the acquisitions process has similar motivations associated with the above goals:

1. Reducing ordering backlogs;

2. Reducing acquisitions cost [staff time and effort];

3. Containing acquisitions cost;

4. Speeding order writing and/or receipt of materials;

5. Improving funds control;

6. Expanding a single-function automated system into an integrated system;

7. Improving management information;

8. Achieving compatability with resource sharing partners; and

9. Committing the library to the use of technology.[2]

Furthermore, an automated acquisitions system, such as the ones integrated into the DYNIX and Gaylord's GALAXY circulations systems, as well as small-utility specialized database programs such as Right On Programs' Acquisitions module should possess all or most of the following features in order to be useful:

1. Integration or connection with other automated functions including circulation, cataloging, serials control, and the bibliographic database

2. Database access

3. Vendor name/address file

4. Electronic purchase order writing (batched or on-demand)

5. Online ordering—electronic interfacing via telephone modem

6. In-process file

7. Claiming

8. Receiving/paying/automatic check vouchering and printing

9. Fund accounting

10. Vendor monitoring (back orders and fill rate, cancellations, receipt time between orders)

The prioritization of the goals mentioned in this chapter's opening paragraph ultimately determines the daily procedures and defines staff tasks, activities, and routines. Presumably, any library involved in acquisitions already has a standardized work flow for materials, from the initial selection and ordering to processing and ultimate shelving for patron access. This flow chart, either in written or unwritten form, probably assumes specific tasks from various personnel. It is important that all staff members understand their role in this process, can track an item through the process, and understand why tasks are being performed in such a manner.

Ted Grieder summarizes the functions of an acquisitions unit as inclusive of five activities, occurring in the following sequence: selecting; verifying (precataloging, searching); ordering; receiving; and recording funds (encumbered money for titles ordered, but not yet received).[3] Rose Mary Magrill and John Corbin's work on acquisitions activities has been enlarged below to detail the specifics of videocassette acquisitions.[4]

Obtaining Information about Titles for Purchase

Verification. Through the use of a standardized order form, the acquisitions staff must obtain from selectors specific videographic information which identifies that title from all others, enabling it to be ordered from a specific vendor. This process may require double-checking various vendor print/microfiche catalogs and searching on-line and CD-ROM databases such as A/V Online, OCLC, Inc., and Gaylord's Precision One. Vendors such as Baker & Taylor Video and Ingram/Commtron provide libraries with free microfiche products listing titles, producer, manufacturer order number, and vendor order number (or ISBN), as well as retail and extended discount selling price. The process of verifying an item against a particular vendor's "catalog inventory" for ordering is somewhat different than bibliographic verification from various bibliographic CD-ROM products and on-line bibliographic utilities such as OCLC and WLN required for cataloging. The downloading of the bibliographic record may occur at the time an order is initiated or it may be done at the point of cataloging, after the item has been received, checked against the invoice, and the invoice paid.

The Order Form. Whether the selector uses a MOF (multiple order form), POF (purchase order form), single order form, an electronic form on a database, or an acquisitions subsystem like DYNIX's Desiderata file to order materials, the order form is often the only communication device between the selector and the acquisitions librarian. This form must contain sufficient information for the order clerk to verify its existence, distinguish it from other titles, permit it to be ordered through regular channels, and/or define the selector's preferences for ordering, cataloging, and classifying as well as its assignment to a particular branch, collection, and type of use. For these reasons, a diverse amount of information should be included on any order form, whether completed on a hard-copy, multiple order form or an electronic equivalent. The type of information included in such a form should be the minimum amount required for the various functions such a form performs related to the acquisitions and cataloging process. First, it can be used as the selectors' method of initiating an order request for specific titles. Secondly, it can be used by the acquisitions staff as a reporting device back to the selector regarding the following information: title and quantity (copies and volumes) that has been ordered, the order date, purchase order (P.O.) number, invoice number, dollar amount encumbered and actually spent, and date that the item was received, cancelled, and/or backordered. Thirdly, the multiple order form can be an important tool for communicating with the cataloging staff, making sure that any cataloging and classification are congruent with the needs of collection. Inclusive of all the aforementioned needs, the order form should have space for the following information:

1. Title (plus any available subtitles).
2. Series.
3. Imprint information to distinguish it from another version with the same title—producer, production company, and copyright date and/or date of release.
4. Number of volumes and/or parts.
5. Vendor information—company name, address, and phone number as well as possible sales representative to which P.O. is to be sent.
6. Vendor order number.
7. Manufacturer's order number (if different).
8. ISBN, when available.
9. OCLC or similar bibliographic utility number.
10. List price (important for acquisitions staff when encumbering funds); extended or expected discount price from vendor and space for recording the actual price.
11. Budget line item from which funds are to be encumbered.
12. Review/selection source citation (important for title verification and vendor double-check, as well as for descriptive cataloging).
13. Selector's name, authorization, and order submittal date.
14. Special instructions for the acquisitions staff in ordering as well as catalogers. This may include information regarding special negotiated replacement prices.
15. Rights delineation—home use, public performance, closed-circuit, duplication (if duplication, how many copies to be duplicated?).
16. How many copies to be ordered? Instructions on copy distribution—how many to what libraries/branches?
17. Does the library already own a copy of this exact title? Is it in the database/catalog? Is this a replacement, a duplicate, or just an additional copy (holdings record)? Space for local automated system bibliographic number, bar code, and classification/call number should also be here.
18. Call, Cutter, or Classification number.

Figures 4.1–4.5 are examples of videocassette order forms used in various public libraries, as well as a Model Order Form which serves as an eclectic composite of elements previously discussed. Many libraries use a generic order form for all materials; others use different forms for print and nonprint materials; still others use different forms for each format. Some libraries use a single order card; others must have a multiple order card consisting of several carbonless copies of the completed form. Although the form originates at the point of selection, each completed form copy has a specific destination and function at that destination. For example, one copy might be retained by the selector as notification of order; a second copy is sent to the acquisitions department for order preparation; a third copy may accompany the received item to technical services, serving as a work slip from which to catalog the item. Oftentimes the cataloger may import a MARC record from a national database into the local database before the item is received. The information on the order form is the only videographic information that the cataloger will possess to facilitate that process; therefore, it must be as complete and correct as possible. Also, dates of ordering and item receipt as well as purchase order and invoice numbers may be recorded on such forms; thus they serve dual roles as status report devices. Even libraries possessing electronic ordering systems may need to utilize some sort of screen form to facilitate ease of ordering. The various order fields available to the selector on any order form directly reflect the complexity of the ordering and reporting mechanism, and the cataloging depth of any library. Librarians should continually monitor their needs in the order and cataloging process and modify order forms and procedures accordingly. Without such evaluation in place, it is easy to create a paper monster or possess overly complex ordering routines. The order form and its electronic equivalent should possess only those fields of information which are needed by all parties involved in the order process.

All five order forms have some fields of information in common. Title, publisher, vendor, vendor address, fund encumbered, price, number of copies, various order numbers, review citations, and date ordered are the major fields where consistent information is requested. From that point, however, each form digresses, becoming responsive, in part, to each library's unique acquisitions and cataloging procedures.

The Model Order Form (Figure 4.1) reflects a format-specific form in that it provides information fields for information encountered only when ordering videocassettes. Special rights such as home-use only (HU), public performance (PP), closed circuit/broadcast television (CB) and duplication rights (DB) are delineated. Special attributes like "closed-captioned for the hearing impaired," "described narration," "letter-box," and "dubbed" should also be noted, as they are helpful for catalogers in describing and identifying the item. Various order numbers such as the manufacturer's number, the distributor/vendor number, the ISBN, and a bibliographic database number are equally important to the order clerk and vendor in distinguishing one title from another. The order

Figure 4.1
Model Order Form

```
               Special Rights: HU PP CB DUP #____

    Call #:                  Attributes: CC  DV  LB

    Title:
    Copyright Date:                      # Vols.:
    Series/Edition:                      List Price:
    Producer:                            Ext. Price:
    Vendor Address:                      # Copies:
                                         Man. #:
                                         ISBN #:
                                         OCLC\LC:

                  Selector:             Fund #:
    P.O.#.:       Date Ordered:         Coll. Placm.:
                  Date Entered:         Priority:
    Inv.#:        Review Citation:

    Date Rec.:           Branch Distribution:
    Special Instructions:
```

may be for an added copy or replacement, and the existence of the videographic record should be noted so that a cataloger will not inadvertently or unnecessarily create a duplicate database record. Various report information such as the purchase order number, invoice number, date ordered and received, and fund number encumbered may also be necessary. Departmental libraries may house collections in specific areas such as popular, local history, or by subject (business, humanities, etc.). For libraries utilizing such departmental delineations, a field for collection placement may prove useful. For libraries utilizing an organized collection development process in a branch setting, a system of routing order forms and denoting branch distribution of ordered copies is a must. In this manner, a significant number of duplicate orders can be avoided resulting in more efficient order preparation and processing time.

The two-part, carbonless form used at the Elkhart (IN) Public Library (Figure 4.2) is media oriented. It contains specific fields necessary for ordering media (compact discs, audiocassettes, videocassettes, kits, etc.) within the library ordering process. This form is also used as a status report form back to the selector and to generate a work slip from which to catalog the item coincidental to ordering. The boxes indicating format as well as the author/composer information and ordering/cataloging priority are essential information.

The four-part, carbonless uniform order form used by the Toledo-Lucas County (OH) Public Library (Figure 4.3) is used for all print and nonprint formats. It has separate sections for title information, fund and price information, and branch/department distribution. It is also used as a report form reflecting

Figure 4.2
Elkhart (IN) Public Library Media Order Form

PO #	AC ☐ MC ☐ CD ☐ VC ☐ Other ☐ _____	
Vendor	AUTHOR/COMPOSER	PRIORITY
Year	PERFORMER	
Publisher	Title	Vols.
ISBN	Edition/Series	
Mfg. #	Fund #	Collection/Class
Vendor #	Publisher's Address	Special Inst.
No. of Copies		
Price		
Cost		
Invoice Date	Selector/Approver/Date	Reviews

Source: Provided by James C. Scholtz, Associate Director/AV Services, Elkhart Public Library, Elkhart, IN, 1994.

price, cost, fund number encumbered, and date of bill. Note that it does not specify a media format or have any field for series information.

Figure 4.4 illustrates the uniform materials order form used by the Cumberland County Public Library & Information Center (Fayetteville, NC). It is similar to the four-part form used by the Toledo-Lucas County Public Library, except that it has some additional fields for classification number, selector identification, date of order and receipt, special instructions, and review source citation information. Because of its single copy format, it is not used as a report form, but as an initial order vehicle and technical services work form.

Figure 4.5 shows a book selection work card utilized at the Phoenix Public Library (AZ), completed for a videocassette order. Note that the ISBN field doubles as a vendor order number field. The selector has provided the acquisitions department with order information from two vendors, Baker & Taylor Video and Ingram Video Services. Thus the acquisitions librarian must decide from whom to order this title. Note that this three-part, carbonless form is suited for use as a report form, containing report information such as call/classification number and fund number encumbered. It also contains valuable identification information for the cataloger such as agency to be assigned, publication date, and special notes.

The Order Process and Specific Tasks. A typical scenario for a multiple order

Figure 4.3
Toledo-Lucas County (OH) Public Library Uniform Order Form

				NEED	REC'D		NEED	REC'D
	Adult [X]	DNC	ART			Lo		
		Ref.	AS			Mau		
Author (Last name first)	Juv.	Circ.	BL			Mot		
	[ ]	Repl.	BUS			Ore		
Title			CR			PP		
			CS			RC		
MCK			HTB			SS		
			Lit-F			So		
Publisher Date		Price	LH			Sp.S		
			Soc.S			SyL		
		Fund	Tech			TatC		
			VisS			T.H.		
Edition No. of vols.		D.H. OK Dir. OK	B			Wash		
			Hed			Wat		
			Hol			WT		
Order No. Dealer No. cop.	Cost	Date of bill	Ka			Corr		
			LgCr			SBL		
							12-52	

Source: Provided by Pat Lora, Toledo-Lucas County Public Library, Toledo, OH, 1992.

form might be as follows: The selector writes/types up order on order form and sends to the acquisitions department, where the multiple order form is completed. To save effort, the selector may complete a multiple order form, keep a single copy for his/her records, and send the remaining parts to the acquisitions department. In a more efficient system, the selector would enter the information into an electronic database where it would be immediately transmitted to the acquisitions department, permitting the printing of multiple order forms and purchase orders. The acquisitions department would complete the order form, adding dates, P.O. number, and other essential information, then possibly route a hard copy back to the selector. In a totally electronic environment, this hard-copy status would not be necessary because the order and its relevant information would be retained within the database, accessible through a variety of search keys. The order would be electronically transferred to the vendor or a purchase order printed automatically after input. Acquisitions receives the multiple order form, verifies title and other order information, encumbers the funds, prints the purchase orders, and transmits the order to the vendor. Date ordered, P.O. number, and extended price, as well as vendor number, ISBN and/or OCLC/LC number should also be indicated on the form, one copy of which is returned to the selector. This information should be recorded in the electronic database. The selector now knows the title has been ordered and files it in an ''on-order'' section of the order file. When the title is received and checked in, a copy of the multiple order form might be used as a cataloging tool, accompanying the title through the cataloging and processing phases, eventually coming home to the department/ branch/special collection where it will be shelved.

Figure 4.4
Cumberland County (NC) Public Library & Information Center Uniform Order Form

R-NC-F-NF-J-GEN-E	Author _____
Classification #	Title _____
_____	_____
AC-REP-ED _____	
Price _____	_____
Your initials _____	Publisher _____
Date Or'd _____	Address _____
Date Rec'd _____	_____
Special Instructions: _____	Date of Pub. _____
_____	ISBN # _____
	Selection Source _____

Total   Copies   HQ   BKM   BORD   EF   E   HM   NW   SL   STED

Source: Provided by Barbara D. Garcia, AV Department Head, Cumberland County
Public Library & Information Center, Fayetteville, NC, 1992.

All information would be completed on the order form including invoice number, date received, discounted price, and call/classification number.

Today there is much emphasis on collection development and satisfying patron demands/needs as quickly as possible. To an extent, the multiple order form or electronic database could be used as excellent cooperative collection development tools. In a typical library scenario, before an order would be sent to the vendor, the order could be automatically/simultaneously routed to other departments and branches. Those departments and branches would indicate how many copies of an item they want and transmit the order back to acquisitions within a specified amount of time, after which the orders would be transmitted to the vendor. By using a scenario such as this, a library can reap several benefits: librarians can rely on the best volume discount from the vendor, save staff time and effort by ordering all needed copies at the same time, and have a good chance that all copies will arrive together, thus saving time and effort on the cataloging and processing end.

In some libraries, especially those possessing computerized circulation/databases, an item may be reflected in the database immediately upon initiation of the order. Commonly called a bibliographic record, this specific title information could be a brief record consisting only of title, producer/production company, and copyright/release date information with an ''on-order'' or similar status attached to a holdings record, or it could contain an entire MARC record, complete with contents, subject heading, and analytical entry fields. The record would probably not be modified or altered to reflect local database concerns

Figure 4.5
Phoenix (AZ) Public Library Book Selection Work Card

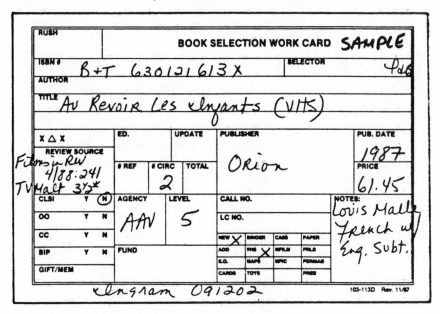

Source: Provided by Phoenix (AZ) Public Library, 1992.

(discussed in Chapter 6) yet, but a holdings record indicating a status of "ON ORDER" or similar status would probably be evident. A computerized database having the capacity to reflect immediate status of an item, whether on order, on shelf, or circulating is termed to be "dynamic," rather than a static database, such as a CD-ROM product, which is not able to detail on-shelf or circulating status. Used in this manner, a dynamic database allows patrons to put holds (also termed reserves) on specific titles which are on order.

Initiating Purchase Orders and the Materials' Purchase Process

As previously discussed, the selector may already have indicated a vendor preference on individual multiple order forms. Library policy may also dictate that the selector must indicate a vendor on each order. It may be the selector's task to locate verification information, including vendor order number and other vendor information, or it may be an acquisitions task. The acquisitions staff may have a set of default vendors used for specific types of materials or when the selector does not indicate a vendor preference on the order. The acquisitions staff must select an appropriate vendor for order fulfillment. Choice of vendor should reflect the library's level of importance given the following items:

1. list price and available discount;

2. number of titles/volumes needed for a minimum order;

3. vendor inventory, especially concerning the subject/genre of title (many vendors specialize in certain titles or genres);

4. order preparation time (can the order be made by telephone, on-line, or by other, more labor-intense means?)

5. order fulfillment (number of back orders, cancellations, titles received), plus average number of days for this process to occur;

6. availability of preprocessing/precataloging (possibly customized);

7. geographic location, ease of ordering (800-number, fax, computer ordering, etc.);

8. company invoicing and returns procedures, back order, and cancellation statements mesh with the needs of the library; and

9. number, frequency, and type of vendor-related problems.

While acquisitions personnel should have the authority to select and/or redirect the order through an alternate vendor, especially after the first back order or cancellation, a standard order hierarchy should be established by mutual agreement between the acquisitions department and the selectors. In this manner, when an item must be reordered, it will not have to cross hands or departments, thus reducing the amount of lag time and chances of lost orders. Titles and their respective quantities must be ordered through a wide variety of means depending upon the existing processes of the library. These may include the manual typing of purchase orders, entry of items into a computerized database, using an acquisitions program to print sorted purchase orders, or ordering direct via fax or voice. As a matter of course, certain forms such as multiple order forms or special vendor order forms may be attached to these purchase orders. Also, funds from an identified line-item budget account must be encumbered for the expected purchase price of the items ordered. Once the order is prepared, it must be dispatched by mail, phone, on-line, or fax.

It is important that the acquisitions staff maintain accurate address files listing vendor names, addresses and important phone numbers, special account numbers, contact/sales representatives, and details and dates of any special problems or special order requirements such as dollar amount purchase minimums, standard discounts, or special shipping and handling information. Some automated acquisitions systems have such an address book/vendor monitoring system component. Libraries not possessing such a system can still rely upon a cardex card file. Today however, there exists a wide variety of low-priced but extremely flexible and powerful personal computer database software like Microsoft Works, PFS First Choice, and PC-File that make building such a vendor file an easy chore. Information for this file can be obtained from a variety of sources including, but not limited to, catalog contracts and invoice statements, and conversations with sales representatives. An excellent, albeit somewhat dated book detailing specific acquisitions information for about 400 audiovisual vendors is J. Michael Pemberton's *Policies of Audiovisual Producers and Distributors: A Handbook for Acquisitions Personnel*, 2nd ed. (Metuchen, NJ: The Scarecrow Press, Inc., 1989).

Maintaining Purchasing/Ordering Records for Materials

This task involves maintaining files, either manually and/or by computer, which show the status of each order. Manual files are very labor intensive, and can usually only be organized so that access is by one limiter such as title, purchase order number, vendor, or date ordered. Automated systems, however, have multiple access points and have the ability to maintain records long-term.

Receiving and Checking Ordered Materials

A fourth responsibility of an acquisitions unit is receiving and checking materials, which involves the following: (1) opening received packages from vendors and checking all titles against the order forms (bibliographic and vendor supplied data) and the vendor invoice and packing slips; and (2) checking the titles for physical damage. This involves an six-point visual check:

1. check case and windows for cracks or separation;
2. check back flap by opening to see if spring is working properly;
3. check for tape and leader secured to each hub;
4. check for tape tightly wound/packed around play hub (The RTI and Paulmar cleaning/ inspection machines are excellent tools for evaluating physical tape damage, cleaning off excess oxide present on many new tapes, and for repacing the tape on the play hub tightly.);
5. check for all labels to be correct and adequately adhered to surfaces; and
6. physical box (cardboard or plastic) should be in good shape, with any artwork and annotation information intact (usable).

Neither magnetic damage nor unplayability because of internal tape defects can be detected by the RTI or Paulmar machines. It is important, therefore, that any visual checking of the title frame and/or credits (using a VCR) for precataloging be done as soon as possible once the items have been received, checked in, and assessed against the six-point check. Most vendors will accept defective tapes as returns and exchange for a replacement, credit, or exchange for another title; however, they do have replacement time limits, such as 30 days. Also, many vendors will not accept defective or incorrect title returns once property/ownership labels and stamps have been adhered. Because of these vendor-imposed conditions, it is vital that purchase contracts be read and that the limits and conditions be followed. All supplemental/accompanying material should be included and complete.

Returns. All returns should be taken care of as close to the date of receipt as possible. Telephone notification of the vendor may also be necessary to authorize return or vendor-paid pickup. Each vendor may have specific forms which must be completed and returned along with specific problems like defective titles, wrongly invoiced titles, and damaged-shipped titles. All paperwork, copies of invoices, and packing slips must be kept together, photocopied, and/or returned with the titles. Titles must be boxed or packaged and returned to the vendor. Records of these returns along with periodic followups as to their filled status must also be kept. A standard form, such as the one illustrated in Figure 4.6, might be used to notify vendors of the type of damage and reason for return.

Authorizing Payment for Ordered Materials Received

Another responsibility of an acquisitions unit is authorizing payment for materials, which involves the recording of the actual price paid for each item, releasing the encumbrance and entering the actual cost of an item in the financial records, and preparing payment or creating the authorization required to release payment for those materials. This process may involve writing some information on the multiple order form such as the amount actually paid, date received, and invoice number.

Clearing Order Records

This process involves recording the receipt date on a multiple order form or electronic receiving screen, preparing an appropriate transmittal record to accompany the material to the next stage of preparation (usually the cataloging department), and possibly changing any database status from "on order" to "in process" or other meaningful status terminology.

Claiming and Cancelling Orders

This task involves monitoring the files for outstanding orders to be claimed cancelled and/or reordered. Each vendor will have a different time period for cancelling back orders, and query letters should be sent at least every three months to these vendors regarding status of back orders and informing them of cancelled items. When cancellation of a title occurs without an order being reissued, it is the task of the acquisitions department to delete that order from the database and send the appropriate forms to the selector. If the ordering process involves downloading various MARC/OCLC or other bibliographic utility records into a local database prior to receipt, and cataloging of the item when an item is not received/cancelled, this record must be deleted. If any holds have

Figure 4.6
Model Library to Vendor Videocassette Damage Return Form

```
VIDEOCASSETTE DAMAGE REPORT FORM

                                          Date _____
Vendor Name _____  Address _____
Title _____
Damage Report:
____ blank                      ____ case damaged
                                indicate parts dam. _____
____ poor quality picture
                                ____ physical tape damage
                                (tape stopped at first damage)
____ no sound                   ____ wrong tape sent

____ magnetic distortion        ____ case mismarked
(tape stopped at first          describe _____
damage point)                   _____
____ other defects _____
____ send to AV for repair      ____ return. OK
____ return to vendor: ____ reorder;  ____ cancel/credit
Date repaired/returned ____     AV technician _____
```

been placed on such a title, the circulation system should automatically produce a notice which can be sent to the patron notifying them of the title's unavailability.

Handling Materials That Need Special Treatment

This task involves a wide array of special situations not limited to maintaining records for and acknowledging gift materials, cooperative purchase materials, depository and leased materials, subscription materials, standing orders, blanket orders, and approval plans. Most acquisitions systems, especially automated ones, are set up to handle title-by-title ordering, with each title purchased at a respective price. Knowledgeable audiovisual librarians are often able to negotiate special purchase agreements for a block of titles from one vendor. Sometimes this involves purchasing a number of titles and receiving a set amount as a bonus. In cases such as these, a negotiated deal with a vendor will require certain wording and prices stated on a P.O. These prices may or may not reflect a set percentage discount. In most automated acquisitions/circulation databases, a list price must be present in the bibliographic or holdings record as a replacement value and an encumbered value. If encumbered at list price, a line item budget would reveal false encumbrances or, if encumbered at a prorated, extrapolated per-title dollar amount, would show a false value in the replacement holdings record. Acquisitions systems requiring order placement on a per-title basis may demand that special P.O.s and orders be manually typed and processed, downloading only a brief record, an OCLC/MARC record, or other bib-liographic record without holding records attached to avoid false encumbrances. Therefore, a method of communication from selector to acquisitions department staff must be developed so that in these special cases, the vendor receives the proper P.O. necessary to fulfill the order at the agreed-upon price and the library both encumbers and expends the correct amounts. In some cases, a prorated amount may have to be input into an automated system for the correct total to be encumbered to that vendor. In other cases, a special replacement cost may be negotiated with the vendor. These special prices should be listed in the hold-ings record, so that the patron is not charged a false dollar amount when the title is lost, not returned, or damaged.

Dealing With Individual Titles That Need Special Treatment

This task involves negotiating credits or refunds for items not wanted, re-ceived in error or in damaged, unacceptable condition, arranging for rush pur-chase and receipt of titles from local video stores or department stores such as K-Mart, Waldenbooks, Target, and Wal-Mart. Prepaying for titles or using credit card payment also falls under this task assignment. Lastly, this task deals with solving dilemmas related to poor vendor performance and finding new vendors.

Developing and Analyzing Performance Standards

A last responsibility of an acquisitions department involves collecting and analyzing various measures of performance used to evaluate budget use and vendor order fulfillment. Previously discussed in this chapter were the various points of importance used in evaluating ordering from a vendor in the first place. These statistics, plus the rate of budget utilization from month to month and current average per-title/volume cost compared with previous years' costs, should also be studied.

Listservs

Today, E-mail listservs on the Internet provide a method of linking librarians across the world, and in all types of libraries, together to share news and con-cerns, and to discuss problems and potential solutions. Video librarians have two such listservs that would prove invaluable for any acquistitions librarian searching for specific titles, subjects, and/or vendor information, as well as just general care and handling information about videocassettes in libraries. The listservs are listed as follows:

- Media-L—subscribe by sending a subscription message {e.g., leave subject field blank; Message: sub Media-L} listserv@bingvmb.bitnet.
- Videolib—ALA Video Round Table listserv. Subscribe by sending a subscription mes-

sage to {leave subject field blank; Message: sub videolib (or videonews) [your full name]} listserv@library.berkeley.edu.

SUMMARY

All methods, processes, and forms shown in this chapter can be easily integrated into any library's acquisitions protocol with the proper planning. The audiovisual department, and all departments and branches or sites that deal with videocassettes as collections, as well as the acquisitions department, should have input into and coordinate the planning process. Policies, workflow diagrams, and task procedures should be drawn up from these plans and updated when necessary. The biggest hurdle to overcome is to allow the selectors of videocassettes to have the freedom to purchase creatively. This may involve one or more of the following purchasing options: using an agency credit card for some 800-number television/radio advertised titles; accepting preview prints sent with an invoice and using the invoice to initiate a P.O.; purchasing from telemarketers on approval; allowing prepayment on some purchases and being quick to prepare that payment; using various approval plans; organizing special buying plans or "deals" with vendors; taking part in special buying plans involving payment to another library, system or regional agency rather than a vendor; leasing collections; and duplicating copies from masters and taping programs off-air. It is vitally important that the avenues to facilitate ease of ordering in these special circumstances are present and that the policies and procedures of acquisitions are flexible enough to accommodate special purchasing arrangements. Flexibility does not mean that consistency of policy application and standards will suffer, but it does ensure that the library will possess an excellent diversity of title types, acquired from a wide range of vendors, for the best possible price.

NOTES

1. Audrey Eaglen, *Buying Books: A How-To-Do-It Manual for Librarians* (New York, Neal-Schuman Publishers, Inc., 1989), p. 106.
2. Richard W. Boss, *Automating Library Acquisitions: Issues and Outlook* (White Plains, NY: Knowledge Industry Publications, Inc., 1982).
3. Ted Grieder, *Acquisitions: Where, What, and How* (Westport, CT: Greenwood Press, 1978), p. 15.
4. Rose Mary Magrill and John Corbin, *Acquisitions Management and Collection Development in Libraries,* 2nd ed. (Chicago, ALA: 1989), p. 1.

5

Copyright Issues within the Acquisitions Process

Even in an academic library setting, it would be fairly unusual to find an acquistions librarian deliberating the copyright laws during the selection/ordering process of print material. But, in that same academic setting, other public service librarians dealing with interlibrary loans and photocopies live and die by the laws governing copyright. Likewise, to librarians ordering videocassettes, the various use goals and objectives of a videocassette collection are reflected in the performance and other rights which those videocassettes possess (or the library can purchase). The acquisition of those rights has a direct effect on the nature, philosophy, policies, and procedures of the acquisitions process. The concept of copyright related to prerecorded videocassettes is perhaps the one of the most misunderstood, misinterpreted, and volatile subjects for librarians as well as people in the film/video industry. By gaining an understanding of terms such as "home-use only," "public performance," and "educational use," the acquisitions librarian will be able to converse intelligently with media librarians and vendors alike, and thus make sure that the video rights needed by the library are the actual ones acquired. Therefore, the purpose of this chapter is to detail, in a practical fashion, some of the main points of United States Copyright law as they apply to videocassettes, and to seek answers to the following questions and statements:

1. Clarify the United States Copyright law in understandable language.
2. Define the terms and vocabulary of use and performance including, but not limited

to, home-use only, public performance, nontheatrical public exhibition, and the public domain.

3. Clarify videocassette use in semipublic and educational institutions concerning the fair use and educational exemption sections of the law.

4. Explain the options for acquiring public performance rights at or after the time of purchase as well as presenting some suggestions and forms to make the process easier.

5. Explain how one can be sure that they are purchasing/have purchased videocassettes with public performance rights.

6. Can libraries tape programs off-air and how long may they keep them?

7. What is meant by off-air taping; does it include cable transmissions and pay TV channels like HBO and Cinemax?

8. Can libraries tape from satellite transmissions?

COPYRIGHT DEFINED

Copyright is a right in intellectual property enacted by Congress stemming from Article I, Section 8 of the U.S. Constitution. In 1976, an omnibus revision of the 1909 U.S. Copyright Law called Public Law 94-553 was enacted, becoming effective January 1, 1978. The following outline (see Table 5.1) details the major sections of the law with their respective descriptions and definitions:

The purpose of copyright protection is to afford authors and other creators of intellectual properties the right to determine when and how their respective works are to be used for a period of time (currently life plus 50 years), in effect giving them a monopoly over their creations for a period of time. The 1978 copyright law recognizes both published and unpublished works in five categories: literary works; musical works; pictorial, graphic, and sculptural works; motion pictures and other audiovisual works; and sound recordings. Copyright law requires that, in order for a work to be copyrighted, it must be original and "fixed in any tangible medium of expression, now known or later developed from which [that work] can be perceived, reproduced, or otherwise communicated, either directly or with the aid of a machine or device."[1] It must be a written-down sequence or array of symbols, a recorded text, or medium. And what is protected against is, at the very least, unauthorized literal copying (i.e., reproduction by others, without permission, of the same sequence or array of symbols).[2] For a copyright to be perfected (i.e., valid), a notice of copyright must be placed on all copies of the work in distribution, with the form of the notice as may be required by the Register of Copyrights, Copyright Office of the Library of Congress. Omission of this information may result in forfeiture of copyright, but does not result in entering the work in the public domain. Copyright, which once protected only against the production of substantially similar copies in the same medium as the copyrighted work, today protects against uses and media that often appear in different formats.[3]

In 1986, a division of the United States government, the Office of Technology

Table 5.1
United States Copyright Table of Contents

Sections	Definitions
101	basic definitions of terms used throughout
102 - 104	works protected by copyright
105	U.S. government works excluded
106	exclusive rights of copyright owner
107	right of fair use
108	reproduction by library or archives
109	effect of transfer of a particular copy
110	performances and displays for non-profit organizations (educational exemption)
111	secondary transmissions
117	computer software
118	noncommercial broadcasting
401 - 406	notice of copyright
501 - 506	copyright infringement
504	innocent infringement by libraries[1]

1. Note that the terms "fair use" and "educational exemption" are not necessarily synonomous, although one may be used as a conjunctive argument for the other. Most often, "fair use" applies to photocopying and use of portions of a work rather than the work as a whole. Fair use and the educational exemption apply to all copyrighted works covered by the First Sale Doctrine. The First Sale Doctrine includes all formats except for computer software, databases, and certain electronically transmitted data and musical performances.

Assessment (OTA), raised the question of whether copyright was proprietary in nature rather than regulatory, ultimately deciding that the law was largely regulatory. As previously mentioned, while the law uniformly regulates the rights of the copyright holder (author), it does not detail the extent and/or nature of the copyrighted work by specific users or uses. The OTA based its decision on definitions, feeling that "if regulatory, private use would not be subject to copyright while, if proprietary, private use would be subject to control."[4] However, this author feels that the law is much more proprietary in nature rather than regulatory precisely because it does delineate the rights of the copyright owner, albeit in general terms, and not the rights of the user. Unlike the American Disabilities Act (ADA), the Copyright Act does not provide specific adherence codification or criteria. The proprietary nature of the law is an important concept to grasp because it forms the underlying premise for all further decisions and discussion. In essense, the copyright law establishes a vehicle for use of copyrighted materials on a contractual basis as long as statutory rights are fulfilled. Examples of such contracts are the so-called "public performance" and "home-use only" rights for videocassettes, as well as various use licenses on computer software. Besides offering legal protection against unauthorized copying, the Copyright law affords the copyright holder certain rights. The rights of the copyright holder (owner) are described below.

SECTION 106

Exclusive rights in copyrighted works. The owner has the exclusive rights to do or authorize any of the following:
1. Reproduce the copyrighted work;
2. Prepare derivative works;
3. To distribute copies;
4. Perform the work publicly;
5. Display the work publicly.[5]

The most important of these rights that is particularly applicable to videocassettes is the "right to perform the work publicly," allowing performance to be regulated through contractual manner by, but not limited only to, the following uses: public performance, nontheatrical exhibition, and home-use only. In reality, this right is most often transferred to the purchaser on a per-title basis in the form of a contractual right for unlimited public performance.

A rule known as the First Sale Doctrine governs the relinquishing of copyright control by the copyright holder on most materials purchased through any legal method as it pertains to private use. Generally, copyright controls over the ownership of the physical medium terminate after the first sale of each and every legally made and acquired copy. The First Sale Doctrine applies unilaterally to prerecorded videocassettes, allowing video stores and libraries to rent and/or loan videos to their customers and patrons. Practically speaking, this means that the copyright holder does not receive any revenue from rentals such as video store rental transactions or library fee-based use. Libraries purchase a wide range of educational and entertainment videotapes for in-library use and for lending to patrons. Copyright makes the distinction between ownership of a physical object (in this case a videocassette) and ownership of the intellectual material contained within (i.e., the program on the tape). Once a legal copy has been sold, the buyer of that copyrighted material enters into a "contract" with the copyright holder, based on the rights granted to that copy in Section 106 of the law. An educational video producer/distributor, Direct Cinema, Ltd., has a unique method of getting around the First Sale Doctrine and thus, retaining more user-performance control over the programs the company distributes because the work does not fall within either the fair use or educational exemptions and is purely contractual in nature. Direct Cinema sells long-term, renewable, seven-year leases on all its programs rather than actually selling the physical videocassette. Therefore, the material never falls within the scope of the First Sale Doctrine, remaining under the owner's jurisdiction for the life of the lease. In the past, based on similar reasoning, Walt Disney and other film companies used to restrict showing of their nontheatrical exhibition 16mm feature films to weekdays, preceded by no public advertising, because they did not want to compete with movie theaters possibly showing the same title for an admission charge. The development of new technologies such as videocassettes and video recorders has exacerbated the conflicts inherent in copyright law. Today, the general public, as well as commercial and noncommercial agencies, has an increased ability to copy, manipulate and change, and transmit information from format to format easily, quickly, and cheaply. This technological revolution has lessened the ability of the copyright holder to enforce their rights. Copyright law has not kept up with the technological wheel and this, in a nutshell, is the total extent of the copyright problem.

PERFORMANCE TERMS DEFINED

Section 106:4, "perform the work publicly," allows performance to be regulated through, but not limited to, the following terms: public performance, nontheatrical exhibition, and home-use only (sometimes called home exhibition) use. One of the major questions librarians ask is: "What constitutes a public performance video, and how does it differ from the rental store (home-use only) type?" A public performance video is, generally speaking, any title for which licensing fees (or contractual arrangements by a distributor) have been paid so that it may be shown in public. But what is the definition of "public?" Section 101 of the law defines "publicly" as a performance taking place anywhere "open to the public or at any place where a substantial number of persons outside of a normal circle of a family and its social acquaintances is gathered."[6]

But how does one know what rights the videocassette they have purchased possesses? Before this question can be answered, one must know specifically what rights are included as well as the terms used in describing those rights. In the past, especially with 16mm films, short/long-term public performance leases or single performance contracts were negotiated. Today, videocassette producers are primarily providing two options: blanket licenses (covering specific titles from specific producers for unlimited showings tied to a specific site) and purchasing public performance rights on a per-title (per copy) basis when the videocassette is first purchased. Single showing and per-title public performance rights can still be arranged, but librarians must be carefully to get such agreements in writing from the copyright holder. Usually, public performances of videocassettes fall in one of three categories: theatrical exhibition; nontheatrical exhibition; and fair use/educational exception (classroom use).

Theatrical exhibition deals with the showing of the video where an admission is charged, while nontheatrical exhibition exclusively limits group performances to nonadmission charging (including donations) situations, usually limited to nonprofit agencies such as schools, colleges/universities, and libraries. The 1976 revised Copyright law includes Sections 106 (Right of Fair Use) and 110 (Performances and displays for nonprofit organizations) to extend performance rights in specific educational settings. Specifically, this applies only to schools and academic institutions; public libraries are not considered to be educational institutions by law.

THE COPYRIGHT NOTICE AND PUBLIC PERFORMANCE

Throughout the evolution of video librarians have expressed concern over trying to figure out just what videocassettes have public performance rights and which ones do not. Many times, the copyright notice on the videocassette case/ container or pre-title frame does not indicate "for home-use only"—it carries only a generic FBI copyright warning. The problem is further exacerbated by the fact that many videocassette distributors (and producers) do not know the rights that the videocassette titles they distribute or represent possess. Therefore, sending a letter to Baker & Taylor Video asking for public performance rights for the videocassette *Who Framed Roger Rabbit?* would not yield any positive results because, as a wholesale "jobber," they have no authority to grant public performance rights. Furthermore, even if Baker & Taylor Video did have rights-granting authority, that purchase order may not be read and signed by personnel within the company possessing that authority. Licensing for public performance rights on videocassettes that these vendors sell should be readily apparent on the extent labeling and provided across-the-board to all purchasers. Tiered pricing for rights is a much too complicated procedure, in terms of sales contracts, advertising, and invoicing, for vendors who make profits from large volume sales. Production/distribution companies like Films Incorporated have muddied the waters further by offering two-tiered and subtle subsidiary-company pricing—one a public performance (or education/institutional) price and the other a home video price. In the past, price was, commonly, a fair indicator of public performance rights or home use (i.e., a high-priced video possessing public performance rights; a low-priced video possessing home-use only rights). But that is not the case today. There are quality videocassettes with public performance rights selling for $9.95 to $800, while the range of home-use only video falls between $14.95 to $99.95 consistently. Generally speaking, videos with public performance rights will state such rights on the video case/container or just before the title frame. Following are two examples of "generic" copyright infringement statements which appear on the labels of videocassettes. Figure 5.1 is from a home-use only video, while Figure 5.2 is taken from a video with public performance rights. Both statements are equally vague, not delineating

Figure 5.1
Generic FBI Copyright Infringement Warning Label

FBI WARNING Federal law provides severe civil and criminal penalties for the unauthorized reproduction, distribution or exhibition of copyrighted motion pictures, whole tapes or video discs. Criminal copyright infringement is investigated by the FBI and may constitute a felony of up to five years in prision and/or a $250,000 fine.

any specific use rights, either contractual or statutory; they do not provide librarians with any indication of private home-use or public performance rights.

The warning statement in Figure 5.3 is much more specific than Figure 5.1, expressly stating that the program is licensed only for home use. Figure 5.4 provides an equally specific statement, but the methods by which the company sells the product, *Hiroshima Maiden* (Wonderworks Family Movie series, Public Media Video/Films Incorporated), compounds the problem.

Public Media Video sells only the home-use rights version. Its subsidiary company, Films Incorporated, sells the nontheatrical exhibition rights to the same title. A library can purchase the same video from Public Media Video and, for a small extra fee (currently $10) at the time of purchase, obtain unlimited public performance rights. The company denotes such performance rights on the invoices and packing slips, as well as providing stickers with hand-written authorization numbers for placement on the videocassette case. However, a jobber such as Baker & Taylor advertises the same videocassette title in their monthly catalog/newsletter/advertisement, the *Video Alert*, with public performance rights, selling it for almost $13 less than the public performance version sold direct by Films Incorporated and about $5–6 less than the home-use version sold by Public Media Video. No authorization label or invoice denotation is provided with the Baker & Taylor Video copies, and the "specific" copyright infringement warning stating "licensed for private home use . . ." appears on every one of the videos. Vendors, especially those special interest vendors who have turned from marketing strictly to consumers to marketing to both the consumer and educational markets, seem to be equally confused. Companies like Finley Holiday Films, International Travel Video Network, MPI Home Video, Atlas Home Video, and Questar all market some video titles with public performance rights. The term most often used around these vendors is "educational rights," essentially meaning "nontheatrical public performance" but stemming from their contractual rights with the copyright holder to sell only to the educational sector (public libraries included in their definition).

BLANKET LICENSING

Blanket licensing (also known as umbrella licensing) for feature films is currently available from two companies. Actually, "blanket license" is somewhat of a misnomer, because not all of one producers' (such as Walt Disney, Touch-

Figure 5.2
Films for the Humanities and Sciences Copyright Warning Label

<u>WARNING</u>

Your use of this videocassette constitutes your agreement to observe the copyright restrictions indicated hereon.

This videocassette is protected under the U.S. and all applicable copyright laws. The duplication, telecasting, cablecasting, or broadcasting of this program or any part thereof, for any reason whatsoever, without the express prior written consent of **FILMS FOR THE HUMANITIES & SCIENCES, INC.** constitutes a violation of federal law. Please note that not-for-profit institutions are not exempt from the provisions of the Copyright Act.

FILMS FOR THE HUMANITIES & SCIENCES, INC. is a participant in AIME, the industry trade association that prosecutes copyright violators.

Source: Insert in videocassettes purchased from Films for the Humanities & Sciences, Inc., 1994.

stone Pictures, and RCA/Columbia Pictures) films are available for licensing. Licenses of this type allow institutions to license various producers' home-use only videocassettes for nontheatrical public performance. Thus, any licensed video title obtained through a legal channel (that is purchased, rented, or borrowed—not copied) can be used to show to groups such as story hours, community groups, brown bag lunch showings, and so on. Licenses such as these are site-specific, meaning that specific buildings and auditoriums are licensed (i.e., authorized to provide public showings of licensed video titles). These licenses restrict public performance to in-house use only and do not allow public performance to patrons off-site. Licensing prices are often based on a combination of five factors: (1) number of locations/branches; (2) number of cardholders; (3) number of VCRs in use (in-house); (4) number of videocassettes in the collection; and (5) population of the service area. Occasionally, it is possible to license an auditorium based on its seating capacity. Licenses can be renewed yearly and have no limit on the number of showings per title during that licensing period. Prices per year average about five to ten cents per cardholder. The two existing companies to contact are: Motion Picture Licensing Corporation, 13315 Washington Blvd., Suite 302, Los Angeles, CA 90066; (310) 822-8855; (800) 426-8855; Films Incorporated, 5547 North Ravenswood Dr., Chicago, IL 60640-1199; (312) 878-2600; (800) 826-3456.

FAIR USE AND THE EDUCATIONAL EXEMPTION

Statutory law provides for some unique, relevant exceptions, including fair use and the educational exemption. Essentially, fair use evolved around the photoduplication of poetry excerpts for class use but has enlarged its intended scope from a historical perspective. Basically, the issues of infringement revolve

Figure 5.3
Another FBI Copyright Warning Label

```
WARNING!  Licensed for private home exhibition only.  All other
rights reserved.  Any public performance, copying, or other use is
strictly prohibited.  Federal law provides severe civil and
criminal penalties for the unauthorized reproduction, distribution
or exhibition of copyrighted motion pictures, videotapes or
laserdiscs.  Criminal copyright infringement is investigated by the
FBI and may constitute a felony with a maximum penalty of up to
five year in prison and/or a $250,000 fine.

Licensed for private home exhibition only.  All other rights
reserved.  Any public performance, copying, or other use is
strictly prohibited.  Duplication in whole or in part of this
videocassette is prohibited.
```

around the following factors, but hinge mainly on the substantiality of the duplication compared with the entire work and the financial potential loss the copyright holder incurred through the loss of sales/royalties through the unauthorized duplication.

The Fair Use exemption provides use of copyrighted materials without the copyright holder's explicit permission in the following circumstances:

SECTION 107

Notwithstanding the provisions of section 106, the fair use of a copyrighted work, including such use by reproductions in copies or phonorecords or by any other means specified by that section, for purposes such as criticism, comment, news reporting, teaching (including multiple copies for classroom use), scholarship, or research, is not an infringement of copyright. In determining whether the use made of a work in any particular case is a fair use, the factors to be considered shall include:

1. the purpose and character of the use, including whether such use is of a commerical nature or is for nonprofit educational purposes;

2. the nature of the copyrighted work;

3. the amount and substantiality of the portion used in relation to the copyrighted work as a whole; and

4. the effect of the use upon the potential market for or value of the copyrighted work.[7]

The educational exemption is broader in scope, allowing public performance of an entire work (specifically a video licensed for home-use only rights) within a classroom setting under the following conditions:

1. The performance must be by instructors (including guest lecturers) or by pupils; and

2. the performance must be in connection with face-to-face teaching activities; and

3. the entire audience is involved in the teaching activity; and

4. the entire audience is in the same room or same general area; and

Figure 5.4
FBI Copyright Warning for Films Incorporated

WARNING: The program contained in this videocassette is fully
protected by copyright under Title 17, U.S. Code, Public Law 94-
553. It is licensed for private home use only and may not be
duplicated, copied, broadcasted, or used for public performance in
any manner without written permission.

Source: On label of home-use version of videocassette, *Hiroshima Maiden* (Wonder-
    works Family Movies series), Public Media Inc., 1992.

5. the teaching activities are conducted by a non-profit education institution; and

6. the performance takes place in a classroom or similar place devoted to instruction,
   such as a school library, gym, auditorium or workshop; and

7. the videotape is lawfully made; the person responsible had no reason to believe that
   the videotape was unlawfully made.[8]

The only instance where a home-use only videocassette could be used in a group
setting within the public library would be if it were used in conjunction with
an educational program, provided by a recognized educational institution such
as a public/private school, college or university, conducted in the library's public
room, following the seven requirements listed above.

In determining if any library falls under the "nonprofit education institution"
guise, the following criteria should be met:

1. Do students receive frequent reading, field, or laboratory assignments, for which they
   are held accountable?

2. Do instructors assign grades based on papers, examinations, oral reports, and other
   reliable measures of pupil performance?

3. Are grades reported to parents, guardians, employers, or other responsible parties?

4. Are transcripts of students' grades available to other educational institutions?

5. Does the course lead to a recognized degree, diploma, license, or certificate?[9]

Because public libraries are not "non-profit educational institutions" by law,
they cannot legally utilize home-use only videocassettes for public performance
showings for story hours, adult programming, film festivals, or the like. Similarly, education institutions are also limited in their use of home-use only videocassettes. They can only be used within the classroom setting, under
face-to-face teaching situations. Showing home-use only videos as extracurric-
ular activities, for entertainment purposes, or not in conjunction with a course
of study, is illegal. In 1990, Senator Robert Kastenmeier (Wisconsin), responsible for negotiating the "Guidelines for Off-the-Air Recording of Broadcast
Programming for Educational Purposes" in 1979, came to an agreement with

the Motion Picture Association of America (MPAA), allowing nursing homes to show "home-use only" videocassettes in their group recreation rooms. Through the business exemption, businesses can now use home-use only videocassettes in a group setting provided that the showing is specifically job-training related and the showing is not open to the public.

The St. Louis (Missouri) Public Library prints a flyer describing their videocassette services which also includes a brief statement on copyright (see Figure 5.5).

The inconsistencies, varying vocabulary, and inaccurate statements made by vendors only serve to exacerbate the problem. The following example from a vendor, Instructional Video, Inc., is excerpted from their *1993-1994 Video & Reviews Catalog* (see Figure 5.6).

When any videocassette possessing public performance rights is purchased from Instructional Video, they will automatically supply a sticker for that video indicating those rights, as well as a packing list that clearly indicates those respective videos and their associated stickers. The statements made by Instructional Video are not necessarily false, but they are somewhat misleading. However, they do showcase the contractual nature of public performance in the delineation of three disparate types of rights (i.e., categories), effectively showing that these rights are neither standardized in wording nor in the rights granted. Therefore, the contractual wording pertaining to each title would have to be examined for specific rights. First, the statements imply that Instructional Video actually licenses, rather than just reports, the various public performance rights offered. Secondly, in the strict context of face-to-face teaching, both the fair use and educational exemptions apply even when using home-use only videocassettes in certain situations. Nontheatrical exhibition rights licensed to specific titles are not normally tied to site use (i.e., a site being "in-house for schools and public libraries"). However, it is common practice with some companies to limit use to in-house group showings only such as with the titles from Video Publishing, Inc. and Video Arts (Chicago-based companies). The fair use and educational exemptions, as well as the negotiated nursing home exemption, also provide a legal public performance avenue in certain situations for various organizations, but do not provide nontheatrical exhibition licences for public libraries and in situations excluded by those exemptions. With respect to Categories 2 and 3, usually nontheatrical exhibition rights are not limited only to nonprofit agencies and apply equally to any agency/business that does not charge admission fees. However, the fair use and the educational exemptions do not generally apply to noneducational organizations. While both the law and the explanations in Instructional Video's catalog have omitted some essential details, the company has provided librarians with a basic understanding of copyright use/licensing and, as such, become an outspoken conduit for selling programming with those rights.

Figure 5.5
St. Louis (MO) Public Library Copyright Statement

<u>Copyright</u>

"For Home Use Only" means just that!
Without a separate license from the copyright owner, called "Public
Performance Rights," <u>it is a violation of Federal law</u> to exhibit
pre-recorded videocassettes outside of a family residence or at a
place where a substantial number of people are gathered beyond the
family members or a close circle of friends. This is regardless of
whether an admission fee is charged or not. Even performances in
semipublic places such as clubs, lodges, businesses, camps,
daycares, senior centers, schools and libraries are "public
performances" and subject to copyright control. This applies to
profit making organizations and non-profit institutions alike. For
such performances to be legal, public performance authorization
from the copyright owner must be obtained.

There is one exception. This is the so-called "face-to-face"
teaching exemption found in Section 110 (1) of the copyright las.
In this case the performance is legal if it is conducted by a
teacher or student, and occurs in the course of a face-to-face
teaching activity in a non-profit educational institution,
classroom or similar place of instruction. Non-curriculum programs
do not qualify for exemption.

Televising of a pre-recorded tape is not allowed. In addition, any
temporary videotaping or copying for later playback of copyrighted
materials readily available by rental, lease or license is an
infringement of copyright and not fair use.

Source: St. Louis Public Library, Audiovisual Dept., St. Louis, MO, 1992.

PUBLIC DOMAIN VIDEOCASSETTES

Ted Turner made a career out of acquiring films in the public domain, co-
lorizing (or otherwise altering and/or restoring them), applying for a new copyright, and then destroying the public domain master. Titles in the public domain
are works for which a valid copyright has never been perfected (e.g., registered),
as well as works for which copyright protection has lapsed. Savvy librarians can
also purchase public domain titles for much less than other home-use only videocassettes. Several years ago, a California company, Video-Sig, was among
the largest distributors of public domain titles; however, they are no longer in
business. Sinister Video, a company specializing in horror and science fiction
titles, possesses public domain titles. Public domain video masters vary widely
in resolution clarity, color brightness, framing ratio, and sound quality. Programs
may simultaneously exist in both the public domain and in copyrighted versions;
only the running time and/or editing may be different. Examples of titles such
as this are Frank Capra's "Why We Fight" series (1941–1945) and *It's a Wonderful Life.* Many vendors advertising videocassettes in the public domain advertise in consumer magazines such as *Video Review* and *Video Magazine,* but
beware of these vendors. Buy only from reputable, well-known vendors. While

Figure 5.6
Instructional Video, Inc. Copyright Categories

EASY-TO-READ
PUBLIC PERFORMANCE
DEFINITIONS

All Videos may be used in Circulation.
No duplication, broadcast, cable or closed circuit is allowed
on any title without copyright owner's written permission.
No admission may be charged for the video(s).

CATEGORIES:

PUBLIC PERFORMANCE CATEGORY (1): Videos may be used in-house for schools and public libraries. Best examples: Children's hour; art promotion week; in-house promotions.

PUBLIC PERFORMANCE CATEGORY (2): INCLUDES CATEGORY 1 USE and allows patrons of schools and public libraries to be able to view the videos in a non-profit setting, e.g. senior citizen centers, retirement homes, non-profit groups, clubs or organizations. Best examples: Travel or craft videos in retirement homes; gardening and flower arranging videos to gardening clubs; sports tapes to Little League coaches.

PUBLIC PERFORMANCE CATEGORY (3): INCLUDES CATEGORIES 1 AND 2 USE and also allows for use in a business or for profit manner, e.g. counseling, private classes, store promotional use. Best examples: Travel videos being shown in travel agency; parenting videos used in private family counseling; sport and photography videos in sporting goods stores.

One of the above categories follows each title description
If the video includes Public Performance rights. Otherwise, the video is Home Use Only.

Public Performance and Home Use Only
prices are the same except where noted.

Source: Instructional Video, Inc., 1993–1994 Catalog. Courtesy of Joe McWilliams,
   president.

neither the media librarian nor the acquisitions librarian should be versed in copyright renewal and exploration, they should have knowledge of two print sources that may help in determining if a title is indeed in the public domain. These titles are *Film Superlist* (out of print) and David Pierce, *Motion Picture Copyrights & Renewals 1950–1959* (Laurel, MD: Milestone, 1992). Milestone, P.O. Box 2748, Dept. F, Laurel, MD 20709. (301) 490-2364. $89.00.

OFF-AIR AND SATELLITE TAPING

The Copyright Act itself does not specifically address the issue of off-air taping. In 1979, a federal negotiating committee deliberating the off-air taping issue developed an eight-point consensus document concerning the application of the fair use doctrine to the recording retention, and the use of television broadcast programs for educational purposes. They recommended specific retention time periods and use of recordings in nonprofit educational institutions. Basically, the guidelines apply only to nonprofit educational institutions and limit program retention to a consecutive 45-day period, with only one showing per class within the first ten retention days.[10] It should be noted that off-air refers specifically to antenna-received broadcasts (and simultaneous cable retransmission). This specifically eliminates taping from channels such as Discovery, A&E, HBO, Cinemax, Showtime, Disney, and other pay TV and cable-only channels, as well as RCA's Direct-TV. It may also prohibit taping from satellite reception dishes. Nonprofit educational institutions seeking off-air taping rights should contact the specific channel for taping and retention permission on an individual program basis. Schools may encounter many instances where the librarian or teacher will tape a program at home and use it in a class. Upon bringing that video to school, it falls under the school's jurisdiction and, as such, is subject to the same retention laws as copies made on school equipment. Thus, the legality of the copy is at question; if the teacher taped a program from HBO at home to use in class, it would probably not be considered a legal copy, especially if the sole purpose of copying it would be for school use.

Figure 5.7 shows a warning label which the Memphis School system places on its VCRs to discourage unauthorized duplication of television programs.

The Congressional committee guidelines make no provisions for educational taping of televised channels received via satellite and decoder/descrambler units. Except for legally authorized educational channels, taping from satellite transmissions is illegal.

OBTAINING PUBLIC PERFORMANCE AND BROADCAST RIGHTS

The next logical question a librarian should have about copyright and use rights is stated in three parts: "If the use rights are not clearly defined on the invoice or the video itself, the video states unacceptable rights, or the library wishes to gain other, additional rights, how do they acquire those rights?" In instances where per-title public performance rights are not clearly defined, the librarian should contact the copyright holder and seek to obtain those rights in writing. As previously mentioned, the copyright holder is most often the producer/distributor. By contacting an educational distributor, if they do not hold the rights, there is an excellent chance that they can provide the librarian with information necessary to contact the copyright holder. However, obtaining public performance rights can be a time-consuming process. Some acquisitions librarians have printed purchase orders stating, "videocassettes purchased on this purchase order will be used for private home use and for nontheatrical exhibition to groups in both curricular and noncurricular settings." This statement implies that fulfillment of the purchase order gives the library or school the right of public performance (excluding school exemption under fair use teaching exemption only for curricular use); however, this practice would most likely not

Figure 5.7
Memphis Schools' Copyright Warning Posted on VCRs

WARNING!

GUIDELINES for VIDEO RECORDING and CLASSROOM USE

"OFF-AIR" RECORDING A television program may be copied off-air and
may be used once by an individual teacher in relevant classroom
instruction for a period of up to ten (10) days following
broadcast. After the 10-day period, the recording must be erased.

RENTED/PURCHASED VIDEO TAPES Tapes marketed for the home-video
market, when rented or purchased by schools, <u>can only be used in
face-to-face instruction in a regular classroom.</u>

Rented/purchased video tapes may never be copied unless the rights
or license to copy has been purchased.

IMS VIDEO TAPES IMS video tapes which <u>may not</u> be copied will be
identified with a DO NOT COPY label. IMS video tapes that <u>may be
copied</u> will be so identified - but <u>must be erased on the expiration
date printed on the cassette.</u>

IF IN DOUBT - DON'T COPY - YOU ARE RESPONSIBLE

Source: Memphis Public Schools, Library Media Center, Memphis, TN, 1992.

be upheld in a court of law. Many distributors sell videocassettes but most of
them do not have the copyright authority to grant public performance rights. It
is analogous to a person writing on an automobile purchase order, "I will drive
this car 80 miles per hour." The fact that the dealer has sold the car to this
person with the knowledge that the person will exceed the legal speed limit does
not serve to hold the dealer liable for the purchaser's illegal actions, because it
is not within the dealer's power to modify the speed limits. Contributory neg-
ligence in these one-party contractual forms is not a factor; responsibility of
legal use rests solely with the purchaser and ignorance of copyright does not
serve as a rationale for illegal use.

The purchase of a videocassette, like any product, is a contractual arrangement
for goods. As such the product ordered should be the product delivered. If a
videocassette arrives possessing incorrect or inappropriate use rights from the
one ordered by the purchaser (as long as the purchaser knows that the vendor
has the authority to grant those rights), that party may return the title to the
vendor for a replacement.

Additional rights for programs such as one-time only nontheatrical exhibition,
archival duplication, or excerpted use extends beyond fair use. Off-air taping,
duplication, and closed circuit television transmission should be requested on a
per-title basis at the time of purchase. However, these rights may also be requested after purchase. Most film and video producers do not automatically grant
closed circuit/broadcast transmission rights upon purchase—these rights must
be negotiated separately as part of the purchase. Most often the rights are not

blanket (all titles of one producer), but are negotiated by individual title per one-time showing. The Media Services Department of the University of Utah initially contacts distributors/producers by telephone to make the request for clearance, then sends a letter restating the verbal agreement. In that agreement, the following is stated:

1. Closed circuit transmission will be limited to those network reception sites that are located on campus.

2. Programs will only be used as part of the curriculum in regular accredited classes.

3. No editing will be allowed.

4. Programs will be played in their entirety including credits.

5. Transmission time will only be announced to members of the classes for which the program is scheduled.

6. Provisions of the Copyright Act will be strictly observed.

VIDEO DUPLICATION AND OFF-AIR TAPING

Videocassette duplication and off-air taping are illegal in most cases, but in certain circumstances both methods can be sources of many free, quality titles, retained for the life of the programs. For example, all National Geographic specials currently aired on a Public Broadcasting Station (PBS), plus those programs rebroadcast on any station, can be copied off-air with one copy retained for the life of the video per site. This does not include the program *National Geographic Explorer*, aired over the Turner Broadcasting Network. In a similar fashion, Great Plains National (GPN) offers off-air taping of their *Reading Rainbow* programs, with retention and subsequent erasure occurring over a three-year cyclical sequence related to the first broadcast date. Occasionally video distributors such as Karol Video and Modern Talking Pictures offer corporate video titles to libraries on a master duplication basis. A master copy is sent to the requesting library, a copy is made, and the master is returned to the vendor. Both PBS Video and Barr Films provide an avenue for purchasing masters with duplication rights. These types of rights are especially valuable for libraries with many branches, campuses, and schools, as well as for seasonal titles such as holiday programs. Multiple copies can be make upon demand and erased whenever necessary to reduce inventory.

Figure 5.8 is a sample form letter successfully used by the Audio Visual Department of the Northern Illinois Library System (Rockford, IL) for requesting a variety of use rights. In a best-case scenario, completed copies of these letters should be retained for the life of the video with the relavent rights and licenses transferred to the video through various typed labels.

Figure 5.8
Sample Copyright Permission Request Letter

(library letterhead)

Dear _____   Date _____

I am seeking permission to acquire and/or use your video title(s),

_____

_____

_____,

as outlined below (Section A). If you are not the person or agency
responsible for rights authorization of this type, please forward
this request to the proper party or return it to us as marked in
Section B.

The Northern Illinois Library System (4034 E. State St., Rockford,
IL 61108) is a non-profit library agency consisting of 130 member
libraries of all types including public, school, academic and
special libraries. We have an in-house collection of about 4,500
videocassettes which is used at no charge by our members on an
advanced scheduled basis. Most of our collection possesses public
performance rights and we adhere to all U.S. Copyright laws,
Sections 101-510, Title 17, U.S. Code, Public Law 94-553. We serve
an area of about 800,000 population. Also, our collection is open
for use by the member libraries and their patrons/students.

SECTION A
The Northern Illinois Library System is seeking permission to
acquire and/or use the video title mentioned above as follows. As
the authorizing agent, please place a check mark in the appropriate
response line indicating the type of use authorization granted.
Thank you, in advance for your prompt action regarding this matter.

Figure 5.8 (continued)

OFF-AIR TAPING/RETENTION RIGHTS

Request Response

____ ____ Yes, you may have permission to tape the program off-air and retain ____ copy for the life of the video, or until such time that the program becomes available for sale in either the educational or consumer market. At that time, any copy(ies) must be erased and a legal, prerecorded copy perchased.

____ ____ No, you may not have permission to tape the program off-air and retain.

PUBLIC PERFORMANCE RIGHTS

Request Response

____ ____ Yes, you have permission to show the program, one-time only, to a group of (number and type)_____ people on (Date) _____.

____ No, you cannot show the program to a group.

____ ____ Yes, we give public performance rights to the program for unlimited showings within any size group as long as there is no admission charge.

$_____ (if any) for public performance rights of this type.

ARCHIVAL COPY

Request Response

____ ____ Yes, you have permission to duplicate one copy and retain for archival purposes. This archival copy is not to be viewed unless the original, legal copy has been damaged or lost.

____ No, you may not make an archival copy.

BROADCAST RIGHTS

Request Response

____ ____ Yes, you have permission to show the program over broadcast/cable transmission for the following show date/or period of time: _____.

____ No, you may not broadcast this program over broadcast television or cable.

114

Figure 5.8 (continued)

_____ _____ Other, special uses, restrictions or limitations:

_____

_____

_____

_____

_____

SPECIAL RIGHTS AND REQUESTS

Request Response

____ ____ _____

_____

_____

_____

_____

SECTION B

TO BE COMPLETED BY AUTHORIZING AGENT

Request Response

_____ _____ We are not the rights authorizing/licensing agent. The
contact is listed below:

      Name: _____

      Address: _____

      Phone: _____

_____ No, permission to use the video(s) mentioned above in the
requested manner is **not** granted.

Once signed, this letter serves as a binding contract between
agencies for the inclusive rights indicated.

Authorizing Agent: _____ Date:
_____

Requesting Librarian: _____

Date:_____

SPECIFIC APPLICATIONS OF THE LAW IN PRACTICE

Public Performance Rights

According to the 1992 National Video Survey, sponsored by ABC-CLIO, almost 60 percent of all libraries purchasing video also acquire videos possessing public performance rights. In-house library programming was standard fare in 38 percent of all libraries, with 46 percent of public libraries reporting use of videocassettes for in-house programming.[11] Previous chapters have shown a direct correlation between increased purchase price and various performance/use rights. It would seem that librarians have looked upon public performance videos as a "value-added service" rather than as a separate service or collection requiring special consideration. Because multiple rights distribution (i.e., public performance and home-use only) is prevalent for many titles today, it would behoove librarians to search out the titles they want possessing only those rights that they need. Obtain public performance rights only where there is sufficient demand to warrant the increased cost of those rights.

Informing Patrons About Copyright

According to an ABC-CLIO survey, 85 percent of responding libraries indicated that patrons were adequately informed about the issue of public performance and home-use only through the FBI copyright statement on each video. As this chapter has shown, that FBI warning label is inconsistent in wording and often generic in rights description, offering little or no information to patrons. Fifty-two percent of libraries said they informed their patrons verbally about copyright; 34 percent did so using a handout, available at the point of circulation; 21 percent informed patrons through posted signs; and 9 percent possessed a check-out pocket insert. Twenty-six percent of libraries did not inform patrons in any way.[12]

The question of whether libraries are required to inform patrons of copyright laws, as well as to the extent the library should police the use of its collection, has been hotly debated over the last five years. Copyright expert Jerome Miller stresses that:

libraries and/or librarians are not liable for copyright infringements on the part of individual patrons. A staff member can inform (and in the case of library-owned VCRs, should probably affix a copyright warning to the machine) a borrower about copyright laws—specifically, injunctions against duplicating and [home-use] . . . but is under no obligation to challenge or cross examine a patron concerning intended use of the program.[13]

However, Mary Hutchings Reed, past legal counsel for the American Library Association, reminds librarians that:

if a librarian learns that a patron is borrowing videotapes and using them for public performances. . . . While there is no clear duty to refuse to lend, there is a point at which a library's continued lending with actual knowledge of infringement cound possibly result in liability for contributory infringement.[14]

With the above statements in mind, and considering the way in which most public libraries use/collect videocassettes, it would probably be sufficient for most libraries to post specific signage recognizing both home-use only and public performance videocassettes within the collection (such as the St. Louis, Missouri Public Library's notice mentioned earlier in this chapter) in the library.

Library videocassette collections should also be clearly labeled and/or designated as either public performance or home-use only categories. Designation of this type would not be considered "labeling" under the Library Bill of Rights and would be condered a positive public relations tool and marketing device by both the library administration and clientele. This can be done using one or more of the following methods: describe on note information (505 MARC field) on the catalog card or on-line catalog; by using various colored or symbol stickers on the extant videocassette cases; by using a predetermined alphamnemonic code placed on the videocassette spine/container, possibly in association with the call number; by using a check-out pocket insert or various in-house library signage; or by separating the public performance collection physically from the home-use only collection.

The Order Process and Order Forms

Regardless of whether a multiple-part, paper order form is used or if the order is generated and sent electronically, each title request should contain some essential information pertaining to use and public performance. At the time of actual title selection, the selector should know if the title ordered possesses public performance, duplication, closed-circuit/cable transmission, or other rights. Selection sources such as *Library Journal, School Library Journal, Booklist, Science Books and Films, The Video Rating Guide for Libraries,* and the *Video Librarian* always list public performance rights in their reviews if available. Vendor catalogs from various vendors such as Instructional Video and Baker & Taylor Video Alert, as well as most educational producer/distributors like AIMS Media, Ambrose Video Publishing, and Phoenix/BFA Films, specifically identify titles with public performance rights. In these cases, public performance most often refers to "nontheatrical exhibition"—no admission may be charged. The order form should have a standard method of delineating those rights which the library wishes to purchase, such as a series of boxes which can be checked off. It is recommended that abbreviations not be used, as these boxes will be used by the vendor to fill the order. Only request those rights which are specified in a review or catalog, or those rights which have been negotiated through a distributor sales representative (such as cable transmission and duplication, or another of public aberrant performance). In the latter instance, the inclusion of the form letter described earlier in this chapter would be a good idea. This procedure is as important in the initial order stage as it is in the receipt/order verification and cataloging/processing stages. The library must be sure that exactly what was ordered was received. The cataloging/processing departments must know how the item is to be treated by type, seeking answers to many questions: Should a note be added to the OCLC [505] field delineating public performance rights? Should a subject heading such as "Public Performance Rights Video Recordings" be added to the videographic record (OCLC [650] field) of those titles possessing such rights? Should the videocassette be put in a different colored box, or have a distinguishing mark or dot placed on it? Should it be duplicated and the master processed differently and physically stored in a different location? In many cases the multiple order form, invoice, and Requesting Rights letter are all that the acquisitions department will possess in making choices for delineated use of the video collection.

SUMMARY

As the world progresses from a format-driven society to an electronic, data-driven one, copyright and media use will become increasingly important. In today's complex society, copyright use cannot be adequately policed, and infringement runs rampant. The library should act as one of the last bastions of copyright compliance. Authors/producers need to be adequately compensated for their efforts; otherwise there is little incentive for them to continue the creation of such works. Society, in the form of libraries and educational agencies, needs a sufficient diversity of materials from which to choose, all sold at a fair price, which is directly tied to sales demand, volume sold, and perceived use. Assuring copyright compliance for videocassettes is an important part of the acquisition librarian's role and, if handled properly, can be a great public relations and marketing device, effectively solving clients' needs/demands for group showings and other, more esoteric, but nonetheless essential needs.

NOTES

1. 17 U.S.C. 102, 90 Stat. 2544–2545.
2. Patrick Wilson, "Copyright, Derivative Rights, and the First Amendment," *Library Trends* 39 (Summer/Fall 1990): 93.
3. Ibid., p. 98.
4. Ibid., p. 102.
5. Pub. L. 54-553, Section 106.
6. Jerome K. Miller, *Using Copyrighted Videocassettes in Classrooms and Libraries* (Salem, MA: Copyright Information Services, 1984), p. 16.
7. Pub. L. 94-553, Title I, Section 101, October 19, 1976, 90 Stat. 2546.
8. Mary Hutchings Reed and Debra Stanek, "Library Use of Copyrighted Videotapes

and Computer Software,'' *American Libraries* 17 (February 1986): special pull-out section, A.

9. Ibid., Section B.

10. James C. Scholtz, *Video Policies and Procedures for Libraries* (Santa Barbara, CA: ABC-CLIO, 1991), pp. 192–193.

11. Jean T. Kreamer, ''Statistical Survey of Video Collections in American Libraries,'' in Jean Thibodeaux Kreamer, ed., *The Video Annual 1993* (Santa Barbara, CA: ABC-CLIO, 1993): 92.

12. Jean T. Kreamer, ''Statistical Survey of Video Collections in American Libraries,'' in Jean Thibodeaux Kreamer, ed., *The Video Annual 1991* (Santa Barbara, CA: ABC-CLIO, 1991): 72.

13. Miller, *Using Copyrighted Videocassettes,* p. 48.

14. Reed and Stanek, ''Library Use of Copyrighted Videotapes,'' Section D.

6

Problems in Cataloging Videocassettes

INTRODUCTION

The cataloging of videocassettes is one of the thorniest issues confronting libraries today. While the actual acquisition of videocassettes is arguably the most intensive library process because of the continuous monitoring of the market, surveying vendor catalogs, and making deals with industry representatives, the process of cataloging those materials is much more detail-oriented and has a greater potential for negative consequences, if not performed to certain standards, than the simple act of purchasing. Lauren K. Lee of Brodart aptly sums up the differences between public services and cataloging by stating, "When I put on my public services hat, I want to be able to order any [material] any time. When I switch to my technical service hat, I feel a need to impose order upon the chaos."[1] In today's electronic, on-line catalog environment, cataloging materials is analogous to putting a jigsaw puzzle together blindfolded. All bibliographic records must be accessible through multifaceted searches in order for patrons to have success. Quality control, standards, and real-time testing are some ways that librarians can use to assure that success. Historically, the number, correctness, and inclusiveness of cataloging records for videorecordings has been less than satisfactory. When these unsatisfactory records are imported into a local database without correction or modification, they can cause substantial difficulty and chaos. Charles Osburn speaks specifically to these difficulties in his five barriers toward acquiring any library item, three of which are appropriate to this discussion:

- difficulty of cataloging [or obtaining cataloging information];
- difficulty in acquiring certain materials [and verifying their existence and vendor availability]; and
- difficulty in processing that item once acquired [i.e., multiple cassettes, multimedia kits, oversized cases, supplemental materials].[2]

In 1989, the Rockefeller Foundation Video Distribution Task Force surveyed a number of libraries across the United States for their views and practices regarding existing videocassette collections. Librarians in charge of the video-cassette collections were in widespread agreement that videos should be cataloged, and many of those libraries were already using OCLC as the major bibliographic source utility for cataloging information. Those same librarians felt that videocassettes acquired from mainstream vendors, rather than those purchased from independents, vanity presses, and other, alternate sources of acquisitions, would require very little original, primary cataloging because of the likelihood of bibliographic record appearance in various national bibliographic databases such as OCLC, NYSCAT, and WLN.[3] Furthermore, the survey indicated that 73 percent of all libraries serving populations of more than 25,000 cataloged their videocassette collections; 46 percent used full MARC cataloging, but 3 to 23 percent of those libraries' video titles required primary cataloging because of their nonexistence in a bibliographic utility.[4] Such non-existence of videographic records and the resultant time-consuming process of primary cataloging is, at the very least, costly for the library and tends to increase the time from actual purchase to shelf-readiness. When a match is found on a bibliographic utility such as OCLC, the record is often done incorrectly and/or is incomplete, thus necessitating local verification of the information and substantial modification of that record. This latter choice may involve considerable time, thus effectively diminishing their acquisition in the first place. Also, a title such as *The Wizard of Oz* may be listed in a database several times because of incorrect cataloging or varying copyright dates/manufacturer information. The cataloger must search a number of records before a "hit" can be found. This process costs the library valuable search time and excessive database charges (e.g., OCLC charges a set fee for each record accessed on the screen, not just the one chosen for local database downloading and eventual modification).

Fully 27 percent of those libraries surveyed in the aforementioned Rockefeller Project felt that it was not necessary to catalog videocassettes. Twenty percent of surveyed libraries chose to produce alphabetical title lists of videocassettes instead of cataloging those titles in a card catalog or public access catalog (PAC).[5] Even today, there is a great need to educate librarians about the philosopy and methods of cataloging all library materials.

The ultimate goal of library acquisitions is to purchase as much of any needed product to satisfy intellectual demand and/or need within budgetary limits. If budgets are mismanaged and community responsive collection development strategies are not followed, the worst that can happen is that certain titles may not be acquired and the collection will suffer. Much more of a travesty, however, is the inaccurate/incomplete cataloging or omission of cataloging for titles already owned by the library. The ultimate goal of any library is to make materials available to patrons. When patrons and library staff alike are not able to locate and access these materials when they need them, the entire fabric of a library's reason for existence is undermined. Ralph Hunzinger, Audio Visual Director for the King County (Seattle, WA) Public Library System, feels that "if an item is not fully cataloged and patrons cannot find it, then the library does not own it."[6] Historically, the fact that has set libraries apart from other information businesses/agencies is that of organized bibliographic access. If this characteristic is compromised for videocassettes, then libraries are on the verge of a great demise.

The cataloging of videocassettes in libraries has advanced much since the early 1980s. The revision of AACR II, new rule interpretations from the Library of Congress *Cataloging Services Bulletin,* and MARC/OCLC format integration have all contributed to the greater availability of cataloging for videocassettes. However, problems still remain in terms of adequately policing databases for record input consistency and standardization and unnecessary duplication, as well as modification of the record on the local end. Because there are many fine textbooks detailing the policies, procedures, and specific rules for cataloging videocassettes, this text will not duplicate those efforts. Instead, this chapter will discuss some of the specific problems related to adapting the videographic record to the local database to produce more refined access points. It will also detail problems in the following areas: (1) the connection between circulation/patron reserves and the videographic entry/holding's record and (2) the consistent use of various fields, as well as standardizing terms and subject headings within those fields. The end result of such cataloging will yield a highly "patron friendly" catalog. This is not an easy task, however, and will require much effort, time, and deliberation on the cataloger's part. While it is recognized that there are many libraries possessing a physical card catalog rather than the electronic equivalent or "on-line database," this discussion will focus primarily upon the unique needs and characteristics of bibliographic records in an electronic environment. Specific examples from OCLC MARC records will illustrate various concepts, but the text will not detail, in step-by-step fashion, the correct methods of cataloging. Furthermore, this chapter will seek answers to the following questions:

1. How much detail in the videographic record, both in book catalogs and other types of on-line catalogs, should be available?
2. To what degree does the cataloger have to go to catalog videocassettes?

3. Are Library of Congress subject headings and other types of subject headings useful, and how can they be modified to be more suitable for the video format?

4. To what degree can the cataloger depend upon the information supplied by the video jobber, distributor, producer, or bibliographic vendor (on-line, CD-ROM or other)?

5. How do book catalogs differ from their card catalog and on-line patron access catalog (OPAC/PAC) counterparts in terms of bibliographic needs and patron access (usefulness)?

For an in-depth discussion and comprehensive training in the cataloging of audiovisual materials, the following texts should be consulted:

Frost, Carolyn O. *Media Access and Organization: A Cataloging and Reference Sources Guide for Nonbook Materials* (Englewood, CO: Libraries Unlimited, 1989).

Intner, Sheila S. and Richard P. Smiraglia, eds. *Policy and Practice in Bibliographic Control of Nonbook Media* (Chicago, ALA, 1987).

Maillet, Lucienne. *Subject Control of Film and Video: A Comparison of Three Methods* (Chicago: ALA, 1991).

Olson, Nancy. *Cataloger's Guide to MARC Coding and Tagging of Audiovisual Materials* (DeKalb, IL: Minnesota Scholarly Press, 1993).

Olson, Nancy, ed. *Cataloging of Audiovisual Materials: A Manual Based on AACR 2.* 3rd ed. (DeKalb, IL: Minnesota Scholarly Press, 1992).

A BRIEF HISTORICAL PERSPECTIVE

Many of the video formats' bibliographic problems stem from the general neglect historically given to audiovisual materials by cataloging departments. In college and university situations, film and videocassette collections/services were frequently developed outside of the library infrastructure. Audiovisual services in these agencies were separate entities from the library with their own budget, buildings, staff, and clientele. It was not uncommon for these audiovisual centers to be managed by non-librarians. Their "catalogs" were printed title listings with brief annotations and sparse subject indexes prepared by clerical staff from vendor catalog information.

During the video explosion of the mid-1980s, patrons thronged to the public libraries demanding videocassettes NOW—they wanted them in great variety and in large quantities. In order to supply the patrons' insatiable demands, these videocassettes were ordered, received, and hurriedly shelved without proper cataloging. To library administration personnel, videocassettes were frequently treated as "ephemeral materials." When audiovisual materials were organized in some fashion, librarians often used homegrown classification and cataloging procedures rather than relying on LC or AACR II standards, or utilizing LC or DDC schemes.

The arrival of the half-inch VHS and Beta formats was to have an unforeseen and profound impact on all libraries and how they dealt with the problem of bibliographic access. The number of videocassettes available for purchase became much larger, patron demand increased dramatically, prices started to drop, and collection sizes soared. A public library that once purchased 30 to 50 16mm films in a year could now purchase hundreds of feature and nonfiction videocassettes. In order to give better service and increase access to these collections the cataloging and processing of these materials had to be upgraded.

Today, there are two philosophies in providing access to nonprint resources: the departmental approach and the "omnimedia," integrated approach. Full cataloging is seldom necessary in the departmental approach, where simple title, series, and/or subject lists have traditionally sufficed. The omnimedia approach, on the other hand, stresses uniform treatment for all types of library materials and continues to influence revision of cataloging rules with respect to nonprint media. It is this omnimedia approach with which this chapter is solely concerned.

On-line public access catalogs are often part of a totally integrated catalog-circulation-acquisition system, offering patrons multiple access points to all library materials.[7] However, regardless of the philosophy or machinery used to catalog videocassettes, the access points are only as good as the information originally input into the title record—the "garbage-in, garbage-out" syndrome. Bibliographic utility records, such as those existing in OCLC, WLN, and their CD-ROM counterparts, should always be viewed and modified after uploading in the local PAC to meet local needs for term inclusion, consistency, and standardization.

WHAT IS CATALOGING AND WHY BOTHER?

Even though many readers of this text may not perform original, primary cataloging of videocassettes, at some time in their career they many be involved in the setup and organization of audiovisual cataloging procedures or be asked to evaluate a library's or a vendor's cataloging performance. From an administrative standpoint, videocassettes are more time-consuming to catalog, which ultimately results in cataloging backlogs, resistance from print-biased catalogers, and a significant time delay in getting the material on the shelf ready for circulation. Usually the cataloging of videocassettes involves much interpretation of cataloging rules rather than just their written application. Standard bibliographic databases such as OCLC and WLN often contain inaccurate and incomplete information, or do not contain the item being cataloged at all. Therefore, knowing something about the process and problems of cataloging videocassettes is helpful in making cataloging policy, procedural, and staff-task decisions.

Cataloging serves two functions within a library. The first, an in-house function, is to provide a comprehensive inventory and bibliographic control. The second, a public service function, is to provide multiple access points within a logical, consistent, and standardized framework enabling patrons to locate library-owned materials. It is in the melding of these two discrete functions that the librarian must find unity and compromise—to provide all the information useful to the librarian while also providing a clear, concise access path for the patron. This juxtaposition of different needs results in a basic conflict—patron needs and demands versus local and international standards such as MARC, LC, OCLC, and AACR II (Anglo-American Cataloging Rules II), revised edition.

The term "cataloging" actually comprises three distinct activities:

1. Descriptive cataloging wherein the actual extant of the item is described in accurate detail. This task also entails describing the contents through a descriptive annotation and choosing analytical entries and added entry points. Descriptive cataloging for videocassettes can present problems because, in some instances, the cataloger is describing attributes of the physical cassette, while other instances demand detail of the intellectual property contained within.

2. Assigning subject headings—Library of Congress, Sears, or other standards.

3. Assigning a classification or accession number. One number/letter sequence which effectively distinguishes a single item from another, possibly placing it within a subject framework like the DDC (Dewey Decimal Classification Scheme, 20th ed.), the Library of Congress Classification scheme, ANSCR (Alpha-Numeric System for Classification of Recordings) and others.

The catalog entry or "record" may be a full MARC record comprised of numbered "fields," or it may be a very brief "short entry" with only bare bones information such as title, imprint, collation, and subject headings in it. This short entry could be in the form of an incomplete MARC or OCLC record, or a local database, nonMARC record. The AACR II recognizes three distinct levels of information inclusion, while the Library of Congress (LC) has adopted a minimum level for cataloging audiovisual materials. The previously mentioned assumption of mainstream titles most likely being cataloged by LC is not valid because LC has not undertaken a comprehensive plan to catalog videocassettes. They have a serious backlog of titles and their cataloging is often incorrect and inaccurate, occasionally to the point where original cataloging at the local level would have been more efficient and cost-effective than searching, choosing, and downloading an inaccurate record. The level of cataloging which the technical services staff selects for a library's videocassette collection can be dependent on several factors:

1. How do the patrons access the collection currently, and what are their needs?

2. How does the video collection fit into the mission of the library?

3. How large is the collection now, and what is its projected growth over the long term (five to ten years)?

4. How is the collection currently displayed/shelved?

5. How is the collection currently circulated, and what kind of automated system is available for use with this collection?

6. What level of cataloging is standard for print materials at the library?

7. What classification system is currently used for features and for nonfiction video-cassettes? Is the same one used for print materials and/or can either be adapted for the videocassette collection?

8. What is the staffing situation? (i.e., the availability of professional cataloging staff)

9. What type of catalog does the library possess?

10. Are there circulation policies that may impact upon the cataloging process or procedures?

11. What kinds of materials are in the collection (features, documentaries, local productions, etc.)?

12. What is the current administrative support for the video collection and service (inclusive of budget, staff, housing, etc.)?

Factor 12 may be the most important in establishing an accessible, professionally cataloged collection. Without the active support of the library's administration and a committment to develop and nourish the collection as an integral part of the library's collection development plan, the videocassette collection will remain "ephemeral." It can be easily cut out of the budget and easily disposed of—after all, who knew the collection even existed without those titles accessible through a "real" catalog?

FINDING AND VERIFYING THE VIDEOGRAPHIC DATA

Prerecorded videocassettes are mediated formats, meaning that they require some form of equipment in order to be viewed—unlike a book, which can be opened and read without the aid of audiovisual equipment. Another problem unique to videocassettes is separating the physical medium from the intellectual material contained within. The videocassette itself is only a format. Very often, the "program" magnetically reproduced on that videocassette is a different format altogether (e.g., any theatrically released feature film is originally produced on 16 or 35mm film) possessing a different copyright date as well as other information. Therefore, many times there is a need to view the video, at least in part, to ascertain some vital pieces of information, even if the only purpose is to compare that information to an already existing videographic record. The AACR II rules acknowledge that fact, requiring information from both the extant (physical videocassette) and intellectual property (program contained within the format). The extant item includes the physical videocassette labels (spine and face) as well as the art box (front and back). The intellectual property information can be found in the opening and closing credits (the title, copyright date, producers, director, and major performers). Table 6.1 is a listing of important information and where it most often can be found (E = extant video; I = the actual program).

Table 6.2 illustrates the findings of a library science graduate student at

Table 6.1
Location of Important Videographic Elements

E,I   Title, variant titles, analytical titles

E,I   Series title(s)

I   Original copyright date

E   Manufacturer's copyright date, manufacturer's order number

E,I   Manufacturer

E,I   Producer/production company

E,I   Director

I   Other important credits - writer, musical producer,
         narrator, etc.

I   Major performers

E   Audience indicators, MPAA ratings

E   Running time

E   Closed captioning

E   Other attributes - color, B/W, letterboxed, dubbed,
         subtitled, etc.

E   Descriptive annotation

E   Titles/pagination of supplementary/accompanying material

Northern Illinois University (DeKalb, IL) regarding the percentage of videocassettes, divided into four disparate "types," possessing certain vital videographic information as well as the time necessary to locate that information.[8]

It should be noted that, many times, there are inconsistencies in the title credits on the intellectual property, the videocassette extant label, and the extant art box. This presents a problem in the discernment and prioritization of the elements concerning which one source to use. As a general rule, AACR II recommends using the information on the credits first, the extant label second, and the art box last.

The AACR II also has a prescribed manual of style determining the order and appearance of the videographic information. Table 6.3 is a brief outline of AACR II rules dealing with videocassettes. Although rule interpretations are not necessarily the same within AACR II and LC, the *Cataloging Service Bulletin* from the Library of Congress and its index should be consulted for further rule clarifications.

Originally developed for physical catalog cards, the electronic equivalent of a main entry card is often reproduced within a PAC system. These elements are outlined as follows:

Figures 6.1 through 6.3 illustrate how a variety of videocassettes might be

Table 6.2
Percentage/Time Table for Specific Videographic Elements*

Documentary -

66%	date only at end; 26% no date
66%	producer name at end
66%	publisher name within 1 min.; 20% at end
66%	title in 1 min. / 33% 2 min.

Features -

73%	title in 2 min.
66%	publisher name in 1 min. / 26% in 2 min.
26%	date in 2 min.
66%	producer name in 2 min.

Children's Videos -

53%	title in 2 min.
47%	publisher in 2 min. / 40% in 1 min.
73%	date at end / 20% in 2 min.
46%	producer name at end / 33% in 2 min.

Instructional "How-to" Videos -

66%	producer name at end
46%	date at end / 20% in 2 min.
53%	publisher name at end / 46% in 1 min.
80%	title in 1 min.

* Indicating percentage of the sample used in the study which had
the characteristics described.   Time needed to locate specific
elements is also indicated.   Total time needed for viewing to
locate all information 20 to 25 minutes using fast-forward and
rewind VCR functions.

Source: Robin C. Leckbee, "A Time Study of Videocassette Cataloging within the Stan-
     dards of AACR2," unpublished LIBS 571 paper, Northern Illinois University, De-
     kalb, IL, December 1989, pp. 1–48.

cataloged using the AACR II second level of cataloging. All catalog card and
OCLC record figures have been created by the author for this text. All the
DYNIX record figures are taken from the Elkart (IN) Public Library database.
Bear in mind that, as a general rule, most videocassettes will have a title main
entry rather than an author (i.e., a performer, producer, or director) entry. There
are three areas of title location on a videocassette. The title frame within the
intellectual property is the primary cataloging source, which is mandated by
AACR II in determining the title main entry. Secondary variant sources include
the commercial packaging and the videocassette label.

Figures 6.2 and 6.3 illustrate the importance of being thorough in both the
description of the intellectual content and the physical item. The notes, annotation, and particularly the tracings are very important as access points. Figure
6.3 possesses three variant titles and has two copyright/production dates under

Table 6.3
AACR II Rule Index for Cataloging Videocassettes

```
AACR II
CHAPTER NO.                 RULE DESCRIPTION


1.0               General rules - where to find sources of
                  information, punctuation, cataloging levels
                  (pp. 13-15).

1.1               Title and statement of responsibility, punctuation,
                  General Material Designator [GMD] (pp. 17-26)

1.4               Imprint information (place, producer, date)

1.5               collation (physical description area)

1.6               Series area (see Appendix D for definition/7.6)

1.9-1.10          Items made up of several types of materials and
                  supplementary items  (see also, series)

2.1               Items without a collective title (7.1)

2.7               Notes area

7.0               Motion pictures and videorecording general
                  information

26.4              Uniform titles
```

different distributors. Furthermore, it is part of a series and has a well-known veterinarian host. The descriptive annotation needs to be very thorough. Writing an annotation which is thorough but brief is an art.[9]

Figure 6.3 shows a videocassette which also is part of two series. Analytical entries play a vital role in linking the four short titles/authors to the main title. The analytics are also mentioned in the descriptive annotation. It is important to note that in many electronic databases, repetition of titles/terms may yield duplicative search results. Thus, putting a title analytic in the MARC 505 field [NOTES][10] and the 740 field [TITLE TRACED DIFFERENTLY] for *Jane, Wishing,* for example, will yield two entries under that title, both leading back to the same videographic entry, *A Tale of Four Wishes.* This is confusing to the patron, and may be avoided by modifying the local database display/search profile.

An issue which catalogers labor over is deciding upon the main entry and the use of uniform titles. To a large degree, the emergence of the electronic catalog has lessened the importance of the main entry and uniform style cards. However, the main entry is also the deciding factor for Cuttering. Also, if the main entry chosen differs from the title on the videocassette label(s) or art box (inclusive of back, front and spine), they must be relabeled to be consistent with the title frame and main entry. Two examples will clearly illustrate the need for this practice. A cataloger views a video with the title frame reading *Walt Disney's*

Figure 6.1
First/Third AACR II Levels of Description

First Level of Description -

Title proper / first statement of responsibility, if different from
main entry heading information or number or if there is no main
entry heading. -- Edition statement. -- Material (or type of
publication) specific details. -- First publisher, etc., date of
publication, etc. -- Extent of item. -- Notes(s). -- Standard
number.

Third Level of Description -

Title proper [general material designation] = parallel title :
other title information / first statement of responsibility ; each
subsequent statement of responsibility. -- Edition statement /
first statement of responsibility relating to the edition. --
Material (or type of publication) specific details. -- First place
of publication, etc. : first publisher, etc., date of publication,
etc. -- Extent of item : other physical details ; dimensions. --
(Title proper of series / statement of responsibility relating to
series, ISSN of series ; numbering within the series. Title of
subseries, ISSN of subseries ; numbering within the subseries). --
Note(s). -- Standard number.

Source: Anglo-American Cataloging Rules, Second ed., 1988 revision., ed. by Michael
Gorman & Paul Winkler (Chicago: ALA, 1988), p. 18.

Cinderella. LC and AACR II treat an entry of this type in a similar manner,
stating: 7.1B1. [New]. When credits for performer, author, director, producer,
"presenter," and so on precede or follow the title in the chief source, in general
do not consider them as part of the title proper, even though the language used
integrates the credits with the title. (In the examples below, the italicized words
are to be considered the title proper.)

Twentieth Century Fox presents *Star Wars*

Steve McQueen in *Bullitt*

Thief, with James Caan

This does not apply to the following cases:

1. the credit is within the title, rather than preceding or following it;
   CBS Special Report
   IBM Puppet Shows

2. the credit is actually a fanciful statement aping a credit; Little Roquefort in Good
   Mousekeeping

3. the credit is represented by a possessive immediately preceding the remainder of the
   title.

Figure 6.2
Sample Catalog Card Main Entry (1)

```
636.7
          The dog owners' manual [videorecording] / [produced by]
             United Media Productions - New York: Maier Group
             Communications, [distributor] c1987.
             1 videocassette (51min.): sd., col., 1/2 in.
          The Doctor Fox Animal series

          VHS
          originally dist. by United Feature Syndicate, Inc.
          1984.
          title on container: Dog Care.
          title on cassette label: A Video Guide to
          Successful Dog Care.
          Producers: Charles Chiara; Annette Van Duren;
          United Media production in association with Actors
          and Others for Animals.

             Summary: Provides information on adopting a pet,
          evaluating a dog's temperament, getting a dog used
          to people, feeding and food supplements, grooming,
          emergencies, the physical exam and preventative
          medicine, illness signs, older dog care and
          neutering. Also includes a special section on
          massage.
          ISBN 0-944623-01-8

          1. Dogs. 2. Dogs - massage  I.  Fox, Michael W. 1937-
          II. Dog care.  III. A video guide to successful dog care.
          IV. Doctor Fox Animal series.
```

Neil Simon's Seems Like Old Times[11]
[Frank Capra's It's a Wonderful Life]
[Walt Disney's Cinderella]

However, even in light of rule 7.1B1, the cataloger has sufficient latitude to determine the main entry along with added entries. A main entry under *Walt Disney's Cinderella* should also have, as an added entry, a uniform title expressed as [*Cinderella*]. In this manner, all Cinderella adaptations could be accessed together.[12]

Although catalogers widely agree, both in practice and theory, that videocassettes should not be given a main author entry, because the responsibility of "authorship" in a video rests in more than one person, they do not often agree on who should be listed in the notes field (found in the film credits). LC provides the following rule clarification:

7.7B6. [Rev]. For audiovisual items, generally list persons (other than producers, director, and writers) or corporate bodies who have contributed to the artistic and technical production of a work in a credits note.

Give the following persons or bodies in the order in which they are listed below. Preface each name or group of names with the appropriate term(s) of function:

Figure 6.3
Sample Catalog Card Main Entry (2)

```
791.456,7
        A tale of four wishes [videorecording] / Bosustow
            Entertainment for CBS Library. - Farmington, MI:
            Family Express Video, 1982.
            1 videocassette (42min.): sd., col.; 1/2 in.

            VHS
            cast: Rick Nelson, Tracy Gold, Bibi Osterwald
            CBS-TV Special
            originally released by Churchill Films, 1981
            Family Hour Specials, Vol. 2

            Summary: A live-action fantasy featuring a girl
            who, unhappy about her homelife and siblings,
            falls asleep and meets Skeeter, a young man
            possessing a bag full of books that seem to
            magically address her problems.  The books come
            alive in colorful animation: Hug Me; The Silver
            Pony; The Man Who Had No Dreams and Jane, Wishing.

    1. Children's Films.  2. Fantasy Films.  3. Children's
        Stories.  I. Sren, Pattie. Hug me.  II. Holl, Adelaide.
        The man who had no dreams.  III. Ward, Lynd. The silver
        pony.  IV. Tobias, Toby. Jane Wishing.  V. Family Hour
        Specials, Vol. 2.  VI. CBS-TV Special.
```

photographer(s); camera; cameraman/men; cinematographer

animator(s)

artist(s); illustrator(s); graphics

film editor(s); photo editor(s); editor(s)

narrator(s); voice(s)

music [composer(s)]

consultant(s); adviser(s)

Do not include the following persons or bodies performing these functions:

assistants or associates

production supervisors or coordinators

project or executive editors

technical advisers or consultants

audio or sound engineers

writers of discussion, program, or teacher's guides

other persons or bodies making only a minor or purely technical contribution[13]

Figures 6.4 and 6.5 dramatically illustrate the wide gap of acceptable cataloging available through OCLC showing MARC records for the same title. The catalogers entering these records could not even agree on the exact title [245], much less the imprint statement [260], notes [520], topical subject headings [650], or added name entries [508, 700]. The general media designator (GMD) in the brief entry was not even correct, being entered as two words rather than the accepted one—"videorecording." Furthermore, the brief entry even left out

Figure 6.4
OCLC Record for *Sesame Street* **Video**

```
OCLC 22747462          Rec stat:        c
Entered:  19901128     Replaced:        19920206    Used:  19921203
Type:      g           Bib lvl: m       Source:   d   Lang:  eng
Type Mat: v            Enc lvl: K       Govt pub:     Ctry:  xx
Int lvl:               Mod rec:         Tech:     u   Leng:  030
Desc:      a           Accomp:          Dat tp:   s   Dates: 1990 ,
    1  040        SGD    c SGD   d JED
    2  007        v  b f  d c  e b  f a    g h    h o    i s
    3  092        b
    4  049        ILCB
    5  245   00  Sesame Street home video visits the firehouse h video
recording / c Children's Television Workshiop.
    6  260        [S.l.] : b Random House Home Video, c c1990.
    7  300        1 videocassette (30 min.) : b sd., col. ; c 1/2 in.
    8  500        VHS format.
    9  508        Producer, Nina Elias; director, Ted May; head writer,
Tony Geiss; writer, Belinda Ward.
   10  650   0   Community life.
   11  650   0   Fire-departments.
   12  740   41  The firehouse.
```

the fact that the video was closed captioned for the hearing impaired. Figure 6.6 is obviously more complete. What is even more amazing is the fact that the more complete videographic record was entered into the database before the brief record; therefore, it can be assumed that the cataloger did not perform a very comprehensive search of the database initially.

CATALOGING VIDEOS IN SERIES

Videocassette titles in series seem to create havoc for catalogers. Before a discussion of cataloging suggestions can be undertaken, it is important to define a series and describe the various series types. Basically, videocassette series fall into four distinct types: a publisher's series; a producer's series; a television serial; and a program issued as a multivolume set (two volumes or more). Examples of a publisher's videocassettes are videocassettes produced by different producers, possibly following a similar "formula" format but packaged to look the same, marketed together and sold as a package. Examples of publishers' series are The Traveloger Collection, National Geographic Society Specials, PBS Video's *The American Experience* series, and National Audubon Society Specials. A producer's series such as Films Incorporated's *The Story of English* or PBS Video's *The Civil War* are examples of a producer's series—dependent and sequential programs dealing with the same subject, all produced by the same company. This type of series may have episode or volume titles. The third type of series is the television serial, possessing an overall serial title with one or more episodes on a videocassette. Each episode may possess its own title. Examples of these titles would be *The Outer Limits*, *The Twilight Zone*, *I Love Lucy*, *The Fugitive*, and *The Prisoner*. Miniseries such as *The Thorn Birds*, *Brideshead Revisited*, *I, Claudius*, and *Shogun* may also fall into the third cat-

Figure 6.5
Second OCLC Record for *Sesame Street* Video

```
OCLC 2236764          Rec stat:       c
Entered:  19901126    Replaced:       19910904    Used:  19921207
Type:       g         Bib lvl: m   Source:   d    Lang:  eng
Type Mat: v           Enc lvl: I   Govt pub:      Ctry:  xxu
Int lvl:              Mod rec:     Tech:     c    Leng:  030
Desc:       a         Accomp:      Dat tp:   s    Dates: 1990 ,
   1  040       MRQ   c MRQ   d YQR   d   SLC
   2  007       v  b f  d c  e b  f a   g h   h o   i u
   3  020       0679808205
   4  037       679-80821-3
   5  082  04   628.922   2   20
   6  090       TH9148   b  .F57   1990x
   7  092       b
   8  049       ILCB
   9  245  04   The firehouse   h videorecording / c Children's
Television Workshop.
  10  260       [United States]  :   b Random House Home Video, c
c1990.
  11  300       1 videocassette (30 min.) : b sd., col. ; c 1/2 in.
  12  440  0    Sesame Street home video visits ; v2
  13  500       VHS format.
  14  500       "679-80821-3."
  15  500       Closed captioned for the hearing impaired.
  16  511  1    Big Bird, Elmo, Gordon.
  17  508       Producer, Nina Elias; assistant producer, Shirley
Abraham ; director, Ted May; music, Steven Lawrence ; head writer,
Tony Geiss; writer, Belinda Ward ; photography, Randy Drummond.
  18  520       This program demonstrates the importance of smoke
detectors, and shows young children three useful safety tips --
yelling for help, getting out fast, and going to the firefighter.
  19  650  0    Fire prevention x Juvenile films.Community life.
  20  650  0    Fire detectors x Juvenile films.
  21  650  0    Puppet films.
  22  650  0    Children's films.
  23  650  0    Video recordings for the hearing impaired.
  24  650  0    Fire prevention.
  25  700  11   Geiss, Tony.
  26  700  11   Ward, Belinda.
  27  700  11   May, Ted.
```

egory if each volume possesses a discrete title, rather than just a multiple set with one title.

Many catalogers have difficulty in determining what constitutes a series title. One example is the proliferous recurrence of the PBS Home Video label in the [440] and [490] fields as a series. A true series is neither a label or a trademark, like PBS Video (under Pacific Arts). The cataloger must decide whether (1) to include the main entry of the series title in the [245] field with each volume listed as a separate title within the [505] and [740] fields or (2) to enter each volume as a distinct videographic record, linked only by the common series field [730]. Depending upon the local database search characteristics and space, the advantages and disadvantages of either choice are as follows:

1. *Advantages:* True series are known distinctly by the series title rather than individual volume titles. Usually, the volumes are closely related in subject content; therefore, individual annotations are not needed. Also, producers and

copyright dates are the same throughout the series. Programs can be listed in any pertinent order, such as alphabetical, volume number, or viewing order within the contents field [505], which may prove helpful to patrons.

Disadvantages: Individual annotations for each volume cannot be entered/ displayed easily. The listing of the individual volumes in two fields simultaneously may result in duplicated listings for a resultant search, ultimately confusing patrons. Each volume is essentially treated like a copy. Many computerized circulation systems such as DYNIX allow holds/reserves to be placed via two methods: (1) first available copy and (2) specific copy. The patron must choose the specific copy if a specific volume is wanted instead of the first available volume. The problem becomes exacerbated when there are multiple copies of each volume. The only alternative to the patron is to put all copies of that specific volume on hold in the hopes of getting one.

2. *Advantages:* Individual MARC records for each series volume, part/title solve the hold/reserve problem mentioned above.

Disadvantages: This form of entry uses much more database space and requires more cataloging time for creation of the records, as well as creating a greater error rate regarding consistent cataloging for multiple entries (however, some systems allow the use of one record as a template to recreate another record). Many times national databases and CD-ROM cataloging products will not have separate records for series titles; therefore, primary cataloging is the only solution. Also, using this method, the series entry cannot not be given a generic annotation.

With the above definitions and discussion of the MARC record and local database search parameters in mind, the following series test is given so that catalogers may find it easier to determine main entry (i.e., 245 field entry).

1. Series with a series title and each title possesses a unique episode title, program number, or volume number (i.e., *Tell Me Why*, *Video Aircraft Report*, National Geographic Society Specials, National Audubon Society Specials). *A decision must be made as to whether all series titles should be shelved together or individually based on their subject content/genre similarity.*

   A. as a group, catalog as in 2A.

   B. individually, catalog under episode title [245] with added under series [440/490]. Include, as part of the title any volume, part, program number, etc. Cutter under episode title.

2. Series with one episode title (subtitle) per video, dealing with the same subject/genre (i.e., needing to be shelved/cuttered together—*The Outer Limits*, *Doctor Who*, plus series with volumes needing to be viewed in sequence). Individual program annotations [520 NOTES] desired.

   A. Catalog under the series title followed by the [GMD] subtitle (episode, program, volume, etc.). Added entries in [740] (episode title) and [440] or [490] (series). Include, as part of the title, any volume, part, program number, etc. Cutter under series title.

3. Series with one episode title (subtitle) per video, dealing with the same subject/genre (i.e., needing to be shelved/cuttered together—"Land of the Eagle" plus series with vols. needing to be viewed in sequence). Individual program annotations [520 NOTES] *not desired.*

    A. Catalog under the series title. Added entries in 740 (episode title with any program, part, volume, number), 440/490, and 520. Cutter under series title.

4. Series with more than one episode title per video, dealing with the same subject/genre (i.e., *The Twilight Zone, The Story of English, Cosmos, The Civil War*).

    A. catalog under the series title followed by the [GMD] : /b the first subtitle (episode, program, volume, etc.); the next subtitle; and so on. Include, as part of the title, any volume, part, program number, etc. Added entries in [740] (episode title) and [440] (series). Cutter under series title.

        It is also recognized that patrons desire the following things:

    A. They want access under title exact/title keyword for certain serial/series titles like *I Love Lucy*, because they will not remember individual episode titles.

    B. On some series (TV fiction programs and same subject series (such as *Doctor Who* and *The Story of English*) titles, the patron must be able to distinguish one unique title from another at the OPAC title list. *Also, there should be no double entries for the same title under the same search list.*

    C. Titles listed under B should be cuttered similarly and shelved together as a group, permitting easy browsing access.

    D. Do patrons desire unique, descriptive annotations (notes) for each title?

In many computerized booking systems, such as Tek Data Systems' DMAX software designed specifically for media, the system allows the input of individual titles with annotations as well as a separate database of series with its own annotations and title listings. These databases are then merged for searching and book catalog production, giving the patron the best of both worlds.

Figure 6.6 shows a record from the DYNIX database of the Elkhart (IN) Public Library, which graphically illustrates the concept of a series main entry for a television miniseries, multivolume videocassette with individual episode titles. Each volume has become a copy in the DYNIX system and is barcoded and circulated separately. Therefore, the cataloging effects the circulation and shelving/arrangement of the title as well as the access points, but the title is cataloged under the series title with one series annotation. Contents notes list individual volume titles.

A local library database record actually has two parts—a bibliographic/videographic record and a holdings record. The videographic record relates descriptive detail to the item for search access, but is not copy specific; the holdings record is copy or barcoded item specific, detailing call number, item barcode, copy number, status (on shelf, out, etc.), and other coded information useful for gathering library circulation statistics. Normally, a copy number refers to multiple copies of the same title. However, some unique circumstances commonly occur in videocassettes to upset this rather straightforward concept. Many

Figure 6.6
Elkhart (IN) Public Library DYNIX/OCLC Record

```
Call Number    Entertainment Video - AV Area    Status: Checked In
               B8514re                           5 other copies

   DYNIX #     333641
   AUTHOR      1) Irons, Jeremy.
               2) Olivier, Lawrence, 1907-
               3) Bloom, Claire, 1931-
               4) Gielgud, John, Sir, 1904-

     TITLE        Brideshead revisited

   IMPRINT    Los Angeles, CA: Virgin Vision, VHS 70144-70149, c1988.
 COLLATION    6 videocassettes (588 min.) : sd., col. ; 1/2 in.

    SERIES    Portfolio Collection

  SUBJECTS    1) Dramtic films

     NOTES    1) Based on the 1945 novel by Evelyn Waugh.
              2) Chronicles a young man's haunting relationship in an
              irretrievably aristocratic world.  The story spans three
              decades from the early twenties to WW II in Charles
              Ryder's relationship with the wild and eccentric
              Sebastian Flyle and the aristocratic Marchmain family.

  CONTENTS    1) v.1. Nostalgia for a vanished past (98 min.) -- v.2.
              Home and abroad. Shadows close in (98 min.) -- v.3.
              Sebastian against the world. Julia blossoms (98 min.) --
              v.4. Julia's marriage. The unseen hook (98 min.) -- v.5.
              Brideshead deserted. Orphans of the storm (98 min.) --
              v.6. A twich upon the thread. Brideshead revisited.
              (98 min.)
Next screen -----

Author    Irons, Jeremy.
 Title    Brideshead revisited                        Holds:  0

#   Call #                              STATUS          BARCODE    LIB
1. Entertainment Video - AV Area        Shelving Cart
   B8514re v.1
2. Entertainment Video - AV Area        Shelving Cart
   B8514re v.2
3. Entertainment Video - AV Area        Shelving Cart
   B8514re v.3
4. Entertainment Video - AV Area        Shelving Cart
   B8514re v.4
5. Entertainment Video - AV Area        Shelving Cart
   B8514re v.5
6. Entertainment Video - AV Area        Shelving Cart
   B8514re v.6
```

times, titles have multiple parts, such as *The Godfather*, issued in two or more separate parts. Even though these parts form the whole and circulate together, libraries may choose to barcode each part for greater inventory control. Series titles such as *The Civil War*, *The Story of English*, and *Brideshead Revisited* possesses multiple volumes, but do not necessarily have to circulate together. Within a local database, circulation is bar code specific. Therefore, it is inherently tied to the holdings record which is accessed (i.e., searchable) through the videographic record. In many cases the patron can actually view the holdings (copies, volumes, parts) and place a hold/reserve on any one copy or all of them. Circulation modules such as DYNIX provide the patron with a "selected copy only" or "first-available copy" selection. As shown in Figure 6.6, the cataloger must make a choice of how the title is to be cataloged relative to how it will be circulated, thus choosing to catalog the entire set under the series title if the series title is better known than its individually titled parts. Each volume would receive analytics and/or a [740] field entry if titled. The collation would reflect the number of volumes within the entire series as well as the series running time. The holdings screen would show the individually barcoded volumes. Advantages to this method are a savings in cataloging time (cataloging a series and adding holdings is faster than cataloging each item in its own videographic record and adding a holdings record) and conservation of database space. If a patron wishes to place a hold on a specific volume, he/she must remember to be copy specific. Furthermore, if multiple copies of one or more volumes are added to the holdings, the patron must be sure to place multiple, copy-specific holds.

As a further example of local database modifications for series, the *Doctor Who* PBS television program is presented: Most OCLC MARC records list the individual episode titles in the [245] field with a series entry in [440/490]. Most patrons do not know individual episode titles and want the entire series shelved/cuttered together. They search under title keyword and title exact for "Doctor Who." It is also important to have a computer default set to recognize "Dr." and "Doctor" as being the same term. Most databases have a string limit on screen/print output when showing resultant search titles. Therefore, it is important that each episode be distinctly identified. Figure 6.7 shows how the Elkhart Public Library has chosen to catalog the *Dr. Who* series.

(Refer to Figure 6.7) In keeping with the series definitions and cataloging recommendations, The Elkhart Public Library has chosen to catalog each episode separately, modifying each OCLC record [245] field (Dr. Who) to contain a title and subfield b title (episode title). A [730] series entry and variant title entries [740] are also entered as well as subject headings [650] for multiple point access. In this manner, all the *Doctor Who* episodes are standardized, containing consistent information and allowing a comprehensive list of all titles in the series be listed at once.

PARTS ARE PARTS . . .

As previously mentioned in the series discussion, it is important to discern a volume title from a series title in both the videographic and holdings records. The practical side of this concept reveals itself when holdings records are attached to single barcodes for circulation. A film such as *The Sound of Music*

Figure 6.7
Doctor Who DYNIX Search—Elkhart (IN) Public Library

```
Your search:  Doctor Who
    AUTHOR                    TITLE (shortened)            DATE
1. Baker, Tom, 1934-      Doctor Who: five doctors /      1989
2.                        Doctor Who: ark in space /      1991
3.                        Doctor Who: the Hartnell years / 1991
4. McCoy, Sylvester       Doctor Who: curse of Fenric /   1991
5. Pertwee, Jon           Doctor Who: day of the Daleks / 1989
6.                        Doctor Who: time warrior        1991
```

```
001      ocm23594036
003      OCLC
005      19921007161921.0
007      vf-cbahou
008      910423p19911973nyu090
020      079395231
040      UAP$cUAP$dIEB
049      IEBF
245 00   Doctor Who: $h videorecording $b time warrior /$c BBC
Enterprises, Ltd.
260      New York : $b Playhouse Video, VHS 5423, $c [1991], c1973.
300      1 videocassette (90min) :$b sd., col. :$c 1/2 in.
440 0    Doctor Who
500      Videocassette release of a 1973 episode of the television
series, Doctor Who.
508      Producer, Barry Lells ; director, Alan Bromly ; writer,
Robert Holmes.
511 1    Jon Pertwee
520      Doctor Who battles to save the entire human race when he
must go back in time to the middle ages. There he faces Linx, a
war-loving Sonlaren fleet commander who is supplying a feuding
medieval man with advanced weapons that could change the course of
history.
650 0    Science fiction television programs.
650 0    Television programs $z Great Britain
700 11   Pertwee, Jon
730 0    Doctor Who (Television Program)
740 0    Dr. Who: The time warrior $h videorecording
740 4    The time warrior $h videorecording
```

may be produced on two videocassettes which need to be circulated together. The videographic collation might read: "2 videocassettes, part I/II (280 min.)." Part I might contain the bar code, with part II rubber-banded to its partner (or boxed together in another manner). A distinction must be made by both the cataloger and the public service librarian in determining a part from a volume, as well as whether to circulate the set as a whole or as separate parts, which will effect both the videographic collation and holdings record. The cataloger cannot always depend upon the wording of the producer/manufacturer in determining volumes or parts. Generally speaking, a volume will have a separate title, possibly be labeled as a volume, and be a unique, separate item with a distinct beginning and ending. A part, on the other hand, may be labeled as such, not have a separate title, and not possess a distinguishable end/credits. Many television miniseries now released on video in multiple cassettes of two or more, such as *North and South*, should be considered parts rather than volumes. When parts constitute more than two physical videocassettes, a decision as to whether they should be circulated separately or as one unit must be made. All parts must be consistently labeled and/or relabeled so that shelvers and other public service staff, as well as patrons, know what they are handling.

FORMAT INTEGRATION

Final implementation of LC's format integration for MARC records is set for 1995, but there are many bugs to work out. Simply put, format integration will allow catalogers the necessary freedom to do a full description of the item and include coded data elements for all aspects of materials, especially useful for kits containing multimedia such as an audiocassette, videocassette, compact disc, books and manuals, and so on. The [740] field will become obsolete, reassigned to 246 [VARYING FORM OF TITLE] and a repeatable 006 [FIXED-LENGTH DATA ELEMENTS—ADDITIONAL MATERIAL CHARACTERISTICS] will be available for different media. Catalogers will not have to determine which type of media is the primary type from which to catalog. While this is an important step in media catalog advancement, it will no doubt cause chaos within a local database. Profiles must be modified to search not only existing [740] fields, but also new [246] fields, or programs globally written to change [740] fields into [246]. Additionally, a 546 [LANGUAGE NOTE] has been added (formerly placed in [500]) as well as a 511 [PARTICIPANT OR PERFORMER NOTE]. Lastly, a 521 field [TARGET AUDIENCE] has been added.[14] Search profiles must be modified, and consistent language developed, to reflect these changes and additions and adapt them for local database use.[15]

TRIAL BY FIRE—TALES OF PUBLIC ACCESS CATALOGS, PATRONS, AND STAFF

In order to develop a useful card catalog, there must be a good match between the needs of the patron and staff and the demands and limitations of the system. This match involves an introspective examination of what the library's clientele and staff need from the catalog and how they perform routine searches. The best way to find out what patrons want is to talk to them about how they use the materials. What would be useful in a catalog that is not there now? What is good (i.e., useful) about what is already in use? Informal conversations with patrons utilizing reference interview techniques will provide surprising insights. Formal in-house use surveys can also be helpful and produce hard evidence to support changes and cataloging policy/procedural modifications.

Talking to staff who deal with the patrons on the front line is probably going to produce the most pertinent information. Public service staff know what patrons want; they know what works and what does not concerning the system already in place. Surveying the staff can also be helpful, especially if they can anonymously and objectively critique current practices. This information gathering is the most important step in the initial planning process and will be very time-consuming and tedious, but will ultimately reap benefits in information access for the staff and patrons. Having a cataloging staff who actually work a public service desk occasionally will help sensitize them to the needs of the patrons as well as make them acquainted with the searching limits and capabilities of the on-line catalog and patron searching patterns and methods.

By far the most difficult procedure in computerizing a library collection is setting up a system profile, or searching program/parameters so that the computer will search, compile, and list the correct MARC record fields for the specific search selected by the user and disregard/not display duplicated information. The computer display must be "user friendly" in that it should display information in an easy-to-read, easily recognizable fashion, such as in standard catalog card format rather than in delineated MARC fields. It should also give the patron information about the media type, displaying the GMD whenever the title is displayed. The inclusion of subfield h in [730] and [740] is vitally important so that all video titles display a GMD.

Today's cataloger of videocassettes must possess an in-depth knowledge of the local computer searching capabilities, but also be able to think like a patron when videographic information must be created, modified, and placed into discrete computer/database fields for search access points. For example, if a user selects a title or title keyword search, the profile might command the computer to search the [245] and [740] fields, as well as the [505] fields. Likewise, series searches might access the [245] and [730], but omit the [505] fields of the videographic record. For the above stated reasons, it is imperative that, whenever MARC records are downloaded into any local system, they are immediately checked for data/field inclusion as well as for field standardization, and modified accordingly. If this is not done, the integrity of the data has been compromised and is of questionable use during a search. Local standardization and record modification can be extremely complex, or as simple as adding a space before and after the GMD so that it does not adversely effect the title filing order.

Catalogers control the search pattern in their inclusion and arrangement of data, as well as in their knowledge of how the local database will search, limit, and display that data. In particular, catalogers should be aware of how their local public access catalog searches data through answers to the following questions and characteristics:

1. Does the system have the following capabilities?

   A. Keywords in titles, summaries, subject headings, and other fields.

   B. Word truncation.

   C. Do browsable and permuted indexes exist?

D. Does the computer allow stop words to be added (words such as a, an, and the) which are not searched?

E. Are Boolean operators used; if so, which ones and how (and, or, not, etc.)?

2. If the MARC record contains the same word, phrase, title, or name in more than one field, and those fields are accessed in the same search, will that search bring up duplicated listings referring back to the same title? This may indicate unwanted duplication in specific fields (e.g., [740] and [505]).

3. How are titles listed on screen as the result of a search? Is GMD (general media designator) shown? Is all, or a portion thereof, of the [245] subfield b, subtitle shown? How many titles/entries are listed on a single screen, and can screens be saved and/ or combined?

   What information stays on the screen during a hierarchical search? How easy/ difficult is it to branch out on a search or retrace steps?

4. Can "see" and "see also" references be placed in these searches?

The trick to having patron-usable cataloging, regardless of what rules and standards are applied, is to choose only one set of rules and standards and stick to them and be consistent in their application. When modifications to those rules are made, they should be documented. Records should be modified globally, if possible, so that access points remain consistent throughout the database, or the entire structure will suffer. The problem with large national and regional databases is that, although they try to adhere to various standards, the sheer number of disparate catalogers inputting records into the database makes conformity impossible. For any given videocassette, there may be as many as eight to ten different bibliographic records for the same item—just cataloged differently. On the local level, the cataloger must search out the title, look at the various record options, and choose the one record that both best suits the needs of the library and will need the least amount of local modification, or choose to perform original cataloging. An on-line circulation, public access database is usually setup or "profiled" to search specific MARC record fields for specific searches, rather than searching the entire MARC record for every search. It is vitally important that the cataloger know what MARC/OCLC fields are used in different searches and, if modified, how that modification will effect other searches and still provide the searcher with succinct, intelligible information.

A CASE FOR SUBJECT HEADINGS

After the video has been physically described, its contents must be conveyed to the user in some fashion. Historically, the contents of any item have been described through subject headings called tracings, which can be terms, word combinations, or phrases. Catalogers have always felt that the distillation of film contents into discrete subject headings was more difficult than describing their book counterparts. Actually, films and videocassettes are not more complex than books to catalog; it is the simple fact that the former can be easily pursued for subject content while the latter must be viewed through a VCR—a time-consuming process. Today, however, most videocassettes are packaged with attractive and descriptive cover art, similar to a book jacket, making content information readily attainable. In 1979, in an attempt to address the complexity of assigning subject headings to films, the National Film Board of Canada developed the PRECIS method. PRECIS was itself a complex system, utilizing keywords from the title and other sources, recombined to produce multiple key phrases. The problem with this system was that there was little consistency or uniformity in phrases and, with so many descriptive terms, a printed catalog quickly developed into a huge, unwieldy, and unusable monster. Today the most commonly used lists are the following: *The ERIC List of Descriptors*, *The Library of Congress Subject Headings*, and *Sears List of Subject Headings*. For an extremely up-to-date, popular listing of subject headings, the reader might try the Hennepin County (MN) Library's *Subject Authorities List* (Minnetonka, MN: the Library). Figure 6.8 details the importance of describing a subject/content video in a detailed fashion; otherwise important information would be lost.

Without the analytic subject headings of the various activities in *The MacMillan Video Almanac for Kids*, this information would be inaccessible to patrons in a card catalog environment. In a computerized PAC environment, if the [505] fields were searched along with the subject heading fields [650] using subject keyword or subject exact searches, the various information included in the summary would not necessarily need to be detailed through subject headings. The development of an up-to-date subject thesaurus which lists terms and phrases in a consistent, standardized fashion is a necessity to accessible subject cataloging. In the omnimedia, integrated catalog environment, it is vitally important that these subject headings be used consistently with nonprint and print titles.

A further example of standardization and consistency in subject heading use is illustrated in Figure 6.9. Four subject headings for videocassettes teaching a foreign language have been chosen to describe the Berlitz video. It is important that catalogers follow this example in duplicating this consistent use of those subject headings for other Spanish language videocassettes as well as any other foreign language videos. In this way, all languages will utilize the same subject headings and will be easily accessible.

Genre Headings for Feature Films

Audiovisual catalogers agree that previously mentioned subject and genre lists do not provide adequate subject headings to describe film genres. In fact, these headings are inconsistent within their own framework. Take, for example, *The Library of Congress Subject Headings* entry for Romance, Historical, Science fiction, and Westerns as a Comparison:[16]

Figure 6.8
Catalog Card Main Entry

```
793.019
          The Macmillan video almanac for kids [videorecording]:
             vol. 1 "rainy day games" / produced by Caravatt
          Communications, Inc. and Macmillan Video.
             Westport, CT: Caravatt Communications, Inc, 1985.
             1 videocassette (60min.); sd., col.; 1/2 in.

             VHS
             based on the book, The Macmillan Illustrated Almanac
             for Kids.

             Summary: This program shows children (ages 8-12) how to
             perform four recreational activities: Soap bubble
             magic; string figures; kite flying and; learning a
             secret language (Ob).
             ISBN 0-02-587490-X

          1. Children - Recreation. 2. Kites. 3. Languages, Secret.
          4. Soap-bubbles. 5. String figures.
          I. Rainy day games (vol. 1)
                         OCLC 19738959
```

Romance drama   Historical drama
Romance fiction   Historical fiction
Romance literature   Historical films
Romances   Historical television programs

Science fiction   Western stories
Science fiction films   Western television programs
Science fiction television programs

There is little uniformity or standardization across genres in Historical television programs and Western (television programs). Romance does not even possess a film or television program equivalent. Thus, libraries have had to create their own genre lists. As with subject headings, it is important that the structure be derived from an existing subject heading, fitting within that genre hierarchy, but modified to fit the genre. The following list details one such genre list currently used by the Elkhart (IN) Public Library to describe genre videocassettes.

When questions arise as to what genre(s) a certain film should be categorized into, it is highly recommend that the following genre guides be consulted: Mick Martin and Marsha Porter's *The Video Movie Guide*, *Bowker's Complete Video Directory*, and *The Video Source Book*. Two of the most extensive reference sources this author has found for classifying movies by genre are *The Motion Picture Guide* (Bowker/CineBooks, 1985+), which is also available on CD-ROM, and *Films by Genre* by Daniel Lopez (Jefferson, NC: McFarland & Co. Publishers, 1993). Remember that the entire purpose of genre categorization is to allow patrons to access smaller groups of the larger video collection whole through standardized topics which are meaningful to them.

Figure 6.9
Partial DYNIX Record, Elkhart (IN) Public Library

```
Call Number     Entertainment Video - AV Area    Status: Checked In
                466 B515v                         3 other copies

    DYNIX #     186322
    AUTHOR      1) Editions Berlitz S.A.

     TITLE         Spanish for travellers

   IMPRINT      New York: Berlitz Publications, c1986.
   COLLATION    1 videocassette (90 min.) : sd., col. ; 1/2 in.

    SUBJECTS    1) Spanish language -- Terms and phrases.
                2) Spanish language -- Videorecordings for English
                   speakers.
                3) Spanish language -- Audio-visual instruction.
                4) Spanish language -- Self-instruction.
```

GENRE HEADINGS FOR FEATURE VIDEOS

Action Films. This includes films where the main plot and characters are involved in relentless action/adventure regardless of the time period (historical period). Includes films with such actors as Clint Eastwood, Chuck Norris, Charles Bronson, Jean-Claude Van Damme, and Arnold Schwarzenegger. Includes spy and espionage films like *The Eiger Sanction,* if action, rather than the solving of the mystery or crime, is the ultimate goal or if there are sufficient "shoot 'em up" action sequences. Includes films such as *Die Hard, Commando, Last Action Hero,* all *James Bond* movies, *Robin Hood, Top Gun, Iron Eagle, Rambo, Lethal Weapon, Cliffhanger,* and *Under Siege.*

Adventure Films. This includes films with adventure, especially outdoor adventure, as the primary plot/source of action. Includes films such as *Grizzly Adams, White Fang, White Fang 2, Courage Mountain, Swiss Family Robinson, Moby Dick, The Incredible Journey,* and *The Adventures of Milo and Otis.*

Animated Films. A full-length feature which uses animated settings and characters exclusively—no (or very little) live action. (I would not put *Who Framed Roger Rabbit?* here!) Full-length and the style of animation (not cartoonish) are keys here. Examples include *The Hobbit, Gulliver's Travels, Fantasia, 101 Dalmatians, Pinnochio, Snow White and the Seven Dwarfs, Beauty and the Beast,* and *Winnie the Pooh.*

Cartoon Films. Basically, what distinguishes an animated feature from a cartoon are three things: the duration of the film (most cartoons are short), the unrealistic, cartoonish drawing style, and the exaggerated intent to make the viewer laugh. All Warner Brothers, MGM, and Disney short compilations (under 30 minutes).

Children's Films. Use this heading for full-length films that do not fit into any other genre (using the subhead "Juvenile") but target children as their main audience. (I can't think of any feature which would not fit into a genre category. This heading should be used sparingly.)

Comedy Films. Where the main characters are involved in a comedic plot and comedy is not an incidental part, but rather an intrinsic whole. Includes The Three Stooges, The Marx Brothers, Laurel & Hardy, and so on. Also includes crossover genres like romantic comedies, musical comedies, and others. However, comedy drama, class in Dramatic Films. Examples include *With Six You Get Egg Roll, Which Way to the Forum?, The Pink Panther, Arthur, Bringing Up Baby, Mr. Blandings Builds His Dream House, Oh, God, The Apple Dumpling Gang, The Naked Gun, Blazing Saddles, Young Frankenstein,* and *What's Up Doc?*

Definition of Feature (Film). For purposes of cataloging, a full-length feature is defined as being a movie released on video that is at least 60 minutes in length, and which has previously been in theatrical release, or is a made-for-video. Made-for-television movies should fall under their appropriate genres, with "Television programs" phrase added to each. *We will use the term FILM after each genre type instead of* videorecording, feature, or other format indicator.

Detective Films. Involves a plot revolving around some type of crime, criminals, and the crime's solution. Characters frequently are police, detectives, private eyes, and other "nosy people." Examples include *The Adventures of Sherlock Holmes, The Alphabet Murders, Double Indemnity, Fatal Attraction, Madame X,* and *Gree for Danger.*

Dramatic Films. A film that does not easily fit into any of the other genres and may contain elements of any or all genres. Examples include *Anastasia, Barry Lyndon, Blackboard Jungle, Champion, The Champ, Giant,* and *Cat on a Hot Tin Roof.*

Family Films. Both "Children's Films" and this subject heading are not necessarily genre-related; rather, they indicate a particular audience. Unlike "Children's Films", "Family" should be used in conjunction with other genre subject headings if possible. All MPAA G-rated films (live action and animated), and possibly some PG films, should fall into the "Family" category. Judgement should be used in assessing whether included titles are appropriate for viewing by the entire family. They should be nonviolent, no-sex, no-blood, and possibly underscore a positive life-skills lesson or message. Examples include *The Bear, Milo and Otis, The Incredible Journey, Seven Alone, White Fang,* and all Disney films (animated or live-action).

Fantasy Films. Fantasy strictly follows a set of laws to create an imaginary world. The rules used may not agree with logic or the laws of nature. Nonrational happenings occur without scientific basis, with magic and the supernatural present. Include films involving mythology here. Examples include *The Neverending Story, Alice in Wonderland, The Adventures of Sinbad, The Dark Crystal, The Hobbit, Watership Down, Time Bandits, Hercules,* and *Jason and the Argonauts.*

Folk and Fairy Tale Films. Adaptations of/or works based on folk and fairy tales by authors such as Hans Christian Anderson and The Brothers Grimm. Includes *The Little Mermaid, Sleeping Beauty,* and *Pinocchio.*

Foreign Films (country). A film produced in a country other than the United States. Many will have narration/dialog in the original language (other than English) and or be subtitled. Others may be dubbed in English. Examples include *Das Boot, Babette's Feast, The 400 Blows, Ran, Intermezzo,* and *Knife in the Water.*

Historical Films. A feature whose plot revolves around an historic event as a central point, using characterizations of real-life people. The story line tries to be as close to the real telling as possible but may take dramatic liberties. Examples include *Lion in Winter, King Lear, Abe Lincoln in Illinois, The Alamo, Henry V, Peter the Great, Quo Vadis, Ben Hur, Martin Luther, Joan of Arc, The Last of the Mohicans,* and *Columbus.*

Horror Films. The matter of horror films is derived from the supernatural and the occult exhibited in very overt terms—ghosts and ghouls, witches and warlocks, vampires and werewolves, monsters and mummies, demonology, black magic and voodoo, and other forms of occult magic. Examples include *The Bride of Frankenstein, Dracula, The Pit and the Pendulum, Fright Night, The Invisible Man,* and all Stephen King movie adaptations.

Musical Films. A feature where the music is an intrinsic and intregal part for the furthering of the plot (story line). Involves not only orchestral music but singing as well. This does not include music videos or operas. Examples include *Band Wagon, Camelot, Carousel, Funny Face, Easter Parade,* and *Sweeney Todd.*

Mystery Films. A mystery is a story of a crime and its investigation involving the police, detectives, private eyes, or other amateur sleths. The solving of the crime is the main plot while the detective is the main character. All Agatha Christie and Sherlock Holmes movies fall into this category. Also included are *Patriot Games, The Big Sleep, D.O.A., The Ipcress File, Klute,* and *The Conversation.*

Religious Films. A dramatic or comedic film where religion (or religious figures, such as King David, Jesus, etc.) plays a prominent and plot-determinant role. Examples include *Moses, The Ten Commandments, The Bible, The Robe, Barabbas, The Last Temptation of Christ, Sister Act,* and *The Bells of St. Mary's.*

Romance Films. A romance is a story (dramatic or comedic) in which the plot revolves around the main character's pursuit of lasting happiness and romantic fulfillment with the opposite sex, regardless of the time period (historical period). Examples include *Idiot's Delight, It Happened One Night, Pillow Talk, The French Lieutenant's Woman, Black Orchid,* and *The Ghost and Mrs. Muir.*

Science Fiction Films. Science fiction is speculative fiction pertaining to potential uses of science and the future of mankind, with its characters and plot obeying all the laws of nature and with scientific knowledge as the base. Examples include *Blade Runner, THX 1138,* all *Star Wars* and *Star Trek* films, *Alien, 2001,* and *2010.*

Short Films. This would be analogous to the term "Featurette" used in the early movie days, where shorter films were butted together or used as a leader into the main feature film. A feature film is over one hour long; anything else is a short. Examples include *The Little Rascals* (*Our Gang* is a Comedy television program), W.C. Fields shorts, and some Laurel and Hardy.

Silent Films. Used for films released without a soundtrack, circa 1898–1928. Videos now include added musical soundtrack but no narration or dialog. These include films like *The Great Train Robbery,* Charlie Chaplin films, Buster Keaton films, and Harold Lloyd films.

Suspense Films. Similar to horror films and possibly involving a mystery and/or the occult, but not relying on overt horror, the suspense film places characters in plots involving extreme physical and psychological tension and terror, and or danger. All Film Noir and the Hitchcock films are examples of this genre. Others include *Basic Instinct, The Silence of the Lambs, Final Analysis, Jacob's Ladder, DOA, North by Northwest, The Birds, Double Indemnity, The Parallax View, Vertigo, Tightrope,* and *The Mechanic.*

Television Programs. Omitting feature films that have been theatrically released and later shown on television, this heading is to be used for *all* television broadcast shows such as made-for-TV-movies, variety shows, TV specials, miniseries, serial compilations and anthologies, and other shows. Examples include *Monty Python's Flying Circus, Black Adder, I Love Lucy, The Jackie Gleason Show, Christmas with the Carpenters, Lonesome Dove, O Pioneers!, Sarah Plain and Tall,* all Wonderworks Family Movies, *The Twilight Zone, The Outer Limits, Roots,* and *The Blue and the Gray* (the latter might be described as an Historical Television Program, a Romance Television Program and a War Television Program).

Subdivision. If a television show is a particular genre as described within the enclosed definitions, that genre should be placed ahead of the heading in the following manner: *Western Television Programs, Science Fiction Television Programs, Family Television Programs,* etc.

In a similar fashion, Children's television programs should be categorized one of two ways: (1) If the genre cannot be easily ascertained: *Television Programs (Juvenile)*; (2) If a genre(s) can be identified: *Western Television Programs (Juvenile), Horror Television Programs (Juvenile),* etc.

War Films. A war film is primarily an adventure story set in a period of war (any period using a recognized war or military action, i.e., Korea and Vietnam) and involving armies, soldiers, and organized military fighting. The war must be the focal point, not just the background, and actions should have military consequences. For example, *Lord Jim* involves an insurrection, but should not be considered a war movie because it is not the focal point of the movie. Examples include *The Eagle Has Landed, The Green Berets, The Killing Fields, Platoon, War and Peace, Tora! Tora! Tora!, Back to Bataan, Platoon,* and *Full Metal Jacket.*

Western Films. Primarily, the Western is an adventure involving cowboys, the frontier, and Indians and outlaws, with the setting and time period set in the American Old West, c. 1789–1900. Examples include *Abilene Town, Big Jake, Comancheros, High Plains Drifter,* and *Angel and the Badman.*

Special Subject Headings

Described Videos. Used as above, this heading delineates those videos having a "described narration" overlaying the soundtrack. Currently, these videocassettes are produced by DVS, Inc.

Public Performance Films. Used in similar fashion to the subject headings "Video recordings for the hearing impaired" or "Closed captioned videos," this heading delineates and groups those titles possessing public performance rights.

Videorecordings. While this heading is currently in use in many MARC records, no other material such as audiocassettes, art prints, or books are so delineated by a similar subject heading. This heading will accomplish one feat—to bring together all titles of one format. However, a search under the [505] field "VHS" string or the [GMD] would yield the same result.

Video Recordings for the Hearing Impaired. Used in place of *Films for the Hearing Impaired, Video recordings for the Hearing Impaired,* or *Closed Captioned Videocassettes.* Use this heading for all videos displaying the CC (closed captioned) trademark. Note that "Closed Captioned for the Hearing Impaired" is appearing much more in both the local SH and notes field than before.

CLASSIFICATION SYSTEMS

Basically, there are two types of classification arrangements: alphabetic and classified. An alphabetic arrangement usually alphabetizes by title. The listing is simple and straightforward, but fragments related genres and subjects. Exact titles are easy to locate but similar genres and subjects cannot be found easily. A classified arrangement shows subject and genre hierarchies, locates related subjects, and allows greater subject depth to be expressed, but searchers must be knowledgeable about the system or first consult an alphabetic index for location information.

Many libraries simply throw videocassettes on the shelf in random order; others use an alphabetic arrangement for features and a classified arrangement for subject-oriented videocassettes. Still other libraries may divide their collections between Children's and Adult, further breaking down each of those collections into broad genre-classified arrangement for features and a number classified system for subject videocassettes. In situations where a two-box system or flat browser-paks (Chicago-One Stop) are used, a classified arrangement many be used with a straight numeric accession system. By using such a system, patrons can easily access titles by genre and subject and staff can maximize space by simply "adding on" to the ends of rows rather than creating space between them for new acquisitions. However, in such a system, care must be taken to identify both dummy and live item with both accession and classified numbers.

This text advocates the use of the same subject classification system used for the book collection at any library for subject "nonfiction" videocassettes. Advantages from using the same system include the cataloger's, processor's, and public desk staff's familiarity with the current system, achievement of consistency between collections, and the patron's possible familiarity with the system. Genre arrangements are fine for libraries with enough space to shelve materials and expand their collection at the same time. However, locating a specific title involves not only knowing the title but also determining the genre designation. The practical purpose of any alphabetic or classified arrangement of materials is to provide some type of logical, repeatable order to a group of materials. To this practical end, they provide an orderly shelving arrangement which accomplishes three functions:

1. facilitates ease of browsing and title location;

2. is organized in a logical manner which is readily apparent to patrons and staff; and

3. is kept as simple as possible but with subject/genre areas sufficiently delineated so as to avoid confusion.

The advantage of using the Dewey Decimal Classification system (DDC) or Library of Congress Classification system (LC) is that staff and patrons will already by familiar with it. A videocassette on travel in Hawaii will have the same DDC number as a book on the same subject. If a library decided to go to an integrated collection, the use of one of these systems would certainly be a necessity. Classification schemes for feature films is more problematic for libraries. DC and LC leave a lot to be desired as far as public libraries are concerned. The fact is that library patrons also use video stores and are used to genre groupings. While librarians may turn up their collective noses at this type of scheme, is it really any different from book collections, where mysteries are frequently pulled out of the fiction section and classified and shelved separately? It is not unusual to find science fiction, short stories, fantasy, and young adult novels separated from the fiction collection in libraries.

Genre classifications are user friendly and are particularly appealing for browsing collections. Obviously, if the feature film collection is part of a university collection that serves a film school, different needs will exist that will necessitate a different approach. American films classed in DDC could go in 813, English films in 823, and so on. Or all the films could go into the 790s. An excellent example of using the DDC number for videocassettes occurs regularly with two series titles, ''The American Short Story series'' and ''Reading Rainbow series.'' The first series is often classed in 808 and the latter series in 372.6. The cataloger must realize that any classification scheme will have hundreds of videocassettes with numbers that are basically only a few digits apart. Workmarks and Cutter numbers with the first four letters of the title might end up being the only discernable difference for many titles.

Librarians possessing small collections may feel that a classified system such as LC or DDC is too complex and may choose to use a few broad subject categories such as feature films, music, documentary, instructional, and children's films. The DDC system provides for an orderly shelf arrangement of subject videos and facilitates transitional continuity from print to nonprint. Alternately, arranging feature films alphabetically by title with genres denoted using colored labels also seems to work well. Genre labels are available from traditional library supply vendors like Demco and Gaylord, as well as video store supply companies such as Video Store Services (6115 Monroe Court, Morton Grove, IL 60053; (800) 325-6867), The Video Store Shopper (8100 Remmet Avenue, Canoga Park, CA 91304; (800) 325-6867) and United Ad Label Company (650 Columbia Street, Brea, CA 92621; (714) 990-2700). These labels facilitate easy location and patron browsing.

Whatever system is decided upon, it is imperative that the selector/acquisitions librarian and the cataloger be on the same wavelength concerning how these materials will be handled as well as who will have the final say on disputed titles.

OPTIONS FOR CATALOGING AND CONVERSION

In the preparation for establishing a cataloging conversion project (or just implementing cataloging for a new collection), it is important to be aware of what choices can be made. Basically there are two options: the library catalogs the materials or an outside contractor does the work.

A library's cataloging department is the first obvious choice for any cataloging. However as mentioned before, backlogs, staffing, or lack of experienced staff may hinder their function as a practical idea. Often, as new materials arrive, they can be more easily cataloged and processed; but conversion of older titles may have to be done on an "as time allows" schedule. If at all possible, it is best to set up monthly quotas and a schedule of which subject areas or titles are to be priorities. A time/motion study might be done to determine an average cost per record for in-house conversion versus the item cost for an outside vendor to do the same task. In many instances, the outside vendor is cheaper; however, quality control is a big issue. Therefore, serious consideration should be given to having an outside cataloging service convert all current holdings with new materials done by in-house staff.

It is very important to consider the cataloging staff's experience and/or expertise in nonprint formats. Before any project can get off the ground, catalogers may have to have some training. The On Line Audio Visual Catalogers group (OLAC) holds annual workshops; the annual ALA conference frequently has cataloging programs; and most states have some sort of local cataloging network that hosts training workshops.

CATALOGING VENDOR SERVICES

As library videocassette collections proliferated, the services offered by cataloging vendors increased to include video as well as books and audio materials. The services available range from the traditional packs of printed catalog cards to full MARC records on tape/disk ready to be loaded onto a local library's automated system. Some of the vendors also sell nonprint materials and ship them to libraries already cataloged and processed, and ready to be shelved. If a library has limited cataloging staff this may be a valid option. It is important to analyze costs compared with the cost of a vendor cataloging and/or processing versus the library doing the work itself.

Following is a selective list of conversion vendors and CD-ROM products that are above average in the media cataloging field. The vendors provide full cataloging and/or processing services, and the CD-ROM products allow low-cost uploading of videographic records because there are no on-line or telecommunications charges, only one-time equipment and subscription fees. Rates will vary and services change from time to time, and the best rule of thumb is to call and get their basic print information and follow up with a telephone call if their services look viable for the library's needs. It is also a good idea to get a list of other libraries that use the services of the vendors and contact them about their experiences.

Vendors—Cataloging/Processing

OCLC Techpro, 6565 Frantz Road, Dublin, OH 43017-3396. OCLC customized contract cataloging and processing service for retroconversion or ongoing cataloging. (800) 848-5878.

Brodart Company, 500 Arch St., Williamsport, PA 17705; (717) 326-2461; (800) 233-8467. MARC records on disc or tape; catalog card kits.

Library Media Service, 109 East Main St., Clinton, CT 06413-2139; (800) 222-8663. MARC format cataloging using LC subject headings with ANSCR, DDC, or LC classification or unclassed. Data supplied on disc, cards, or MARC tagged edit sheets.

Professional Media Services, 19122 S. Vermont Ave., Gardena, CA 90248; (800) 223-7672. Comprehensive cataloging for videocassettes using the most inclusive database for audiovisual materials. Catalog cards, custom MARC records on tape or disc, and custom processing are available.

Vendors—CD-ROM Products

Bibliofile with A/V Access. The Library Corporation, Research Park, Inwood, WV 25428; (800) 624-0559. Around $5,269 for a total 3-year subscription. The database contains over 100,000 popular titles; all with full-level cataloging by Professional Media Service Corporation.

NICEM A-V Online. 600,000 individual MARC records representing over 340,000 titles from the world's largest bibliographic database of audiovisual materials. (National Information Center for Educational Media, Division of Access Innovations, Inc., P.O. Box 40130, Albuquerque, NM 87196; (800) 468-3453).

Precision One, MediaSource. Brodart Automation, 500 Arch St., Williamsport, PA 17705; (800) 233-8467 ($395 per disc/site). A joint effort of the Consortium of College & University Media Centers and Brodart, this CD purports to be the most comprehensive film and videocassette CD currently in production.

GUTENBERG AND THE PRINTED CATALOG

Once upon a time, in 16mm film library land, there was the printed catalog. This catalog, approximately the size of the New York City white pages, was an alphabetically-arranged-by-title body with descriptive annotations, including a complex subject index, which was distributed to schools, YMCAs, community centers, churches, schools, and individuals. Since many libraries and media centers did not perform traditional cataloging of films and videocassettes, this was the only point of access to the collection. Now as more libraries put their collection "on line" via automated systems and/or media booking systems, the question arises about the need for a printed catalog. With the number of videos being collected increasing dramatically, the ability to keep a print catalog current becomes problematic. Also, the cost of printing a large catalog with full annotations and subject index can become too expensive. After all, there is not a printed catalog of the book collection, and no longer even printed catalog cards.

The arrival of the personal computer certainly made it easier for libraries to add to and delete materials from a master list of materials. Many libraries make money producing and selling simple title lists of their videocassette holdings.

Automated booking (aka media scheduling) systems, such as Tek Data's DMAX and Paulmar's SAM systems, usually provide an option for easily printing out a camera-ready copy for duplication. For stand-alone media centers such as school cooperatives and some college/university centers, either of these options may be perfectly suited to their needs. The problem arises when the collection becomes so large that printing a catalog is no longer feasible. A printed catalog must not be just an 8 1/2" by 11" duplication of catalog cards, which would be entirely too unwieldy. In order to be viable, it must be physically pleasing and easily handled, presenting selected information to the reader. Annotations are very important; series titles and their groupings, along with separate titles, are also valuable. Audience indicators and a usable subject index that is sufficiently descriptive, grouping titles into broad categories rather than disparate, isolated subject headings, is vital to patron satisfaction. An index without "see" and "see also" references is not much use. Buying an automated system with home computer dial-access capabilities which permit both database searching and on-line scheduling, holds and/or reserves is one of the technological options toward circumventing the traditional printed catalog. The hard-line fact is that, at some point, printed catalogs will no longer be available because of increased production costs and update difficulties. Patrons will have to either dial into the database and search for the materials they need and place the reserve/booking themselves or they will have to come to the library and use the catalog on site to find their materials. For those librarians and patrons used to having a printed catalog in hand, this seems like a step backward; the counterbalance being the availability of much more information on a professionally produced, dynamic database possessing many more search options than are available in a static printed catalog.

SUMMARY

This chapter has attempted to outline and discuss some of the problems in cataloging videocassettes and also provide some solutions. The cataloger's role in making videographic information available in a palatable and usable form for both patrons and public services staff is a crucial one. Videographic records unloaded onto local databases are most often not complete or correct and may need substantial modification to meet local needs and system profile standards. The cataloger must carefully match the actual item in hand to the videographic record, viewing it if necessary. The cataloging of videocassettes involves more "exceptions to the rule" and rule interpretations than most print materials; therefore, it is a more detail-oriented, exhaustive, time-consuming process. Audiovisual catalogers must become proficient in knowing and applying those rules on a daily basis, as well as developing an in-depth knowledge of the library's local database structure and search engine methods. The public service librarian and cataloger must work together to provide consistent and standardized cataloging which will be usable to patrons.

NOTES

1. Lauren K. Lee, "The Collection Manager's Hat Rack," *Library Journal* 119 (November 1, 1994): advertisement, opposite p. 51.

2. Charles B. Osburn, "Impact of Collection Management Practices on Intellectual Freedom," *Library Trends* 39 (Summer/Fall 1990): 168–169.

3. Randy Pitman, "Rockefeller Foundation Videocassette Distribution Task Force, Final Report—Library Market," unpublished report, June 30, 1989, p. 2.

4. Ibid.

5. Ibid.

6. Ralph Hunzinger, King County (Seattle, WA) Public Library System, [presenter] National Film and Video Market panel on Video distribution, Mesa, AZ, October 29, 1993.

7. Alan L. Kaye, "Video and Other Nonprint Resources in the Small Library," Small Libraries Publications—No. 16 (Chicago: ALA, 1991): 7.

8. Robin C. Leckbee, "A Time Study of Videocassette Cataloging within the Standards of AACR2," unpublished LIBS 571 paper, Northern Illinois University, DeKalb, IL, December 1989, pp. 1–9

9. Sheila S. Intner, a library science professor at Simmons College, describes how to write summaries in an excellent article, "Writing Summary Notes for Films and Videos," *Cataloging & Classification Quarterly* 9 (1988): 55–72.

10. After the inital mention of MARC/OCLC bibliographic field numbers and names, subsequent references to those fields will be placed in brackets for easy identification. Thus the 505 notes field will be shown as [505].

11. Robert M. Hiatt, ed., "Library of Congress Rule Interpretations (LCRI)," *Cataloging Service Bulletin* 13 (Summer 1981): 15.

12. It should be noted here that keyword searching in the electronic catalog environment has largely eliminated the need for duplication of words and terms found in other fields. However, in titles such as *Asphet's Daughter* (Davenport Films) and *Cindy Eller,* which are modern retellings of the Cinderella tale, it may be wise to include them as a uniform title so that a title search will be productive to the patron through many search patterns.

13. Robert M. Hiatt, ed., "Library of Congress Rule Interpretations (LCRI)," *Cataloging Service Bulletin* 22 (Fall 1983): 21.

14. Anne L. Highsmith, "Format Integration: An Overview," in Karen Coyle, ed., *Format Integration and Its Effect on Cataloging, Training and Systems* (Chicago: ALA, 1993).

15. An excellent monograph to consult regarding format integration is Karen Coyle, ed., *Format Integration and Its Effect on Cataloging, Training and Systems* (Chicago: ALA, 1993).

16. Subject Cataloging Division, Processing Services, *Library of Congress Subject Headings,* 10th ed. (Washington, DC: Library of Congress, 1986), various pages.

Selected Bibliography

"Copyright: What Every School, College and Public Library Should Know" (30 min. video) (Elkhart, IA: Association for Information Media and Equipment, 1988).

Dessauer, John P. *Book Publishing: A Basic Introduction.* New expanded ed. (New York: Continuum Publishing Co., 1989).

Dewing, Martha, ed. *Home Video in Libraries: How Libraries Buy and Circulate Prerecorded Home Video* (New York: G.K. Hall & Co., 1988).

Eaglen, Audrey. *Buying Books: A How-To-Do-It Manual for Librarians* (New York: Neal-Schuman Publishers, Inc., 1989).

Ellison, John W., ed. *Media Librarianship* (New York: Neal-Schuman Publishers, Inc., 1985).

Frost, Carolyn O. *Media Access and Organization: A Cataloging and Reference Sources Guide for Nonbook Materials* (Englewood, CO: Libraries Unlimited, 1989).

Grieder, Ted. *Acquisitions: Where, What, and How* (Westport, CT: Greenwood Press, 1978).

Handman, Gary, ed. *Video Collection Management and Development: A Multi-type Library Perspective* (Westport, CT: Greenwood Press, 1994).

Intner, Sheila S. and Richard P. Smiraglia, eds. *Policy and Practice in Bibliographic Control of Nonbook Media* (Chicago: ALA, 1987).

Kaye, Alan L. "Video and Other Nonprint Resources in the Small Library." Small Libraries Publications—No. 16 (Chicago: ALA, 1991).

Kreamer, Jean Thibodeaux, ed. *The Video Annual 1990* (Santa Barbara, CA: ABC-CLIO, 1990).

Kreamer, Jean Thibodeaux, ed. *The Video Annual 1991* (Santa Barbara, CA: ABC-CLIO, 1991).

Kreamer, Jean Thibodeaux, ed. *The Video Annual 1992* (Santa Barbara, CA: ABC-CLIO, 1992).

Kreamer, Jean Thibodeaux, ed. *The Video Annual 1993* (Santa Barbara, CA: ABC-CLIO, 1993).

Magrill, Rose Mary and John Corbin. *Acquisitions Management and Collection Development in Libraries.* 2nd ed. (Chicago: ALA, 1989).

Maillet, Lucienne. *Subject Control of Film and Video: A Comparison of Three Methods* (Chicago: ALA, 1991).

Miller, Jerome K. *Using Copyrighted Videocassettes in Classrooms and Libraries* (Salem, MA: Copyright Information Services, 1984).

Olson, Nancy. *Cataloger's Guide to MARC Coding and Tagging of Audiovisual Materials* (DeKalb, IL: Minnesota Scholarly Press, 1993).

Olson, Nancy, ed. *Cataloging of Audiovisual Materials: A Manual Based on AACR 2.* 3rd. ed. (DeKalb, IL: Minnesota Scholarly Press, 1992).

Pemberton, J. Michael. *Policies of Audiovisual Producers and Distributors: A Handbook for Acquisitions Personnel.* 2nd ed. (Metuchen, NJ: The Scarecrow Press, Inc., 1989).

Pendergrast, Mark. "A Window on the Video Price Wars." *Library Journal* 115 (May 15, 1990): 32–34.

Pitman, Randy. *The Video Librarian's Guide to Collection Development & Management* (New York: Macmillan, 1992).

Pitman, Randy, Sally Mason-Robinson, and Pat Lora. "AV Frontier." See issues of *Wilson Library Bulletin,* June 1988–October 1993.

Public Library Association, AV Committee, ed. *Policy Questions for Audiovisual Services in Public Libraries* (Chicago: PLA, 1986).

Reed, Mary Hutchings and Debra Stanek. "Library Use of Copyrighted Videotapes and Computer Software." *American Libraries* 17 (February 1986): special pull-out section, A.

Salce, Joanne. "Video Distribution: The Maze Made Manageable." *Library Journal* 115 (July 1990): 40–45.

Schmidt, Karen A., ed. *Understanding the Business of Library Acquisitions* (Chicago: ALA, 1990).

Scholtz, James C. *Developing and Maintaining Video Collections in Libraries* (Santa Barbara, CA: ABC-CLIO, 1989).

Scholtz, James C. *Video Policies and Procedures for Libraries* (Santa Barbara, CA: ABC-CLIO, 1991).

The Survey Center. *Summary Report and Data Tables—1990 National Library Video Survey* (Santa Barbara, CA: ABC-CLIO, 1990).

The Survey Center. *Summary Report and Data Tables—1992 National Library Video Survey* (Santa Barbara, CA: ABC-CLIO, 1992).

Index

About the Author

JAMES C. SCHOLTZ is director of the Yankton Community Library in Yankton, South Dakota. He has previously worked as the AV department head in a public library, as an audiovisual consultant at a regional library system in Illinois, and as a community college library director. He has authored three books and numerous professional articles.